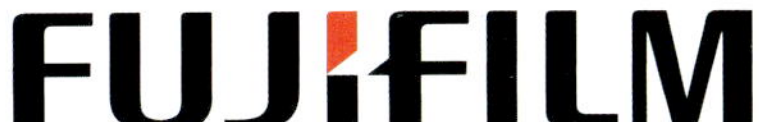

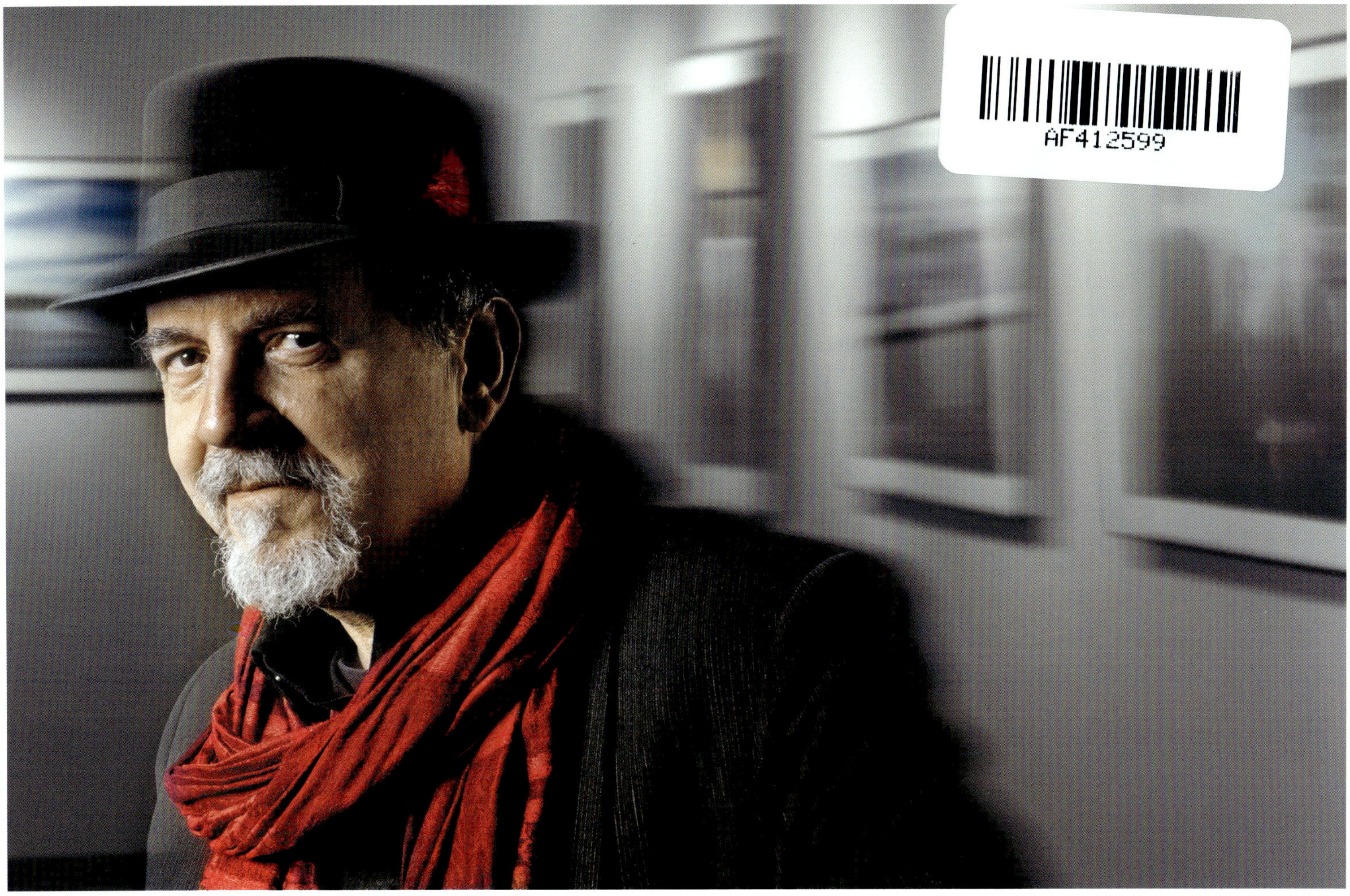

Portrait - Lee Varis, Author of Skin: The Complete Guide to Digital Retouching.

@2014 Bobbi Lane | FUJIFILM X-T1 Camera and XF56mm Lens at 1/8 sec at F9, ISO 200

The **camera** you carry is as important as the **images** you make

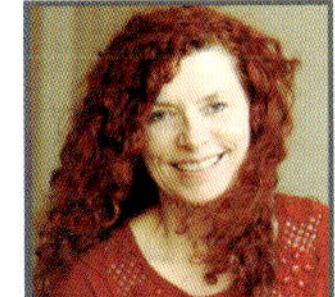

"The new FUJIFILM X-T1 is my new camera of choice. It's a light weight camera with DSLR quality. My goal always as a photographer is to use the tool that is appropriate to my vision, so whatever gear I need to get the job done, is the right tool. The X-T1 is good, really good, far better than I expected from a small camera."

-Bobbi Lane / Commercial Photographer

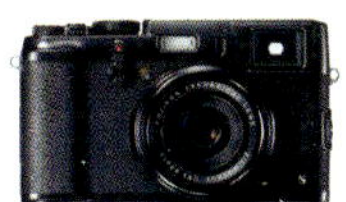

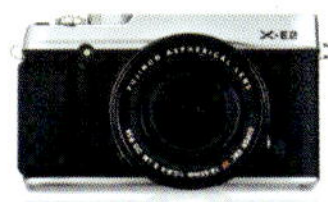

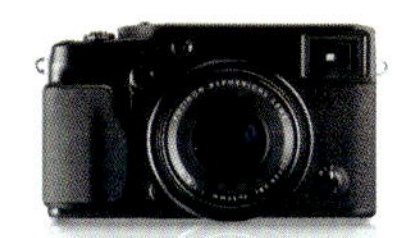

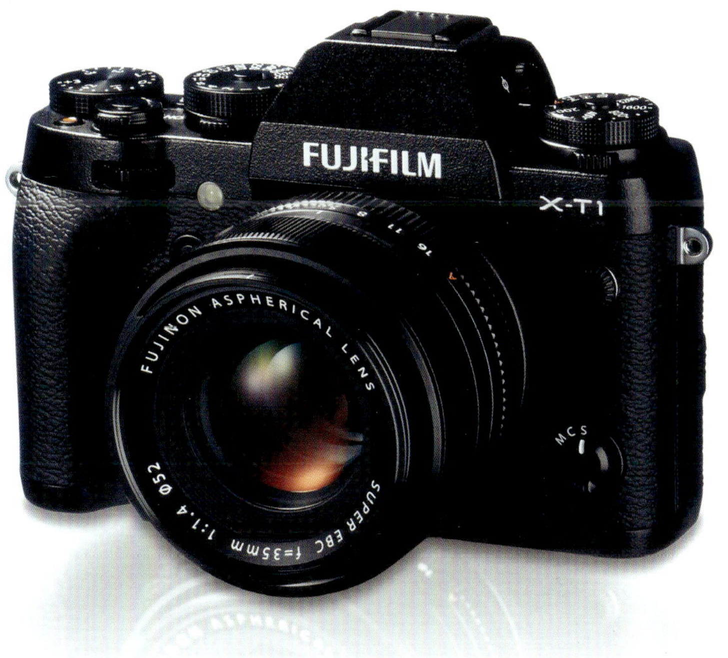

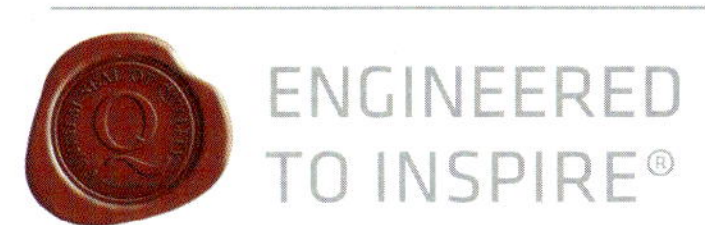

www.FujifilmExpertXT1BLane.com
facebook.com/fujifilmcameras
FujifilmUS

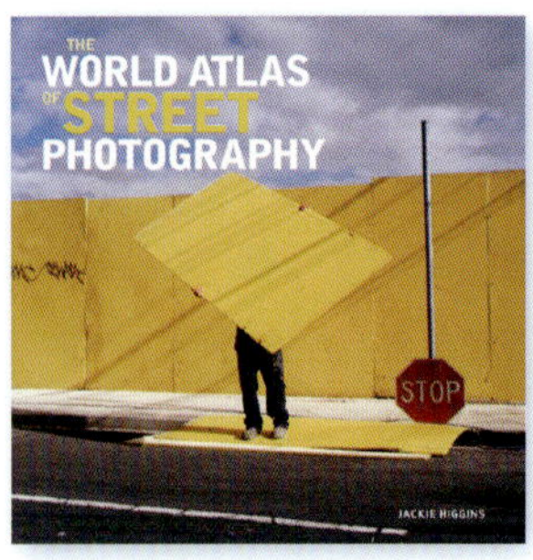
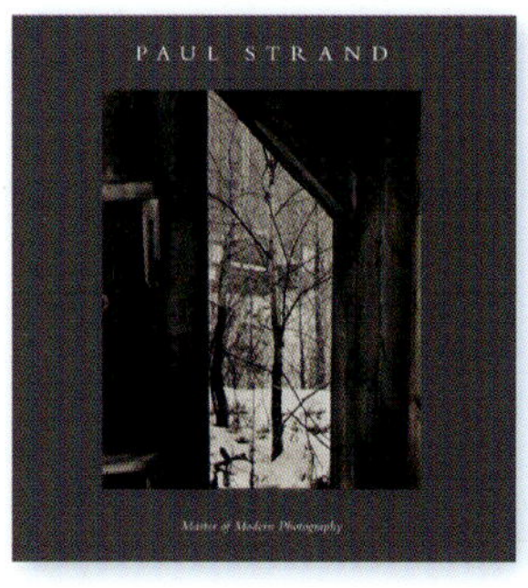
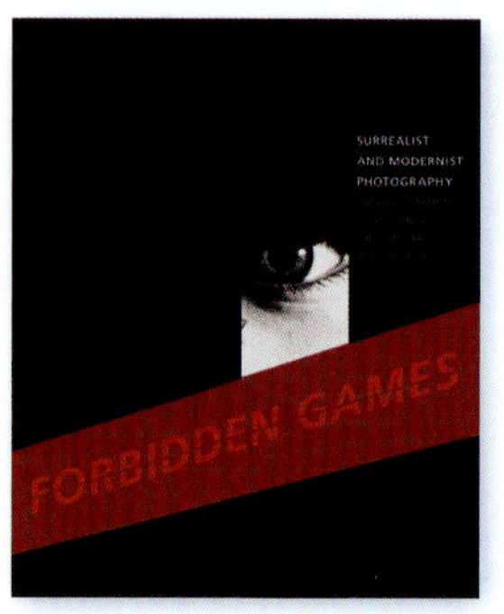
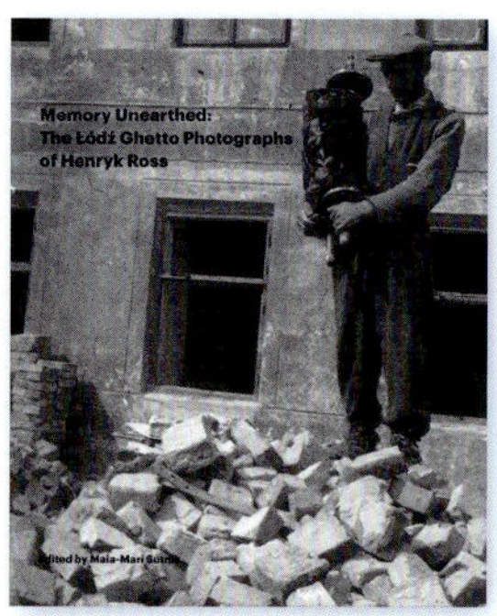
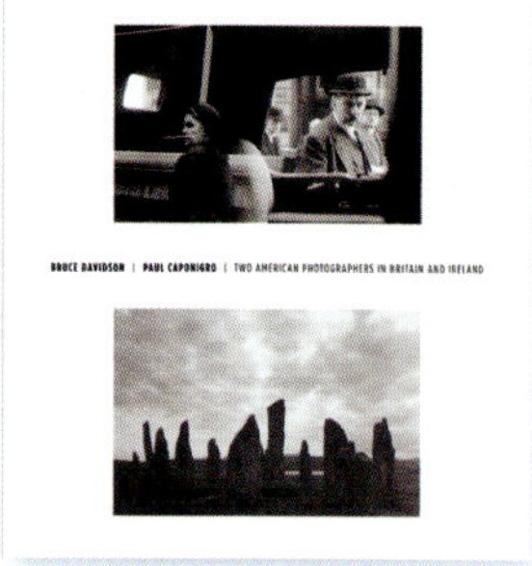

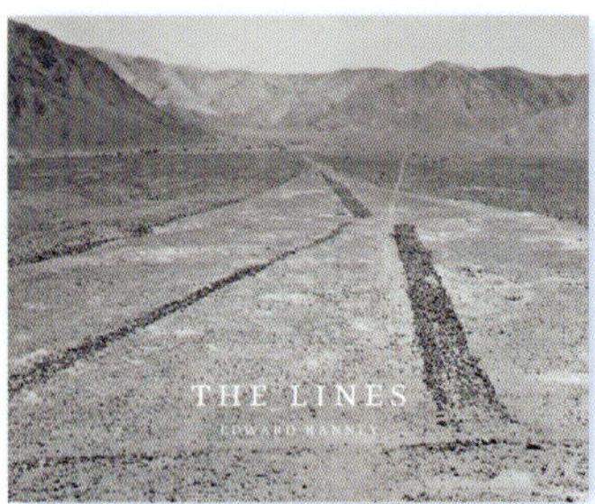

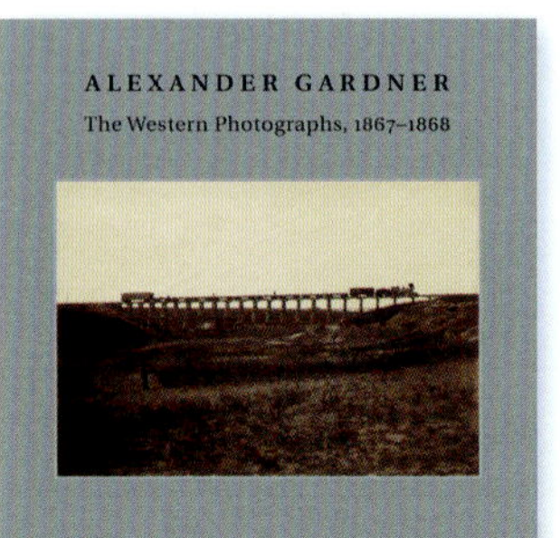

The World Atlas of Street Photography

Jackie Higgins

With a foreword by Max Kozloff

This impressive compendium features over 700 stunning images, assembling the vibrant and varied expressions of street photography, both staged and improvised, from cities around the world.

The Lines

Edward Ranney

With an essay by Lucy R. Lippard

Edward Ranney's evocative photographs of ancient geoglyphs in Peru and Chile reveal their enigmatic beauty.

Distributed for the Yale University Art Gallery

Alexander Gardner

The Western Photographs, 1867–1868

Jane L. Aspinwall

With a preface by Keith F. Davis

This remarkable volume offers an extraordinary glimpse into the transformation of the American West through startling photographs of the frontier landscape and the rich culture of rapidly marginalized American Indian tribes.

Distributed for the Nelson-Atkins Museum of Art

Sarah Charlesworth

Stills

Matthew S. Witkovsky

This landmark publication presents the influential Pictures Generation artist's arresting large-scale 1980 photographic series for the first time.

Distributed for The Art Institute of Chicago

The Home and the World

A View of Calcutta

Photographs by Laura McPhee

With a preface by Amitav Ghosh and an essay by Romita Ray

The unique and vibrant city of Calcutta comes to life in an intriguing array of captivating and visually striking photographs.

Paul Strand

Master of Modern Photography

Edited by Peter Barberie with Amanda N. Bock

With essays by Peter Barberie and Amanda N. Bock

Roundtable discussion with Peter Barberie, Martin Barnes, Karen Beckman, Amanda N. Bock, Tsitsi Jaji, and Maria Antonella Pelizzari; Chronology by Samantha Gainsburg

This catalogue presents a fresh account of the career of one of the 20th century's most important photographers.

Published in association with the Philadelphia Museum of Art

Forbidden Games: Surrealist and Modernist Photography

The David Raymond Collection in the Cleveland Museum of Art

Tom E. Hinson, Ian Walker, and Lisa Kurzner

Handsomely illustrated, this volume is the first publication of the Surrealist photography collection of David Raymond, whose eccentric eye for collecting befits the spirit of this radical art movement.

Distributed for the Cleveland Museum of Art

Memory Unearthed

The Łódź Ghetto Holocaust Photographs of Henryk Ross

Edited by Maia-Mari Sutnik

With essays by Maia-Mari Sutnik, Bernice Eisenstein, Robert Jan van Pelt, Michael Mitchell, and Eric Beck Rubin

Henryk Ross's photographs, covertly taken during World War II, capture both intimate and quotidian moments in the Łódź Ghetto in Poland.

Distributed for the Art Gallery of Ontario

Bruce Davidson/Paul Caponigro

Two American Photographers in Britain and Ireland

Jennifer A. Watts and Scott Wilcox

Photographs taken by Bruce Davidson and Paul Caponigro in Britain and Ireland during the 1960s and 1970s are brought together for the first time into a dramatic visual dialogue.

Published in association with the Yale Center for British Art

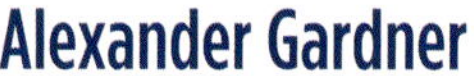
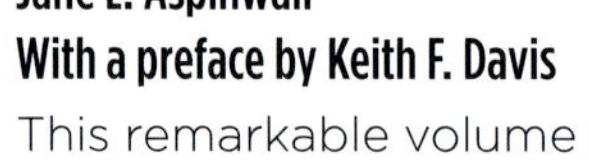
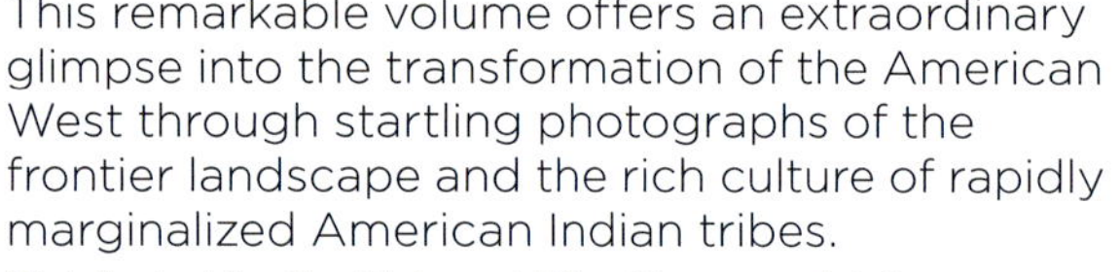
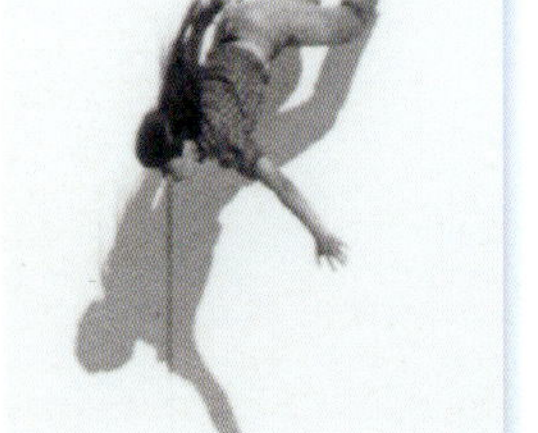
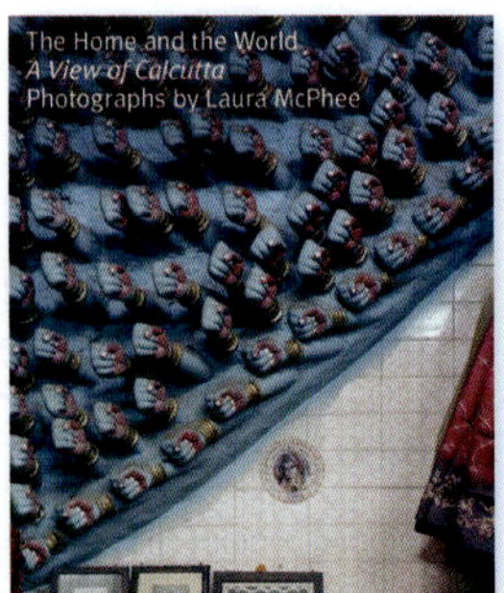

Art | Basel
Miami Beach | Dec | 4–7 | 2014

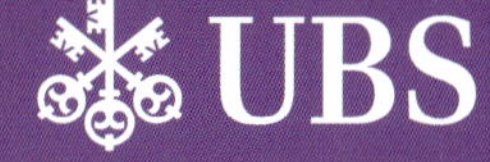

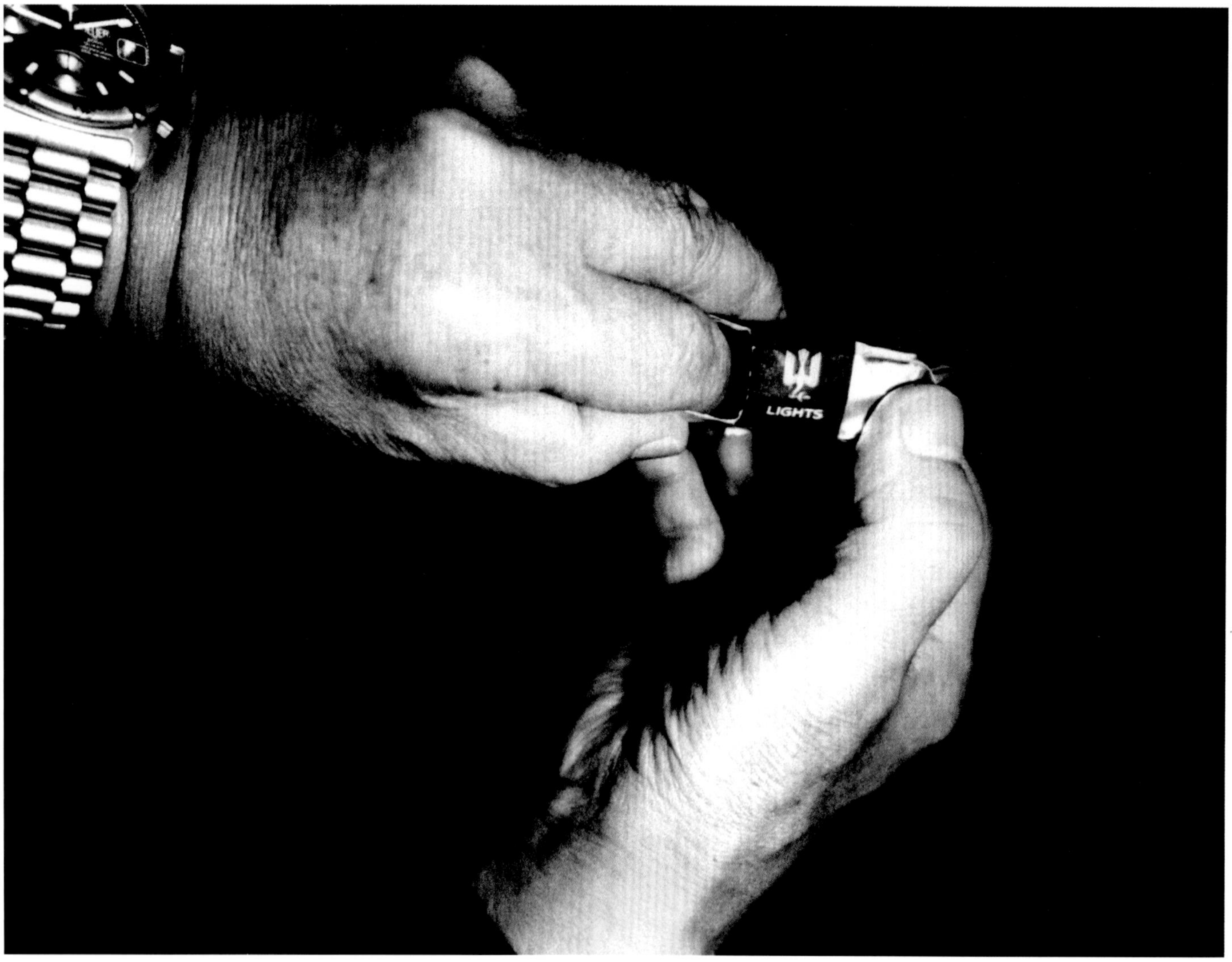

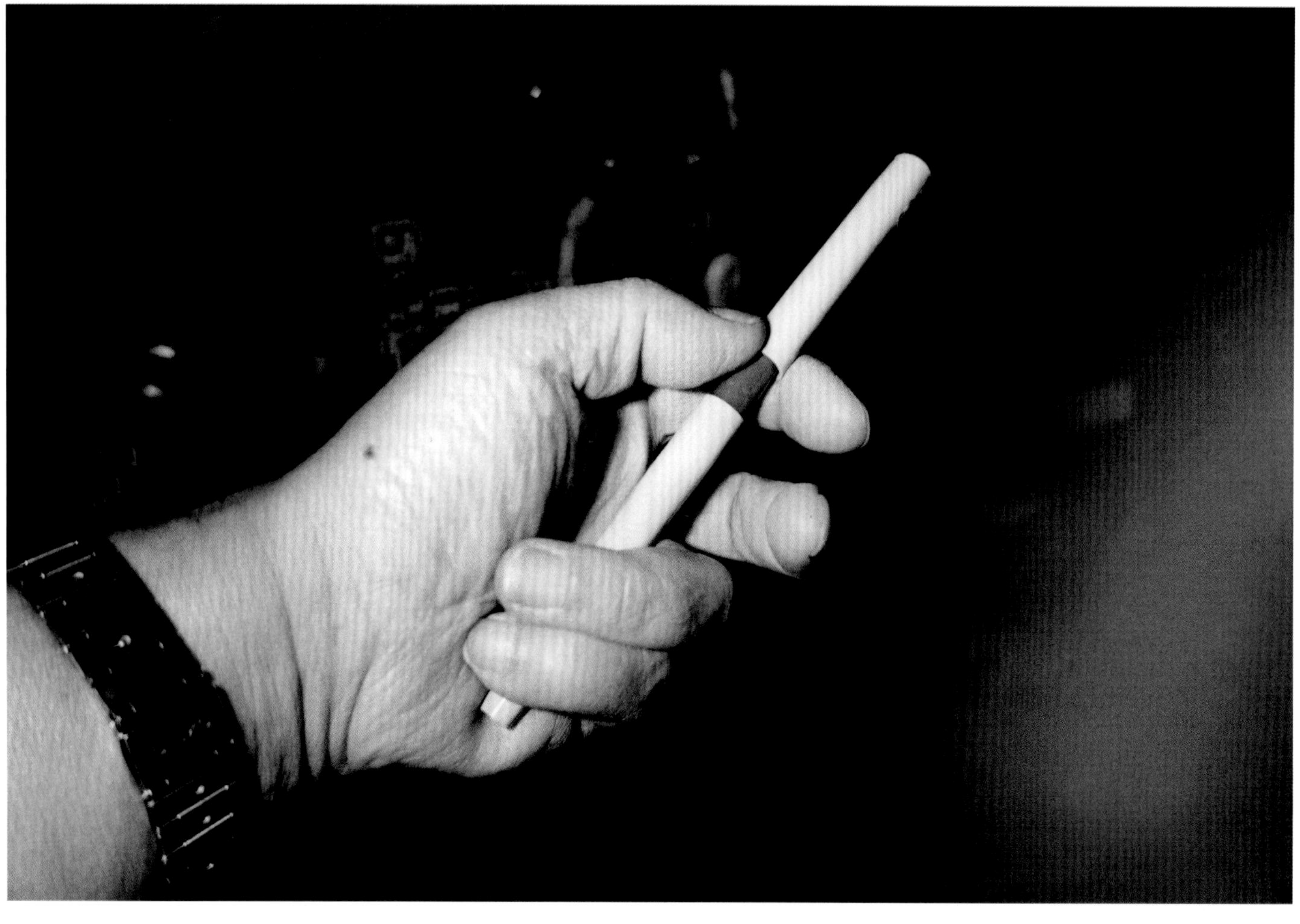
LIGHTS

Winter 2014

Words

Pictures

Front

Back

Opposite:
Kobo Abe, *Untitled*, n.d.
© Kobo Abe and courtesy
Neri Abe

Front cover:
Moyra Davey,
Bio, 2013 (detail)
C-print with tape,
postage, ink
Courtesy the artist and
Murray Guy, New York

Aperture, a not-for-profit foundation, connects the photo community and its
audiences with the most inspiring work, the sharpest ideas, and with each other—
in print, in person, and online.

Aperture (ISSN 0003-6420) is published quarterly, in spring, summer, fall, and winter,
at 547 West 27th Street, 4th Floor, New York, N.Y. 10001. In the United States,
a one-year subscription (four issues) is $75; a two-year subscription (eight issues)
is $124. In Canada, a one-year subscription is $95. All other international subscriptions
are $105 per year. Visit aperture.org to subscribe. Single copies may be purchased
at $24.95 for most issues. Periodicals postage paid at New York and additional offices.
Postmaster: Send address changes to *Aperture*, P.O. Box 3000, Denville, N.J. 07834.
Address queries regarding subscriptions, renewals, or gifts to: *Aperture* Subscription
Service, 866-457-4603 (U.S. and Canada), or email custsvc_aperture@fulcoinc.com.

Newsstand distribution in the U.S. is handled by Curtis Circulation Company,
201-634-7400. For international distribution, contact Central Books, centralbooks.com.

Help maintain Aperture's publishing, education, and community activities by joining our
new general member program. Membership starts at $75 annually and includes invitations
to special events, exclusive discounts on Aperture publications, and opportunities to meet
artists and engage with leaders in the photo community. Aperture Foundation welcomes
support at all levels of giving, and all gifts are tax-deductible to the fullest extent of the
law. For more information about supporting Aperture, please visit aperture.org/join or
contact the Development Department at membership@aperture.org.

Library of Congress Catalog Card No: 58-30845.

ISBN 978-1-59711-282-6

Printed in Turkey by Ofset Yapimevi

Aperture magazine is supported in part by an award from the National Endowment for
the Arts and with public funds from the New York City Department of Cultural Affairs
in partnership with the City Council.

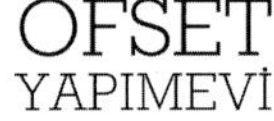
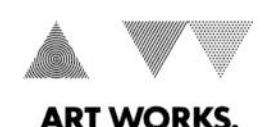

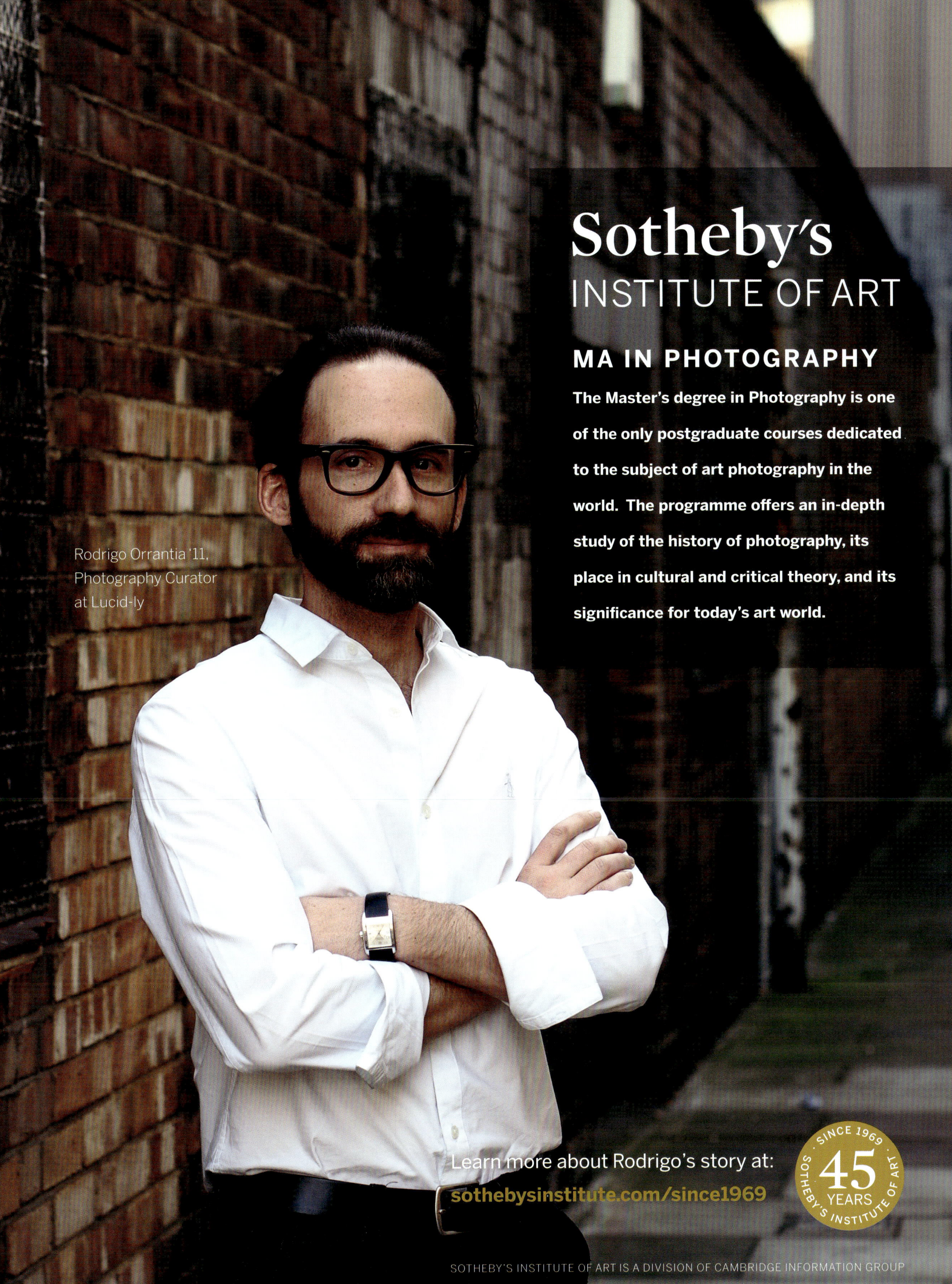

Sotheby's
INSTITUTE OF ART

MA IN PHOTOGRAPHY

The Master's degree in Photography is one of the only postgraduate courses dedicated to the subject of art photography in the world. The programme offers an in-depth study of the history of photography, its place in cultural and critical theory, and its significance for today's art world.

Rodrigo Orrantia '11,
Photography Curator
at Lucid-ly

Learn more about Rodrigo's story at:
sothebysinstitute.com/since1969

SINCE 1969
45
YEARS
SOTHEBY'S INSTITUTE OF ART

SOTHEBY'S INSTITUTE OF ART IS A DIVISION OF CAMBRIDGE INFORMATION GROUP

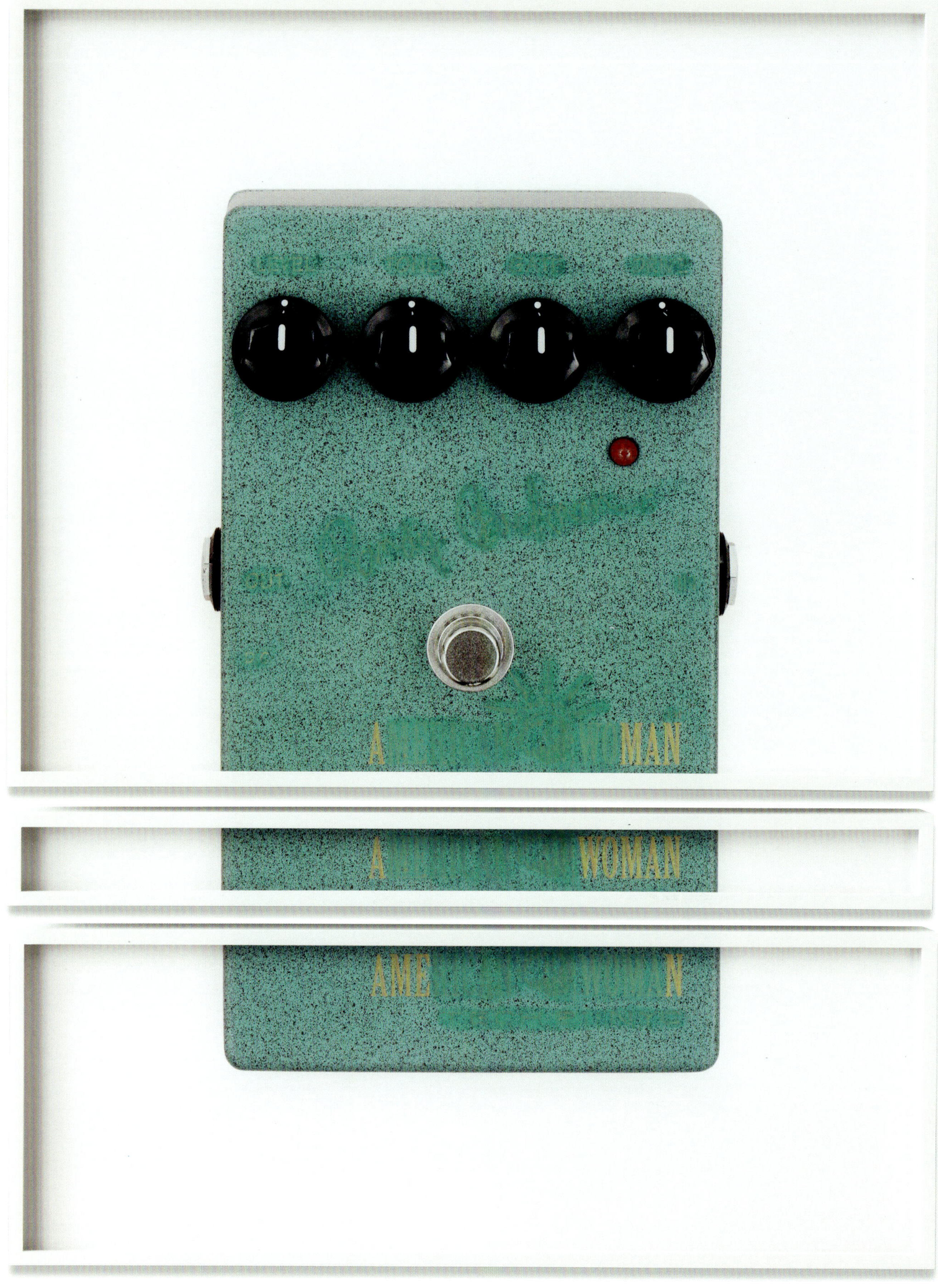

a man
a woman

a men

Lit.

Are images trumping the written word? Even in the age of instant visual communication via Instagram and Snapchat, this isn't a new question. Photography critic and curator Nancy Newhall wrote in 1952, in the first issue of this magazine, of which she was a founder: "Perhaps the old literacy of words is dying and a new literacy of images is being born. Perhaps the printed page will disappear and even our records [will] be kept in images and sounds." Penned more than sixty years ago, Newhall's words sound remarkably prescient now that photographs have come to be described as "chatter" and the culture of books and reading is shifting. A *New Yorker* blog post earlier this year detailed how smartphone pictures had superseded note taking in one writer's process; a recent *New York Times* article proclaimed that "The Emoji have Won the Battle of Words," referring to the popular pictograph lexicon used in text messages.

We hope (and are fairly certain) that the latter isn't true, but this issue is set against a backdrop where images are, arguably, placing significant pressure on the written word, whether or not this is a new or old problem. The prolific French writer Hervé Guibert, an accomplished photographer in his own right, prophetically feared that photography could "quickly turn to madness, because everything is photographable." He is joined in this issue by William S. Burroughs and Kobo Abe, novelists who moonlighted as photographers. Writers Geoff Dyer and Janet Malcolm never developed a practice as photographers, but both have thought deeply and written extensively about images, navigating the tricky business of translating the visual into the verbal. A group of contemporary fiction writers offer varying takes on the pressure images place on what they do—Lynne Tillman smartly reminds us that "fiction is another form of image making," and Teju Cole makes a case for poetry and lyricism in the age of automated images. Gus Powell, Moyra Davey, Sarah Dobai, and Eamonn Doyle have all looked to works of literature to inform their work as image makers, whether by adopting a formal constraint, borrowing snippets of language, or riffing on a theme. Taking a cue from Burroughs, creator of the "cut-up," Natalie Czech and Erica Baum reanimate found language—from tactile, printed book pages to unlikely commercial objects (like the effects pedal opposite)—prompting viewers to reflect on how language can be both read and seen.

Words as inspiration for image making, words as images, images as open-ended fictions, documentary under the influence of fiction—as in the case of Walker Evans and his interest in writing and French literature, explored here by David Campany—are just some of the ways in which image and language brush up against each other in these pages. Perhaps novelist Tom McCarthy gets it right when he says, "in the end the difference between image and word isn't relevant because ultimately it's all scriptural…photography is a branch of writing." — The Editors

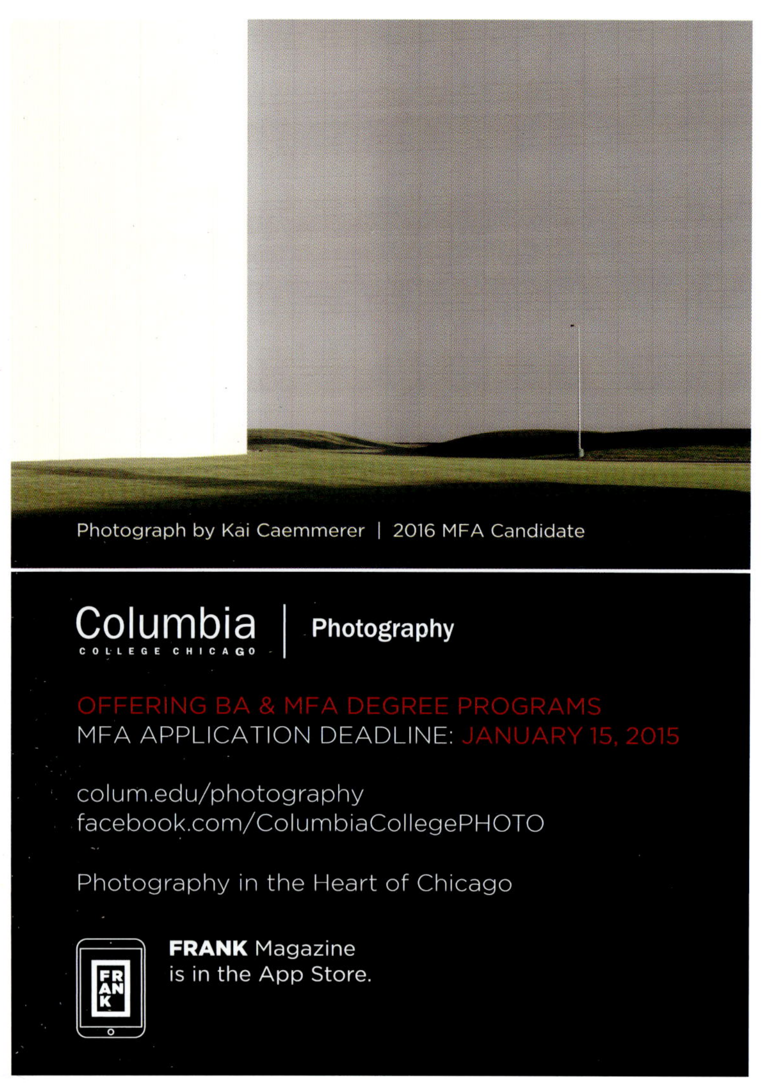

Photograph by Kai Caemmerer | 2016 MFA Candidate

Columbia
COLLEGE CHICAGO | Photography

OFFERING BA & MFA DEGREE PROGRAMS
MFA APPLICATION DEADLINE: JANUARY 15, 2015

colum.edu/photography
facebook.com/ColumbiaCollegePHOTO

Photography in the Heart of Chicago

FRANK Magazine
is in the App Store.

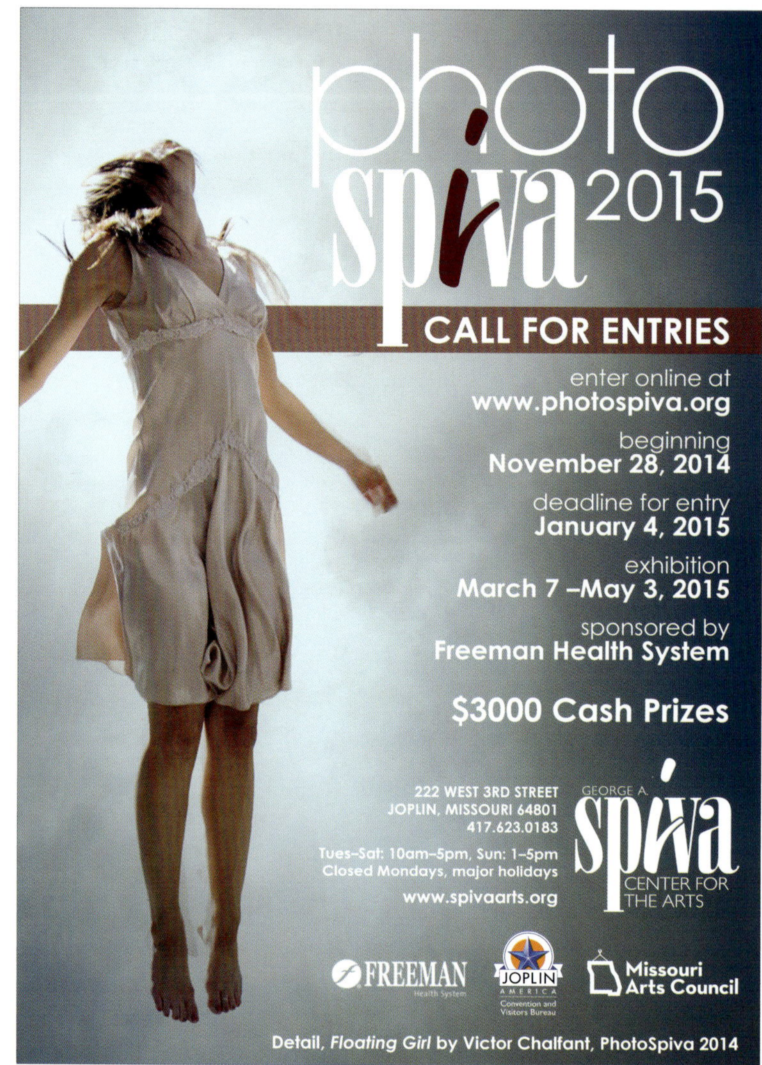

photo
spiva 2015
CALL FOR ENTRIES

enter online at
www.photospiva.org

beginning
November 28, 2014

deadline for entry
January 4, 2015

exhibition
March 7 –May 3, 2015

sponsored by
Freeman Health System

$3000 Cash Prizes

222 WEST 3RD STREET
JOPLIN, MISSOURI 64801
417.623.0183

Tues–Sat: 10am–5pm, Sun: 1–5pm
Closed Mondays, major holidays

www.spivaarts.org

GEORGE A.
spiva
CENTER FOR
THE ARTS

FREEMAN
Health System

JOPLIN
AMERICA
Convention and
Visitors Bureau

Missouri
Arts Council

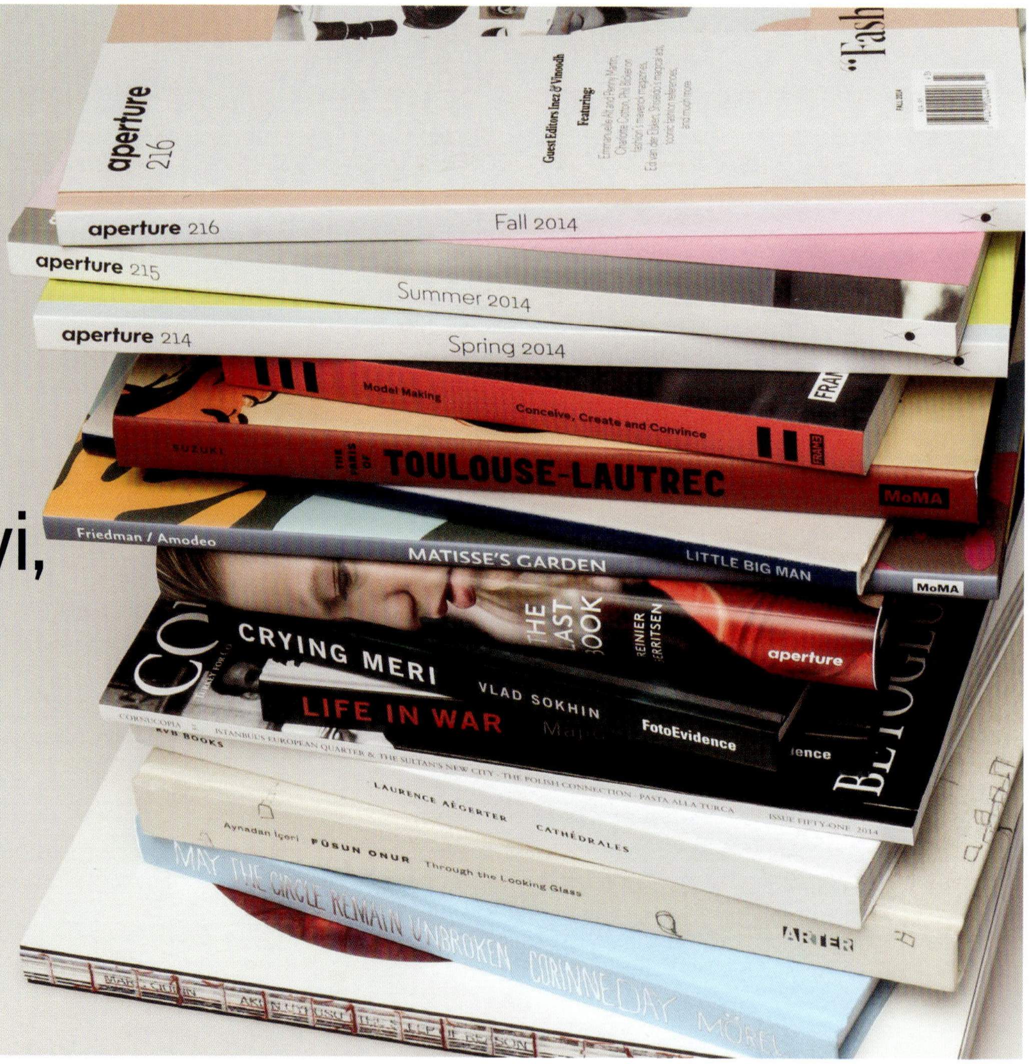

Detail, Floating Girl by Victor Chalfant, PhotoSpiva 2014

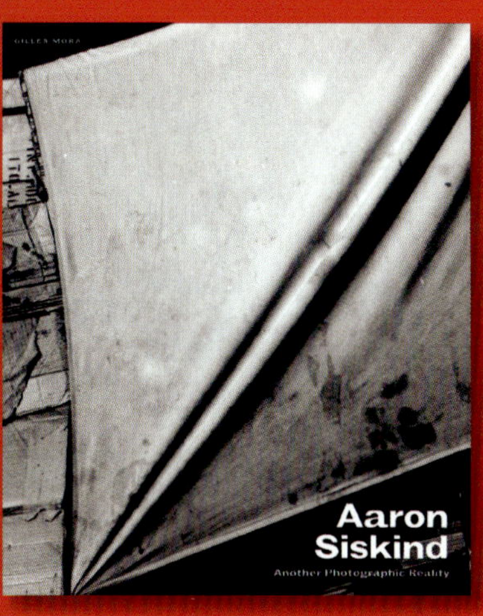

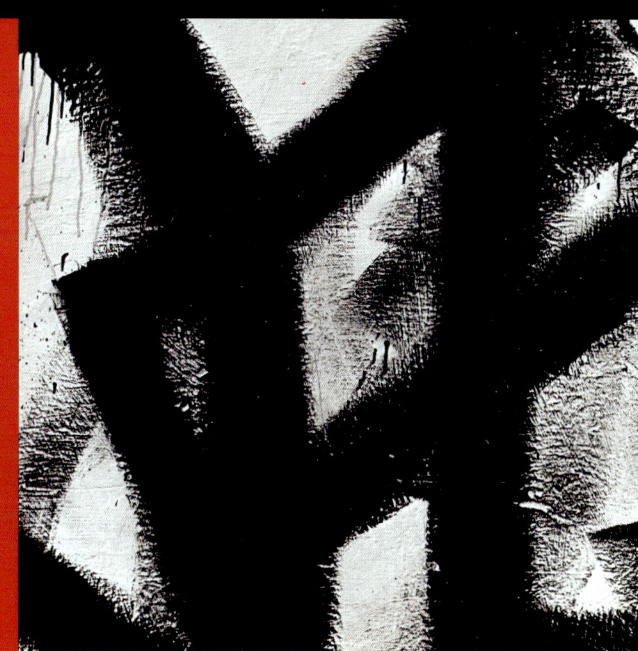

Aaron Siskind: Another Photographic Reality

INTRODUCTION BY GILLES MORA
TEXT BY CHARLES TRAUB

The first true retrospective of a towering figure in American photography and the only book on Aaron Siskind currently in print, this volume features important, rarely published work and an authoritative text by noted photo historian Gilles Mora.
150 doutone photos
$65.00 hardcover

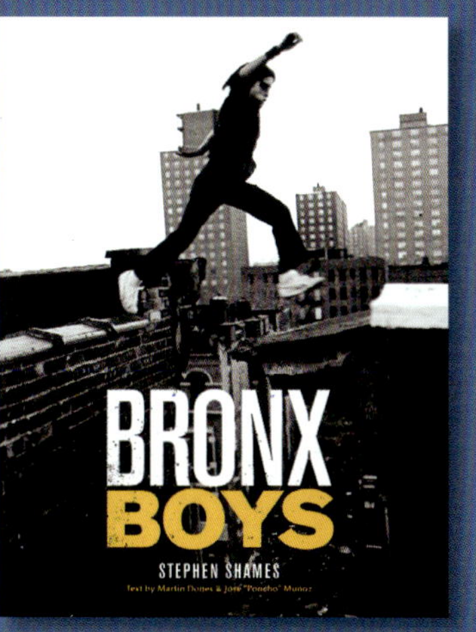

Beyond the Forest
Jewish Presence in Eastern Europe, 2004–2012

BY LOLI KANTOR
INTRODUCTION BY ANDA ROTTENBERG
AFTERWORD BY JOSEPH SKIBELL

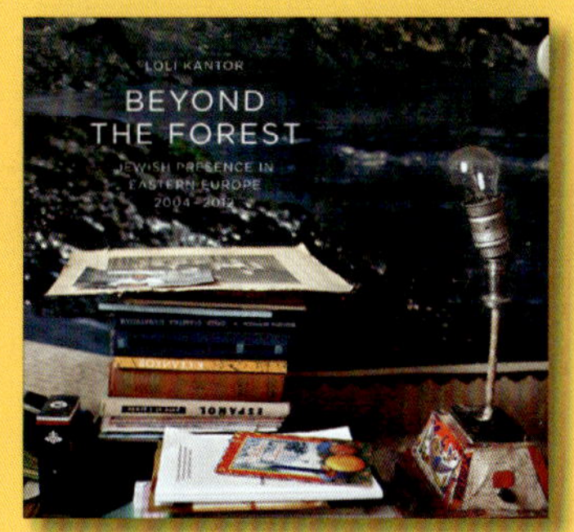

This evocative photo essay explores how Jewish communities in Ukraine, Poland, Romania, and the Czech Republic are reclaiming their history, rebuilding their communities, and revivifying their Jewish identity following the Holocaust and decades of Soviet domination.
68 color and 44 в&w photos
$60.00 hardcover

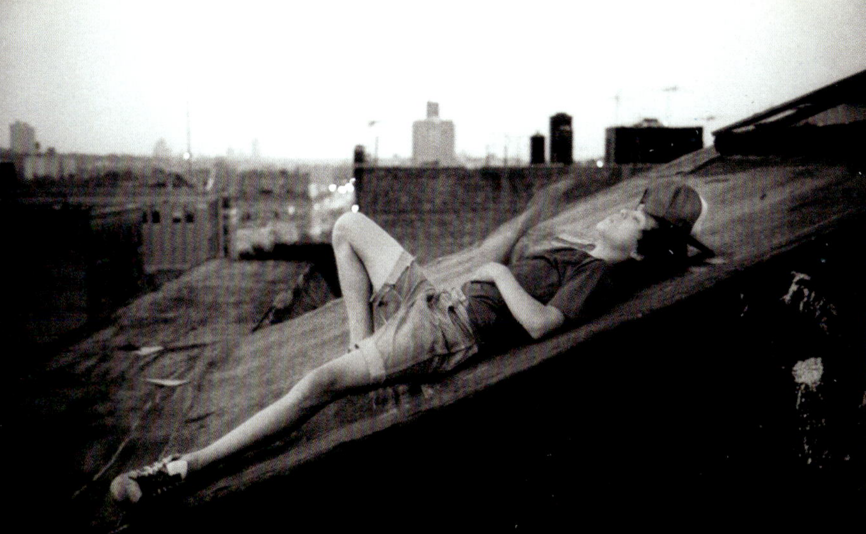

Bronx Boys

BY STEPHEN SHAMES
TEXT BY MARTIN DONES
AND JOSÉ "PONCHO" MUÑOZ

Bronx Boys captures the violence, resilience, and hope of young men growing up in what was one of the toughest and most dangerous neighborhoods in the United States.
123 duotone photos
$50.00 hardcover

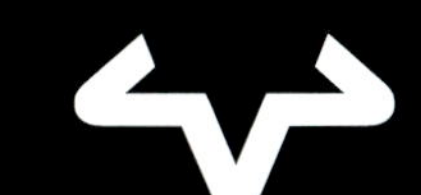

utexaspress.com

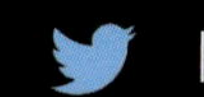

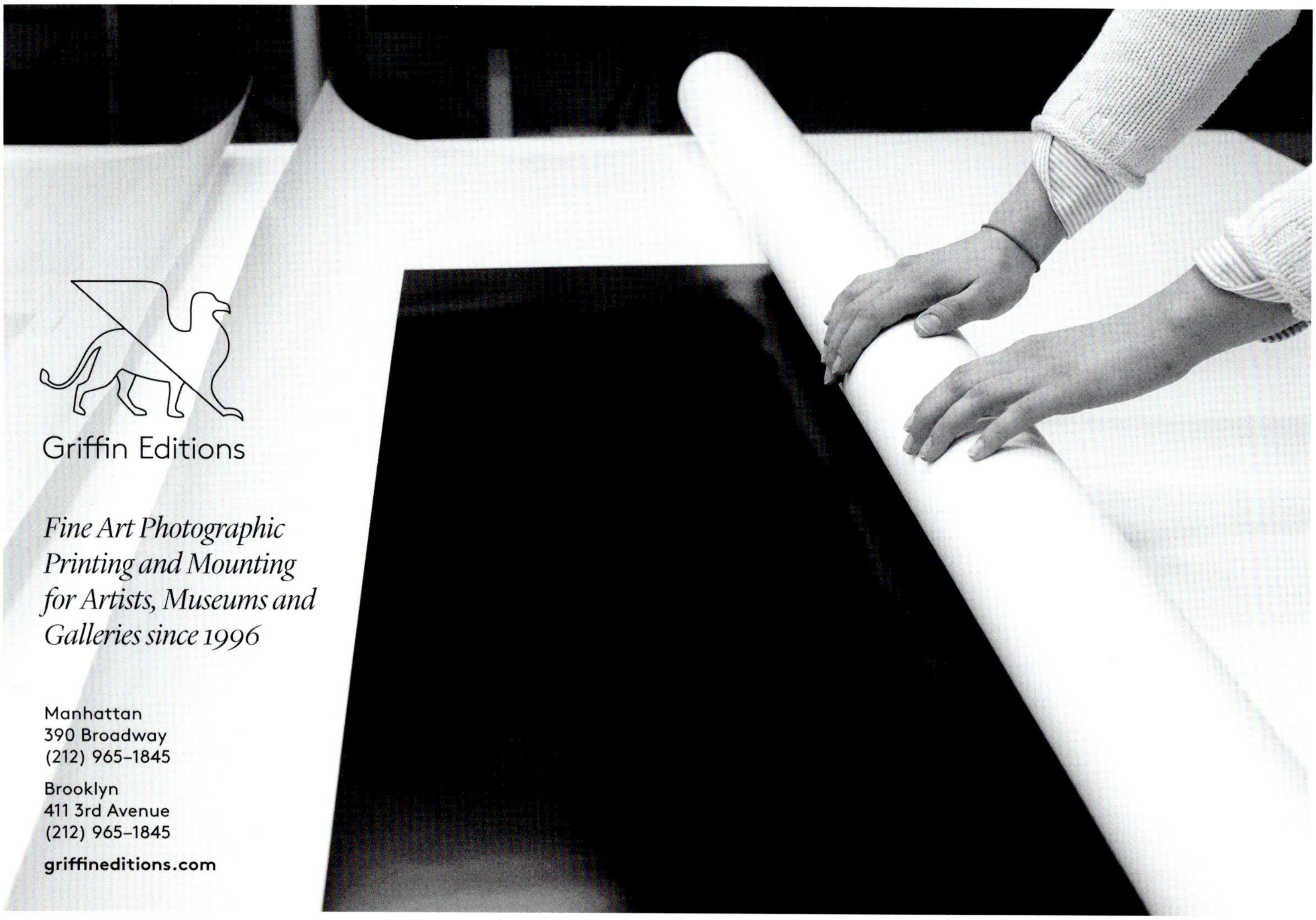

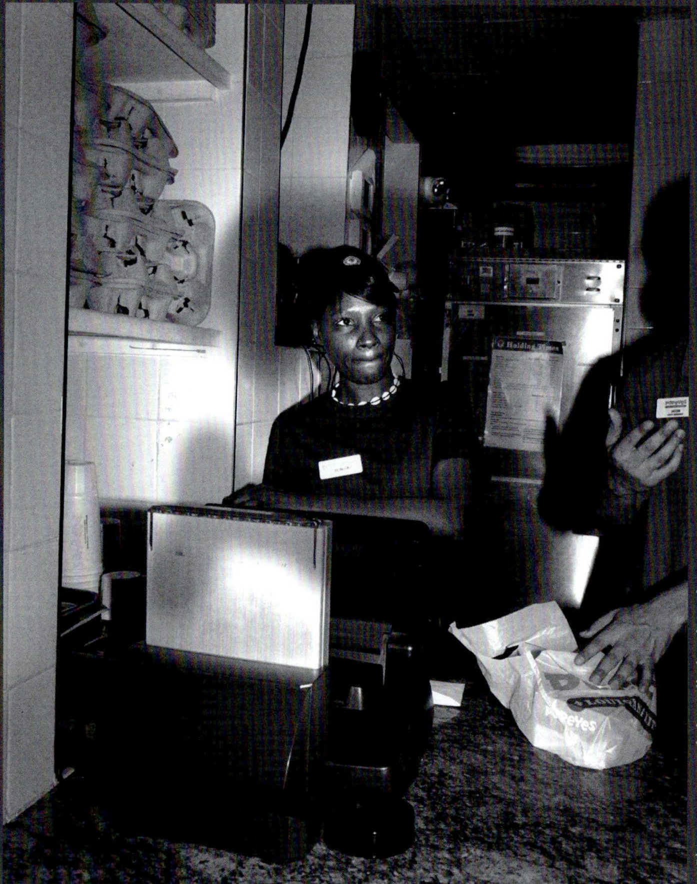

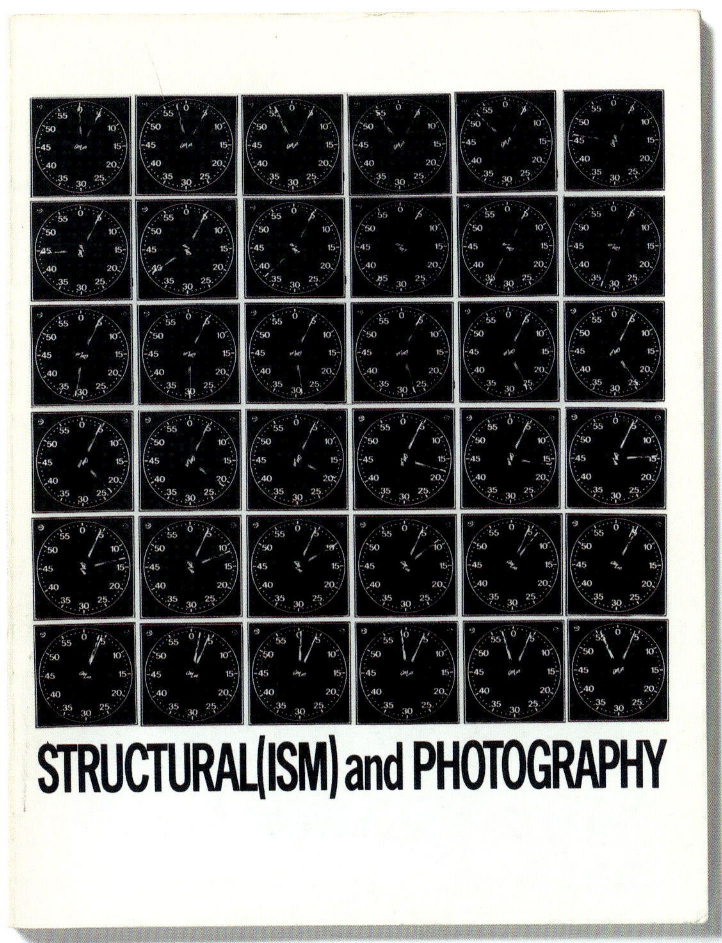

Lew Thomas's *Structural(ism) and Photography*
Erin O'Toole

Lew Thomas came to photography late, when he was already in his thirties, and never quite shed his outsider status among the photography establishment of his native San Francisco. An influential figure in the Bay Area art scene in the late 1970s and early '80s, Thomas, aside from making and showing his work, also organized group exhibitions for local nonprofit art spaces and museums, and published books with Donna-Lee Phillips under the imprint NFS (Not-For-Sale) Press. Although curator John Szarkowski included Thomas's *9 Perspectives* (1972) in his key 1978 exhibition *Mirrors and Windows* at the Museum of Modern Art in New York, Thomas's work has not been widely exhibited outside of San Francisco. Recently, however, a younger generation of curators, collectors, and gallerists interested in points of conversion between photography and conceptual art has discovered his early work, and in the spring of 2014 it was the subject of an exhibition at Cherry and Martin in Los Angeles.

Thomas received a BA in English literature from the University of San Francisco in 1962, and his first jobs out of college were in book sales. It was while managing the Patrons of Art and Music Bookstore at the California Palace of the Legion of Honor Museum in San Francisco, which he established in 1964 and ran until 1982, that Thomas first discovered photography through books. He soon determined it would be the best medium for expressing his own unrealized artistic ideas, and in the late 1960s enlisted Joe Schopplein, a free-lance photographer who documented artwork and exhibition installations for the Legion and the de Young Museum, to teach him to shoot and do his own printing in the darkroom.

A great admirer of Walker Evans, Thomas began by photographing in the documentary style, but with the birth of his daughter, Kesa, in 1971, his life became more domestic and his work took a conceptual turn. That year, inspired by observing his daughter's incremental efforts to understand the world around her, Thomas had what he considered to be a major creative breakthrough with *BLACK & WHITE*, a piece that boiled photography down to its most basic elements. Composed of two prints—one all black with "BLACK" typeset in white letters across the center, and the other all white with "WHITE" across it in black—the work set Thomas on a new course. The process of producing it "made it clear that I did not need a reflected, pictorial image to make a photograph," Thomas wrote in his seminal text *Structural(ism) and Photography*, and he began to consider the operations of photography in radically simplified terms. "I did not need to go somewhere to take a photograph," he asserted. "In fact all the content I would ever need for photography was already with me."

Structural(ism) and Photography, published by NFS in 1978, documents the body of photographs and installations that followed from *BLACK & WHITE*. Concerned primarily with time, duration, and sequence, the work was guided by Thomas's distinctive gloss on Structuralist

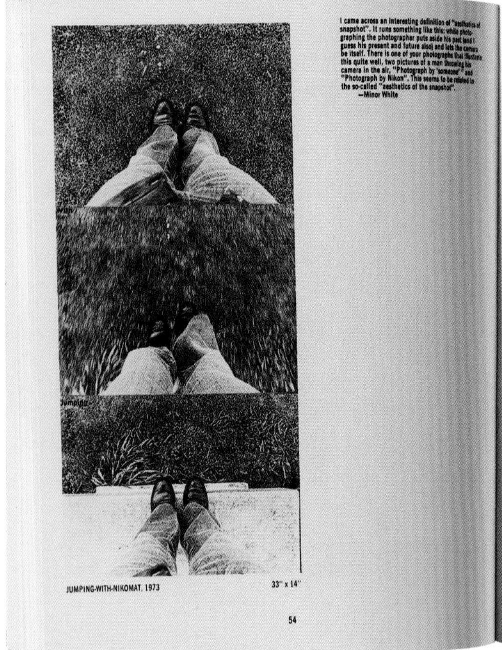

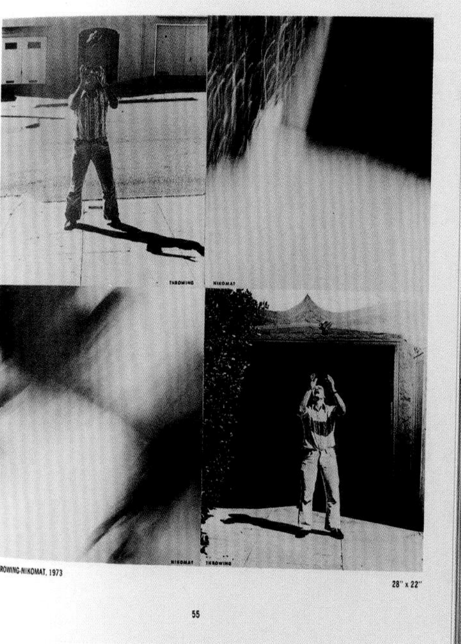

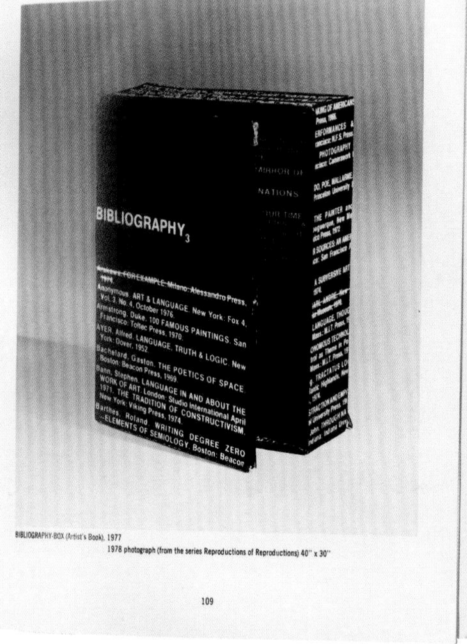

Pages from Lew Thomas, *Structural(ism) and Photography* (NFS Press, 1978)

Thomas's camera to the front of his house, showing incremental adjustments in focus from near to far. Documentation of installation pieces staged at various Bay Area institutions, including several involving the arrangement of a set of entirely black and entirely white prints on the gallery walls, make up the last part of the book.

While Thomas's work is strictly photographic and is concerned with the mechanisms of the medium and the limits of photographic representation, it is informed less by the history of photography than it is by conceptual art, literary theory, semiotics, modern poetry, and film theory. Dense with transcriptions of correspondence with curators and other artists describing his idiosyncratic approach to the medium, explanations of individual works, statements of purpose, and quotations by Thomas's favorite philosophers and poets, *Structural(ism) and Photography* is as much a manifesto as it is a monograph. The book culminates in a series of bibliographic pieces that list authors as diverse as Gertrude Stein, Mel Bochner, T.J. Clark, Alain Robbe-Grillet, Michel Foucault, and Kazimir Malevich, and pointedly omit names such as Beaumont Newhall, Ansel Adams, and even Lewis Baltz. Like much of the text in the book, these bibliographic works serve both as evidence of Thomas's wide-ranging interests and influences and as a rejection of what he saw as the insularity and anti-intellectualism of mainstream art photography.

Structural(ism) and Photography is worth revisiting today because it explores ideas about photography, such as its complex relationship to time, which remain central to contemporary practice, even after the advent of digital. At a moment when many young artists and photographers are investigating the nature of photographic seeing in their work, Thomas's elegant and often slyly humorous photographs look as fresh and relevant as ever.

thought. "Letting the object express itself is what Structuralism is all about," Thomas told me recently. "I was just a witness. You have to accept what the object tells you." Shot either at his home, at the Legion, or along 34th Avenue between Geary and Clement streets, the photographs explore, among other things, how the camera registers depth of field, perspective, and the passage of time. Grids of thirty-six prints—representing a full roll of film—follow the hands of a darkroom timer as they clock a minute, for example, or trace the movement of light across a parquet floor over the course of a day. A ten-part horizontal series follows a length of masking tape extending six feet from the lens of

Erin O'Toole is associate curator of photography at the San Francisco Museum of Modern Art and is currently organizing a retrospective of the work of Anthony Hernandez, scheduled for fall 2016.

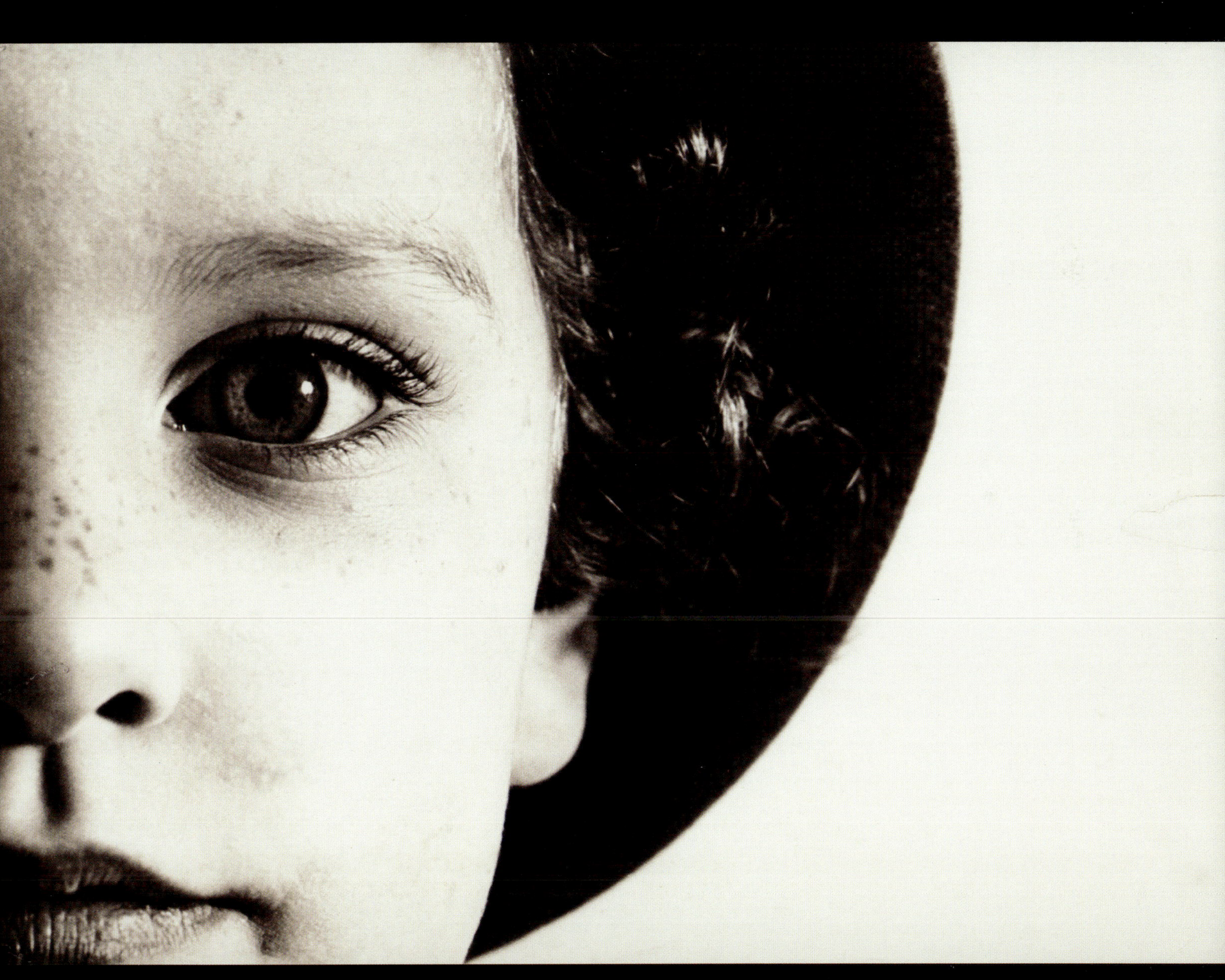

Modern Photographs
From the Thomas Walther
Collection, 1909–1949

Opens Dec 13

MoMA

Visit MoMA.org/ObjectPhoto
for an in-depth look at the
collection. A related publication

THE MUSEUM OF
MODERN ART
11 West 53 Street
MoMA.org

The Thomas Walther
Collection Project is made
possible by The Andrew W.
Mellon Foundation.

Max Burchartz. Lotte (Eye).
1928. Gelatin silver print.
The Museum of Modern
Art, New York, Thomas
Walther Collection. Acquired

Curriculum
A List of Favorite Anythings
by James Welling

PBS Documentaries
In the late 1960s, PBS aired a series of documentaries on contemporary art. These beautiful thirty-minute black-and-white films introduced me to the work of Frank Stella, Andy Warhol, Robert Rauschenberg, and Barnett Newman. I took the train to New York from Hartford, Connecticut, and saw Rauschenberg's *Inferno* drawings at MoMA, Barnett Newman's last show at the Knoedler Gallery, and Frank Stella's retrospective at MoMA. I put away my watercolors and my emulation of Edward Hopper and Andrew Wyeth and began reading *Artforum*. I remember the distinct feeling of newness and change when I first encountered Richard Serra's *Splashing Lead* on the cover of the February 1969 issue of *Artforum* in the high school library.

1. *Artforum* Special Film
Issue, September 1971.
Cover: Scene from
Ken Jacobs, *Tom, Tom,
The Piper's Son*, 1969

2. Paul Strand, *Rebecca's
Hands*, 1923

3. Merce Cunningham and
Meg Harper in a perform-
ance of Cunningham's
RainForest at the Brooklyn
Academy of Music, 1968.
Photograph by James
Klosty

4. Maurice Merleau-Ponty,
The Primacy of Perception
(Evanston, Illinois:
Northwestern University
Press, 1964)

5. Morton Subotnick at
his Bleecker Street studio,
1966. Photographer
unknown

6. Marion Faller, *Portrait
of Hollis Frampton
(directed by H.F.)*, 1975

7. Wallace Stevens,
The Necessary Angel
(New York: Vintage, 1965)

Strand: © Aperture
Foundation, Inc., and
Paul Strand Archive;
Klosty: © and courtesy
James Klosty; Subotnick:
Courtesy Morton Subotnick;
Faller: Courtesy Burchfield
Penney Art Center Collection,
Buffalo, New York

Annette Michelson's "Bodies in Space: Film as 'Carnal Knowledge'"
In my freshman year at Carnegie Mellon in Pittsburgh, I encountered "Bodies in Space: Film as 'Carnal Knowledge,'" an extended essay on Stanley Kubrick's film *2001: A Space Odyssey* written by Annette Michelson in 1969. Michelson's writings introduced me to her idea of "radical aspiration" in the world of New York experimental film and dance. Michelson's consideration of Kubrick and the links she made between his work and the New York avant-garde were an intense eye-opener. Up until that point I only vaguely understood what the avant-garde might stand for; that it could extend from Hollywood film to the Judson Church Theater was thrilling.

Publishers' Logos
In the early 1970s the most cited writer in *Artforum* was the French phenomenologist Maurice Merleau-Ponty. So I sought out Merleau-Ponty's books published by Northwestern University Press. After some struggle I realized I couldn't make sense of his ideas. But I came to love his publisher's distinctive interlocking arrows on the front cover, and the interior layout and typeface. So I looked for other books published by Northwestern. When I was in New York I'd visit Papyrus Books near Columbia University and spend the evening reading philosophy and poetry in the aisles. Then I'd carefully select one volume to buy. Like Northwestern's arrows, each publisher had a distinctive, memorable logo. Vintage Books had a fiery, anthropomorphic sun on its spine; Hill and Wang's logo comprised interlocking black letter initials; George Braziller's clean serif-type name locked down the title page; Grove Press placed a funny *Y* on the spine. Each publisher's logo held the promise of an exciting and different intellectual journey.

Hollis Frampton and Structural Film
Shortly after reading Michelson, *Artforum* ran a special film issue that introduced me to Structural film. The Structural filmmaker Hollis Frampton was a frequent contributor to *Artforum* and his articles on Edward Weston and Paul Strand tipped me off to modernist photography. Frampton was a witty and erudite writer, and his film work bristled with literary allusions and humor. On holidays from Carnegie Mellon, and after visiting Papyrus, I would see Structural films at the Anthology Film Archives in the Public Theater on Lafayette Street. Over the course of the next year I saw films by Joyce Wieland, Michael Snow, Peter Kubelka, and Frampton. Once I overshot my subway stop at Astor Place and ended up on Canal Street. As I walked up Lafayette Street to the Public, I passed the loft on Grand Street I would inhabit a decade later.

Merce Cunningham Company's *RainForest*
My world of contemporary art expanded dramatically when I saw Merce Cunningham's dance company perform with John Cage in Pittsburgh in 1970. Cunningham rehearsed, gave master classes, and danced, and I was in the first row at every public event that week. The company performed *RainForest* at the Carnegie Museum, with Warhol's Mylar pillows floating on and off the stage, and *Tread*, with a décor of standing fans orchestrated by Bruce Nauman. I rushed to the library and started reading back issues of *Dance Magazine* to understand where Cunningham fit in. Cage and Cunningham became my two aesthetic mentors for the next few years as I experimented with chance procedures to make different types of artwork.

Morton Subotnick and Electronic Music
At the performance of *RainForest*, David Tudor and Cage performed Tudor's score with an orchestra pit full of electronic devices. I was mesmerized by Cage and by electronic music. I listened to everything I could find by Cage and Tudor in the Carnegie Mellon arts library. The University of Pittsburgh had a strong electronic music department, and a year later I attended a memorable outdoor concert there by Morton Subotnick. Later at CalArts, I heard live works by Max Neuhaus, Harold Budd, and Charlemagne Palestine. In 1972, Philip Glass and his ensemble performed "Music in Changing Parts" in the main gallery at CalArts, and when that extremely loud forty-five-minute piece ended abruptly, I experienced the sensation of levitating for a few seconds.

Paul Strand Retrospective
At CalArts I began to gravitate toward photography. But after a couple of years of photo-conceptualism I was aching for something that had more seriousness and gravity. My big insight arrived when the Paul Strand retrospective came to the Los Angeles County Museum of Art. In the consummate perfection of Strand's composition and printmaking, I discovered that there was a lot to learn from and emulate. A year after encountering his work I purchased a 4-by-5-inch view camera and began making my own photographs. In an act of youthful rebellion, I put aside my interest in the New York avant-garde (Rauschenberg, Cage, Cunningham, Serra, Michelson, Frampton) and moved heavily into 1930s modernist photography as an area of intense study.

It would take me a few more years to synthesize the divergent strains of avant-garde dance, film, and music with the modernist photography I discovered in Los Angeles. I combined all these early influences in 1980–81 to create a group of abstract photographs that combined the chance procedures of Cage and Cunningham, the jewellike perfection of Paul Strand, the erudition of Hollis Frampton, and the radical aspiration of Annette Michelson.

James Welling is a professor in the department of art and the area head of photography at the University of California, Los Angeles.

In 2013, a major traveling survey, *James Welling: Monograph*, was organized by the Cincinnati Art Museum, accompanied by a catalog published by Aperture Foundation.

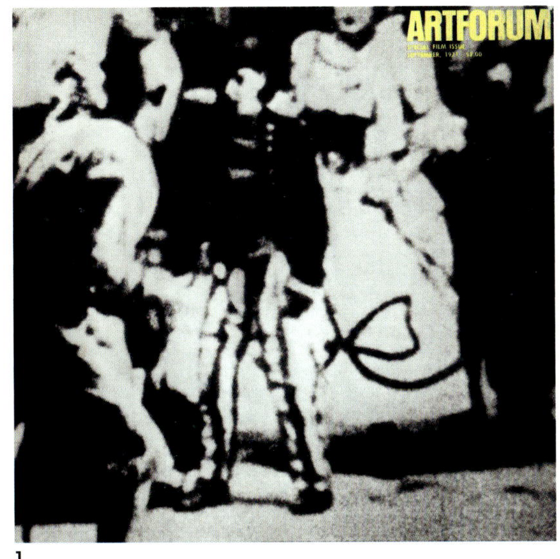

1

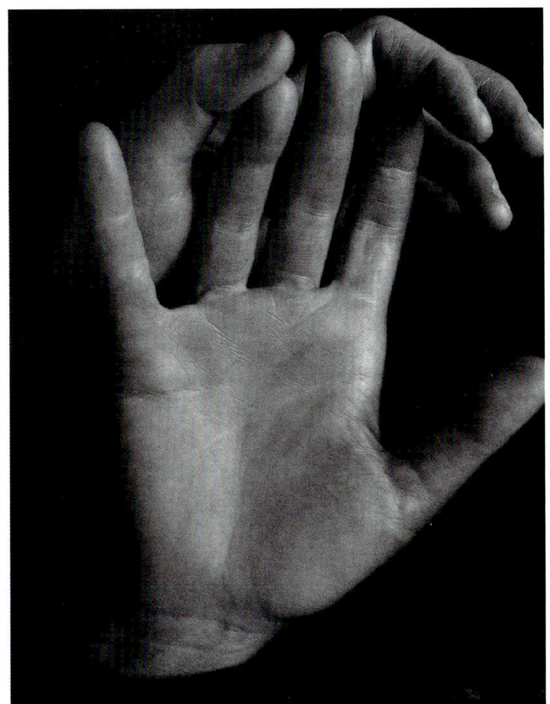

2

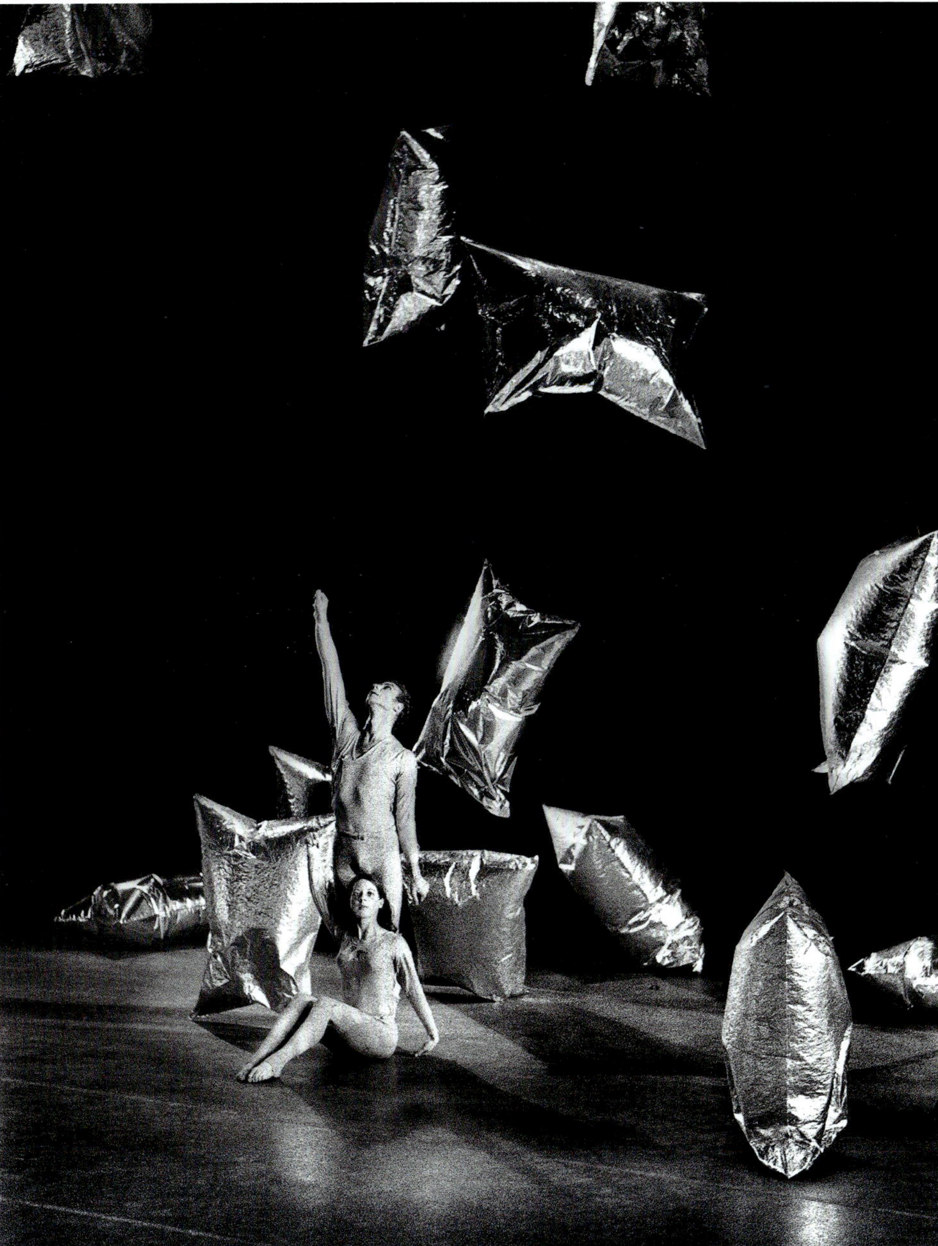

3

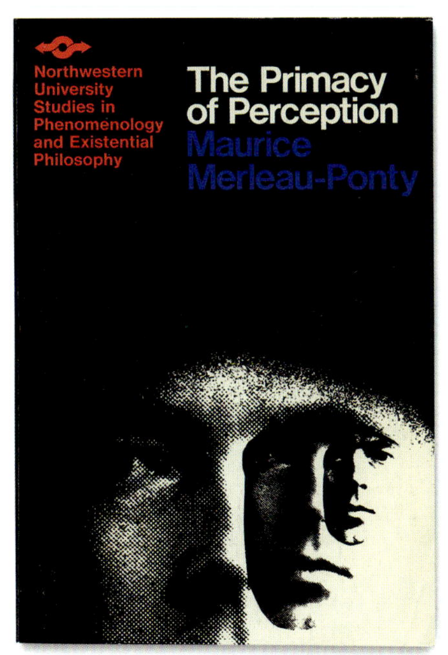

4

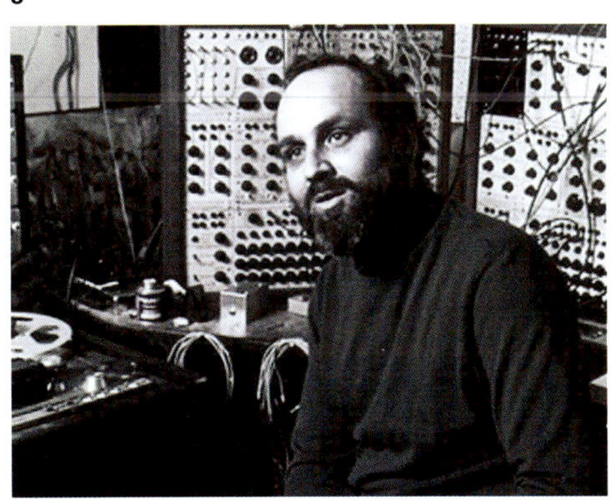

5

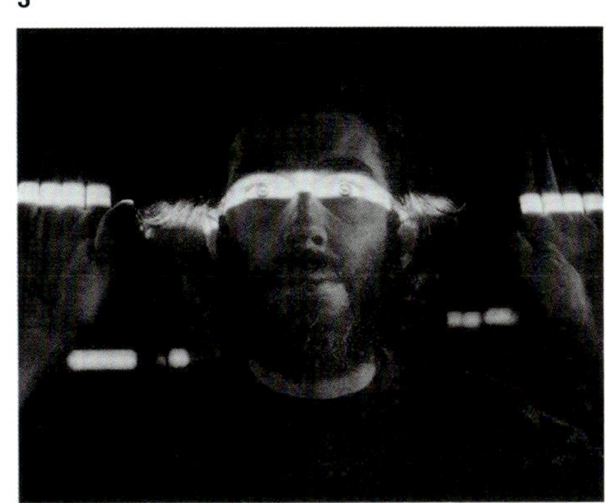

6

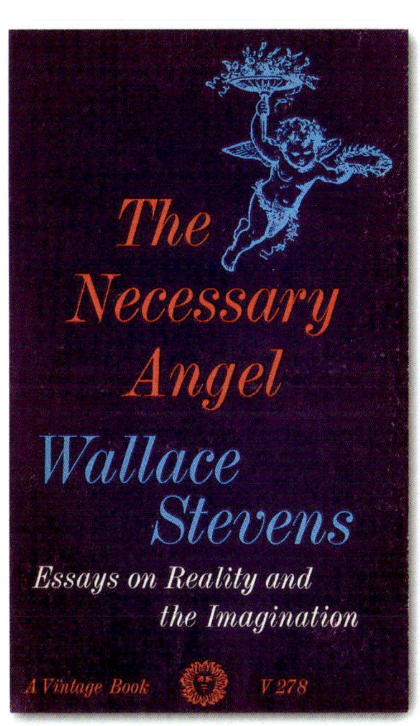

7

Collectors
The Poets
On Recent Acquisitions

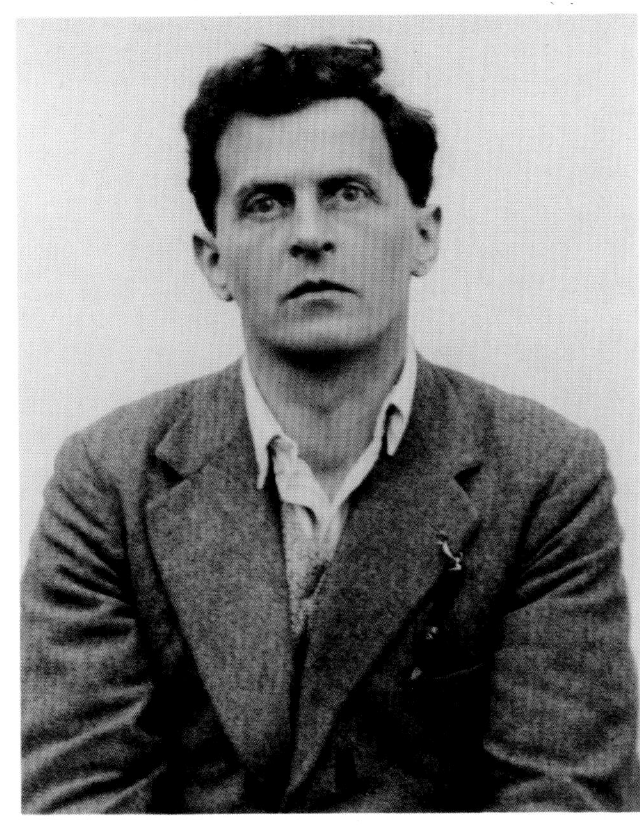

The Fellowship Photograph (Portrait of Ludwig Wittgenstein), 1929.
Photographer unknown

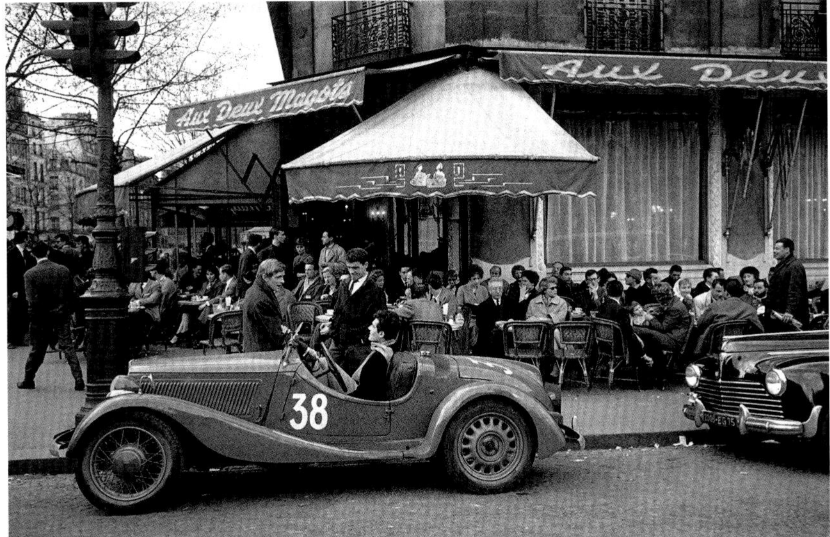

Sergio Larrain, *Boulevard Saint-Germain, Before the Deux Magots Café*, 1959
© Sergio Larrain/Magnum Photos

John Ashbery

I lived in Paris mostly from 1955 to 1965. This photograph, called *Boulevard Saint-Germain, Before the Deux Magots Café*, Paris 1959, is by Sergio Larrain. The Café Deux Magots was a favorite hangout of mine, at least when I was flush enough to afford it. I could conceivably have been there when the picture was taken. The photograph sums up beautifully the atmosphere of Paris on a rather chilly autumn afternoon, with well-dressed and well-behaved tourists sipping their *café exprès* and two fashionable cars, a sports car and a sedan. The three people chatting around the sports car are almost crystallizations of Parisians of that now-distant era. The young man at far left, with his back to the camera, is an iconic silhouette of the time, with pleasantly rumpled clothes and both shoes planted firmly on the pavement. I keep this card tucked into a picture frame over my desk to remind me of the past in all its melancholy variety.

John Ashbery is the author of more than twenty volumes of poetry. He has been the recipient of a Pulitzer Prize, a National Book Award, and a MacArthur Grant, among many other honors.

Ann Lauterbach

I live in an old schoolhouse, built in 1885, in Germantown, New York. It has a large room with south-facing windows. Along the walls, above wainscoting, at about waist height, there is a very narrow, slightly indented shelf that, I am told, once held chalk.

It now supports my collection of poetry chapbooks and the occasional postcard portrait of writers: Proust, Samuel Beckett, and this startling one of Ludwig Wittgenstein, known as *The Fellowship Photograph*, taken by an unknown photographer. It was sent to me some years ago by the poet Mónica de la Torre, with a note about a piece of mine she was publishing in the *Brooklyn Rail*. For so many years, postcards stitched us to one another and to the world! The Wittgenstein photograph is unsettling; it's as if he can barely see out from his mind's fervent activity. There's something eerie about looking back at him, into his uncomfortable, intelligent eyes, and thinking about the silence that every photograph compels us to acknowledge. I think about this silence often, and the indifference of images to it, and the ways in which captions try, but ultimately fail, to undermine it. Wittgenstein thought a lot about the relationship of silence to words, which is probably why so many poets cherish his writing. He is very good company.

Ann Lauterbach received a Guggenheim Fellowship in 1986 and a MacArthur Grant in 1993. Her most recent book is *Under the Sign* (Penguin, 2013). She teaches at Bard College.

Richard Howard

I have lived with this photograph taken by the artist David Alexander for the last five years. It consists of a repetitive frieze of three horizontal rows of the same alternating pair of dogs' *faces* beneath a slender horizontal strip of what is too severely cerulean to be an indubitable sky. The two dogs' multiplied faces stare straight ahead, interrupted only on the lower right corner of these repeating posters by four identical placards of an oddly shrimplike image which eclipses all but the sable ear tips of one puppy and the even sabler nose and chin of the other. In front of the dogs is an alluring fire hydrant which offers a curiously practical attraction to the multiple pairs of dogs. Considering the shiny wet surface in which the hydrant stands, it is possible, even likely, that all the poster dogs have already taken advantage of the opportunity.

Richard Howard, as you can tell, is a devoted dog lover as well as a teacher and translator, notably of works by Baudelaire and Barthes. He was awarded the Pulitzer Prize in 1970 and a MacArthur Grant in 1996. His latest book of poems, *A Progressive Education*, was released this fall by Turtle Point Press.

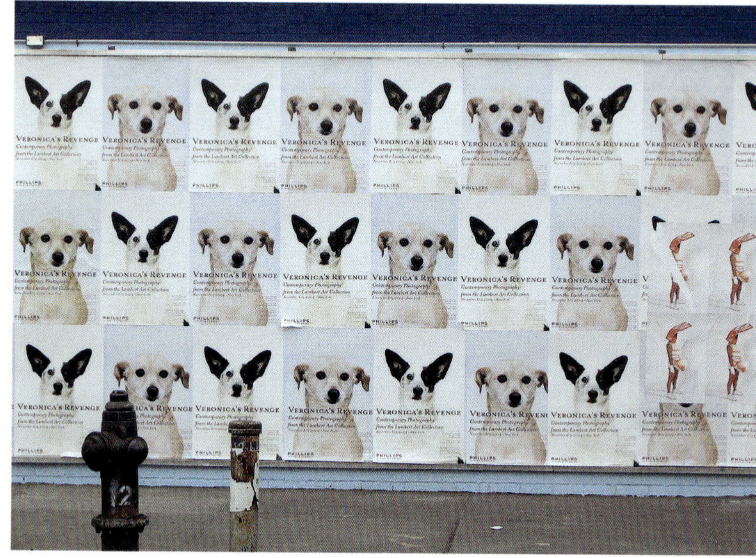

David Alexander, *Dogs and Hydrant*, 2014 Courtesy the artist

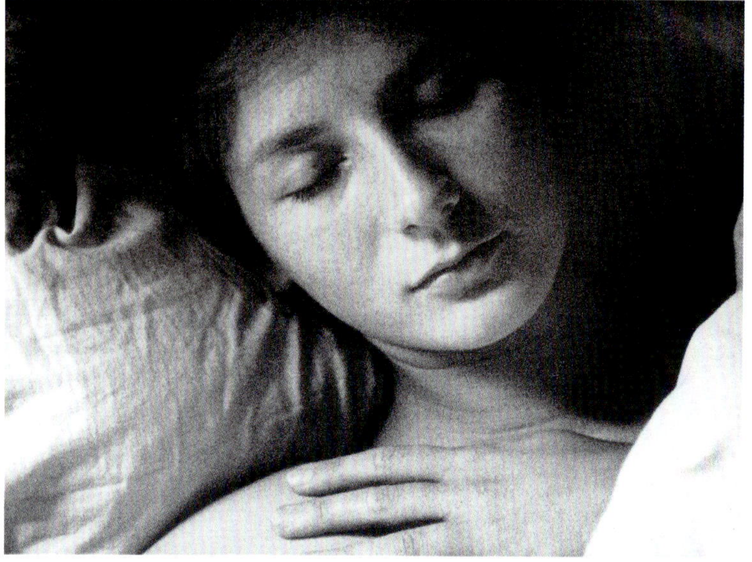

Stills from Chris Marker, *La Jetée*, 1962
Courtesy Argos Films

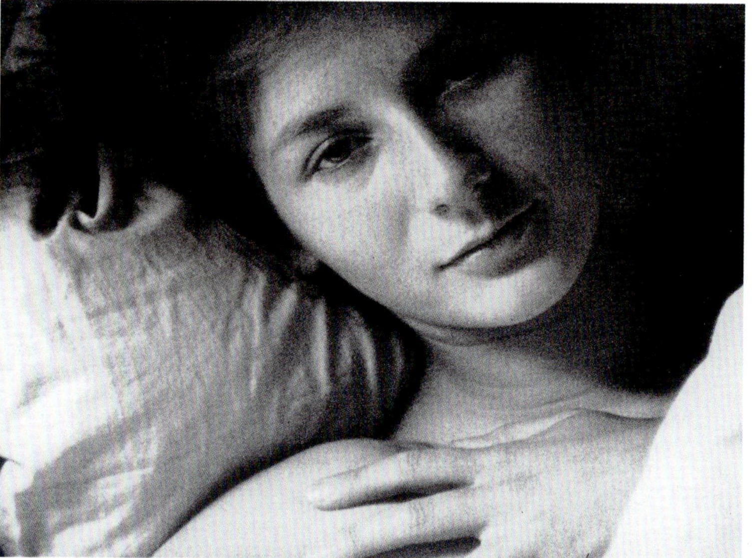

Ben Lerner

Chris Marker's *La Jetée* is composed entirely of stills—save for one brief shot of a woman opening her eyes. This image—the last shot in the photomontage before it briefly becomes a "motion picture"—is a photograph on the verge of becoming film, a flickering between media and their distinct temporalities. I've had various images of the image: a cellphone capture of it from a screen, a page in the book version of *La Jetée*—and what I find most haunting about the photograph is that I always feel her eyes are about to open, to look at me. All photographs I can think of are in the past tense, even if it's the instant past of Instagram—except for this one, which I feel like you have to be careful not to wake.

Ben Lerner is the author of three books of poetry, and the novel *Leaving the Atocha Station*. His second novel, *10:04*, was released by Faber/FSG in September.

Patron
LARS WINDHORST

Special thanks to

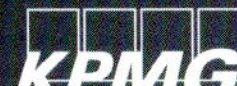

KPMG

LOTTO
STIFTUNG
BERLIN

We
Turn
You
On

Opening Amerika Haus
The Place for Photography
30 October 2014

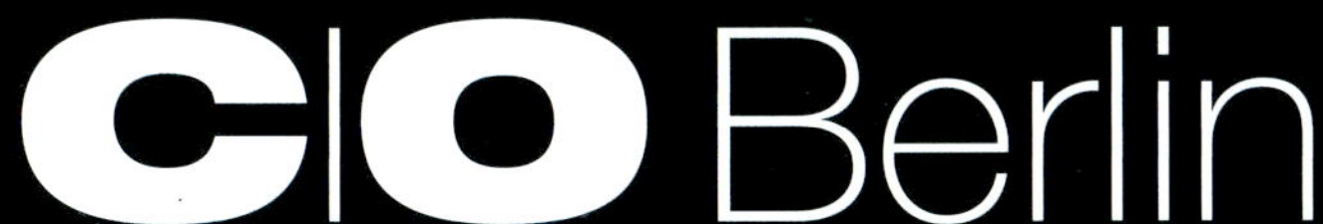

C|O Berlin

Amerika Haus
Hardenbergstr. 22–24 . 10623 Berlin
www.co-berlin.org

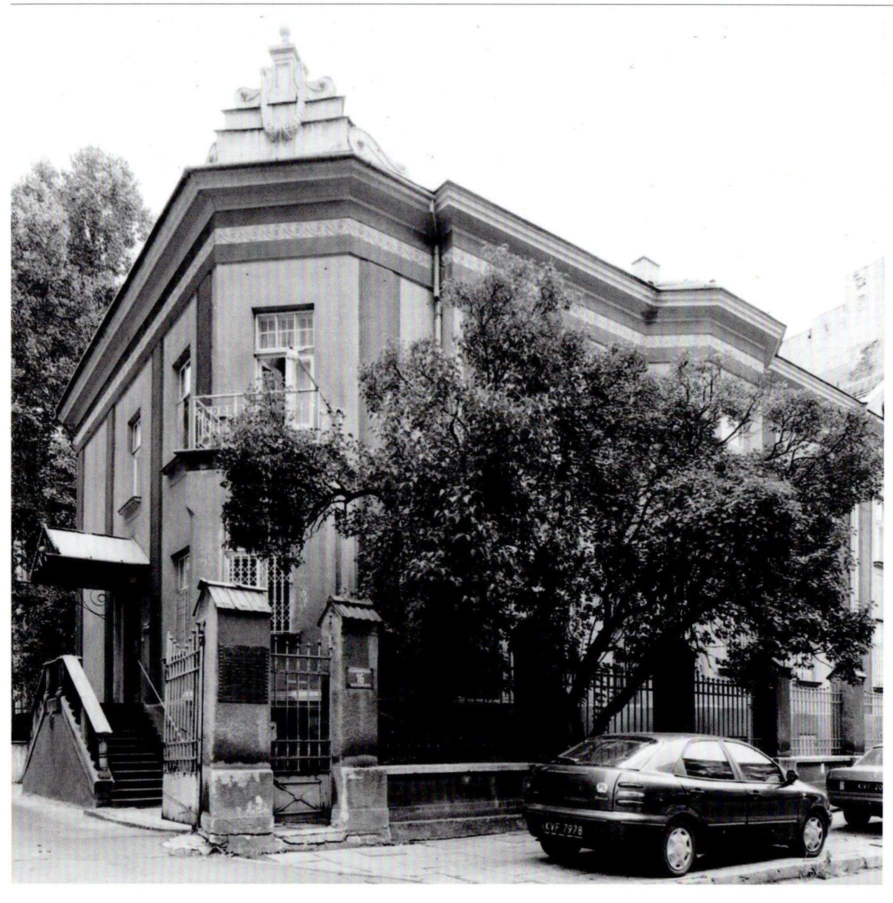
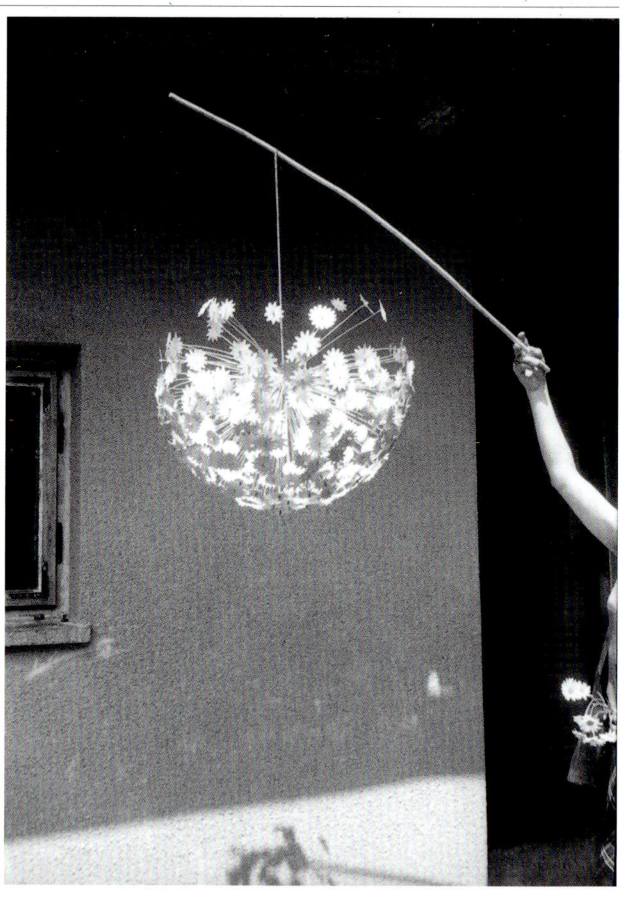
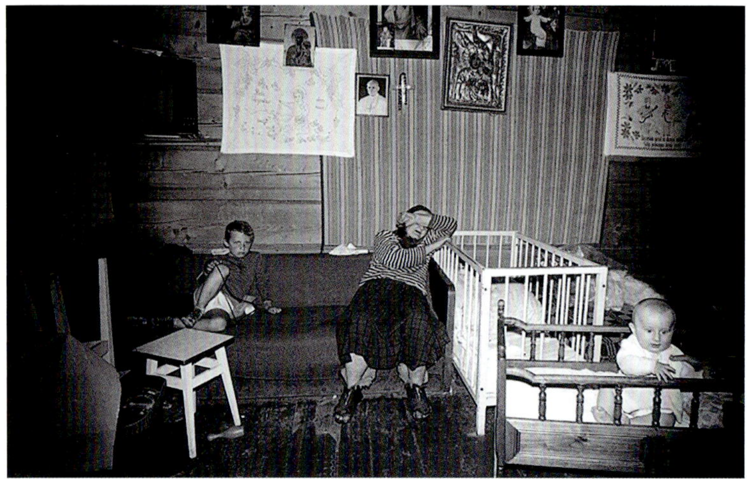
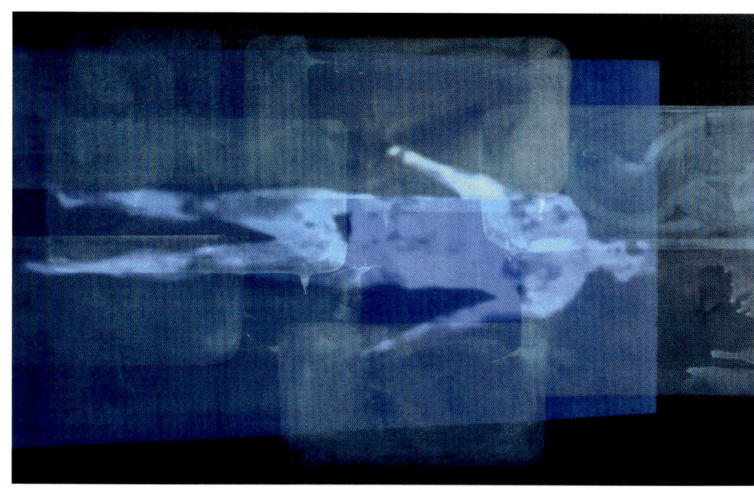
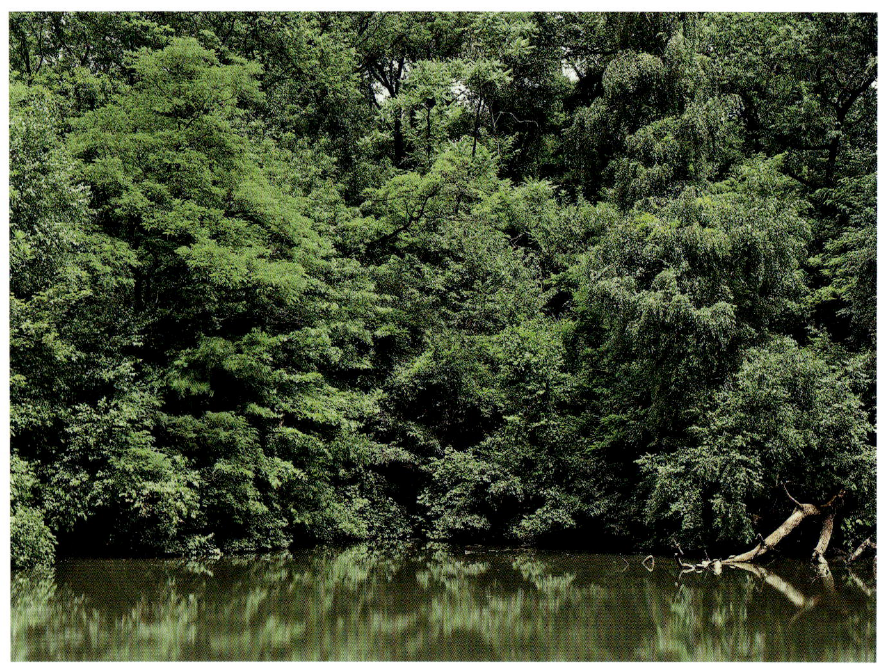
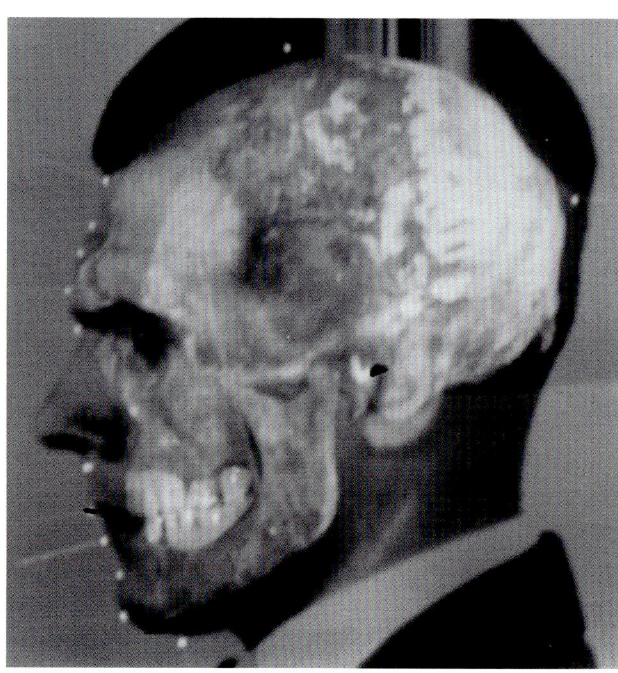

Wojciech Nowicki on Krakow

Opposite, clockwise from
top left:

Exterior view, Museum of
the History of Photography,
Krakow, Poland
Courtesy Archive of the
Museum of the History of
Photography, Krakow, Poland

Untitled, 2014, from the
series *FOLK: A Personal
Ethnography*, 2014.
Photographer unknown
© Aaron Schuman

Dominik Lejman,
Nothing to Add, 2011
Courtesy SOR Rusche
Sammlung, Berlin

Thomas Keenan, *Face-Skull
Superimposition of
Josef Mengele*, 1985
Courtesy Maja Helmer

Trevor Paglen, *Angelus
Novus*, 2012
© Trevor Paglen

Zofia Rydet, Biały Dunajec
region, Poland, 1985. From
the *Sociological Record*
project, 1978–90
© Zofia Augustyńska-
Martyniak

Krakow, Poland, is called a "festival city," and indeed, the city hosts many: literature, film, music (from classical to contemporary), and, finally, Photomonth, the most important photography festival in the country. After 1989, i.e., following the fall of communism, the Krakow photography scene was reborn, along with the rest of the country. Until then the city had one gallery specializing in photography, belonging to the Polish Photography Artists' Union (ZPAF), a sort of professional photographers' association, which was open to few prior to 1989 and which distributed privileges, including official commissions. (This small gallery, which has undergone various changes and management, is today back in the hands of the union.) Krakow is also home to the Museum of the History of Photography, founded in 1972— Poland's only museum exclusively devoted to the medium, with a permanent exhibition on the history of photography. Its collection includes a good deal of photography equipment and a sizable group of autochromes; works by members of the Polish Photoclub, an organization founded in the 1930s; and work by avant-garde artists of the latter half of the twentieth century. And yet, surprisingly, the venue is not an important site on the cultural map. Situated somewhat out of the way, in a cramped little palace, and lacking decently sized galleries, the museum attracts few visitors and little media attention.

Thus the Photomonth festival, organized by the Foundation for Visual Arts, has come to occupy a central role in Krakow's photography scene. From its humble beginnings twelve years ago, the festival has since developed relationships with Krakow's most important museums and galleries, including the National Museum, the Museum of Contemporary Art, the Ethnographic Museum, the Manggha Museum of Japanese Art and Technology, and Starmach Gallery, all of which participate in the festival by offering exhibition space. Photomonth has at times taken on organizing themes such as "Fashion" or "Alias," the latter an ambitious play on artistic identity curated by the photography team Adam Broomberg and Oliver Chanarin in 2011. It eschewed a thematic structure in 2012, when the whole program was programmatically unprogrammed and included a broad spectrum of work from Rodchenko to the recently deceased Polish avant-gardist Jerzy Lewczyński, and other exhibitions that might not have fit earlier themes. This intense engagement with photography is further augmented with portfolio reviews, film screenings, slide-show presentations, and numerous social events held across this medieval city that doesn't sleep—and those who aren't sated by the festival's ample offerings can look to the additional spin-off exhibitions staged around the city, some facilitated by Krakow Photo Fringe.

This year, Photomonth's main program was curated by Aaron Schuman, an American photographer residing in London, and the editor and publisher of *SeeSaw Magazine*, an online publication. Titled *Re:Search*, the festival was a self-described "celebration of photography…as an autonomous form of study, investigation, and pursuit." It explored the connections between photography and science, and featured work by Taryn Simon, Clare Strand, Trevor Paglen, and Schuman, as well as theorists Thomas Keenan and Eyal Weizman. The "experimental" section, titled *Echoes* and organized by Jakub Woynarowski, a Polish interdisciplinary artist, designer, and curator, dovetailed with the presiding theme: it was a meditation of sorts on the translatability of the language of photography into senses other than sight.

The Foundation for Visual Arts has more brewing than this ambitious festival. In 2013, the organization joined Krakow's Zofia Rydet Foundation in

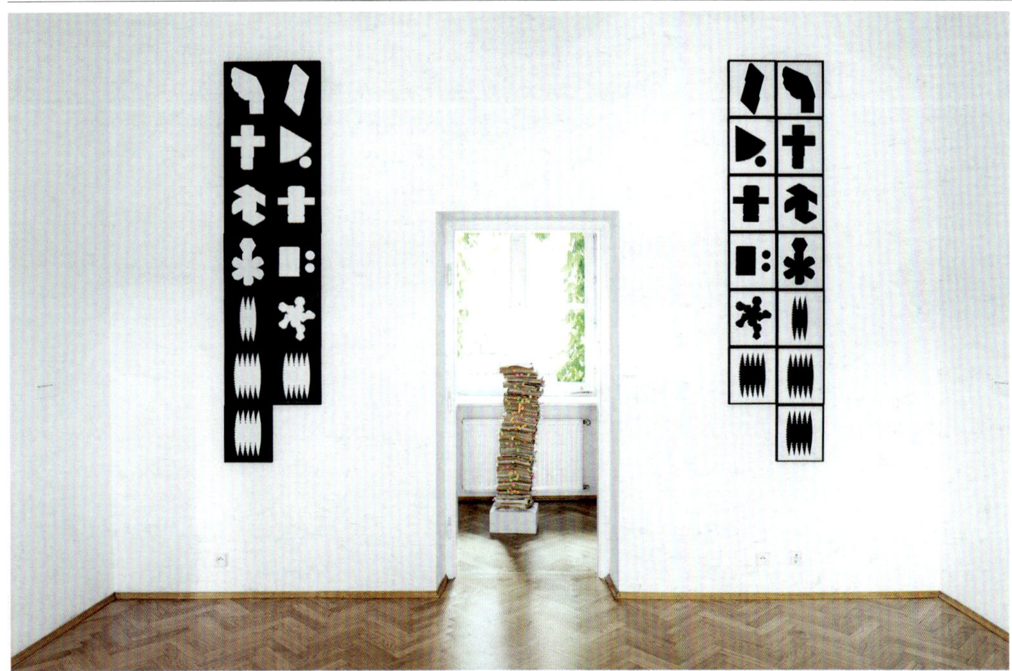

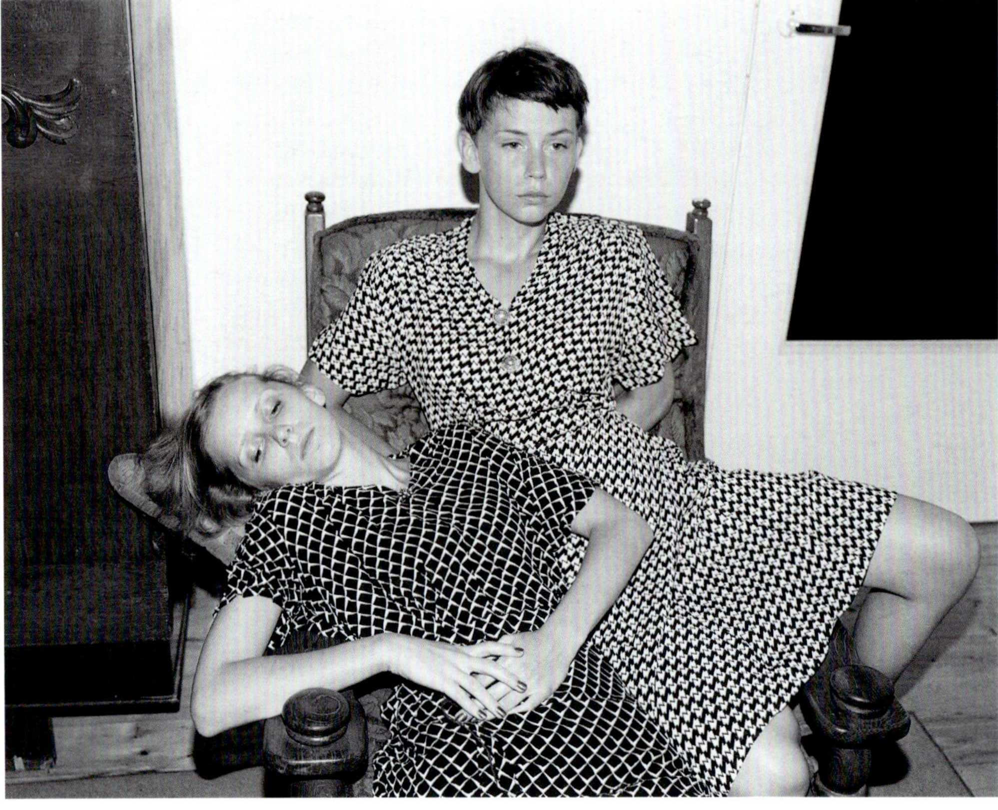

Top:
Installation view of
Clare Strand's exhibition
Further Reading, at the
Szolayski House, National
Museum, Krakow, Poland,
2014, part of Krakow
Photomonth 2014.
Photograph by Studio Luma
© Studio Luma

Bottom:
Joanna Piotrowska,
Frowst XXIV, 2014
Courtesy the artist

doors internationally for young artists. Though photography is taught in Krakow at the Academy of Photography, where the lecturers are well-established Polish photographers, curators, and art historians, young Poles (and older ones too) increasingly study abroad. The Institute of Creative Photography (Institut tvůrčí fotografie) in Opava, Czech Republic, is a popular destination among schools, but many relocate to Berlin or London, like Joanna Piotrowska, who studied at the Royal College of Art, and whose photobook *Frowst* recently received the First Book Award, a prize created three years ago by the National Media Museum in West Yorkshire, England, in partnership with MACK books.

The growing interest in photography as an artistic medium means that several galleries have begun organizing exhibitions and selling photographs in the city, among them Dyląg Gallery, Zderzak Gallery, and ZPAF Gallery. State institutions—this includes the National Museum in Krakow, the Ethnographic Museum, and Manggha Museum—are also catching up, slowly making visitors accustomed to the regular presence of photography in their displays. Partly as a result of the difficult situation currently experienced by press photographers due to the field's changing economy, photography in Krakow operates more independently within a fine-art context and is less tied to the large state institutions.

After years of documenting, by official request, the alleged successes of the Communist model on the one hand, and, unofficially, the dark side of life in a Communist state, as well as those fragments of religious life that didn't fit the guidelines of Communist propaganda (large-scale masses, papal pilgrimages), today documentary photography in Krakow is more likely to concern corporate life or intimate expressions of private life. The greatest change, however, is in the way photography is produced and encountered: it has migrated from newspapers and magazines to the walls of galleries and online. Not that there is anything particularly regional in this change. It just means the world has greater access to Polish photographers, and vice versa.

tackling the digitization and release of a monumental unfinished series by Zofia Rydet, titled *Sociological Record*, created between 1978 and 1997. This project is a record of families in interiors, generally with a backdrop of a country house, showing a Poland of the past: a poor country of peasants dressed in humble clothing. The project exists as a website (zofiarydet.com) and will be exhibited in the future at Warsaw's Museum of Modern Art and packaged as a major publication.

Indeed, the pace of change and political transformation that occurred in Poland over the last quarter-century has been significant, opening many

Wojciech Nowicki is
a Krakow-based writer
and curator.

Moyra Davey,
Valerie Plame, 2013
(detail)

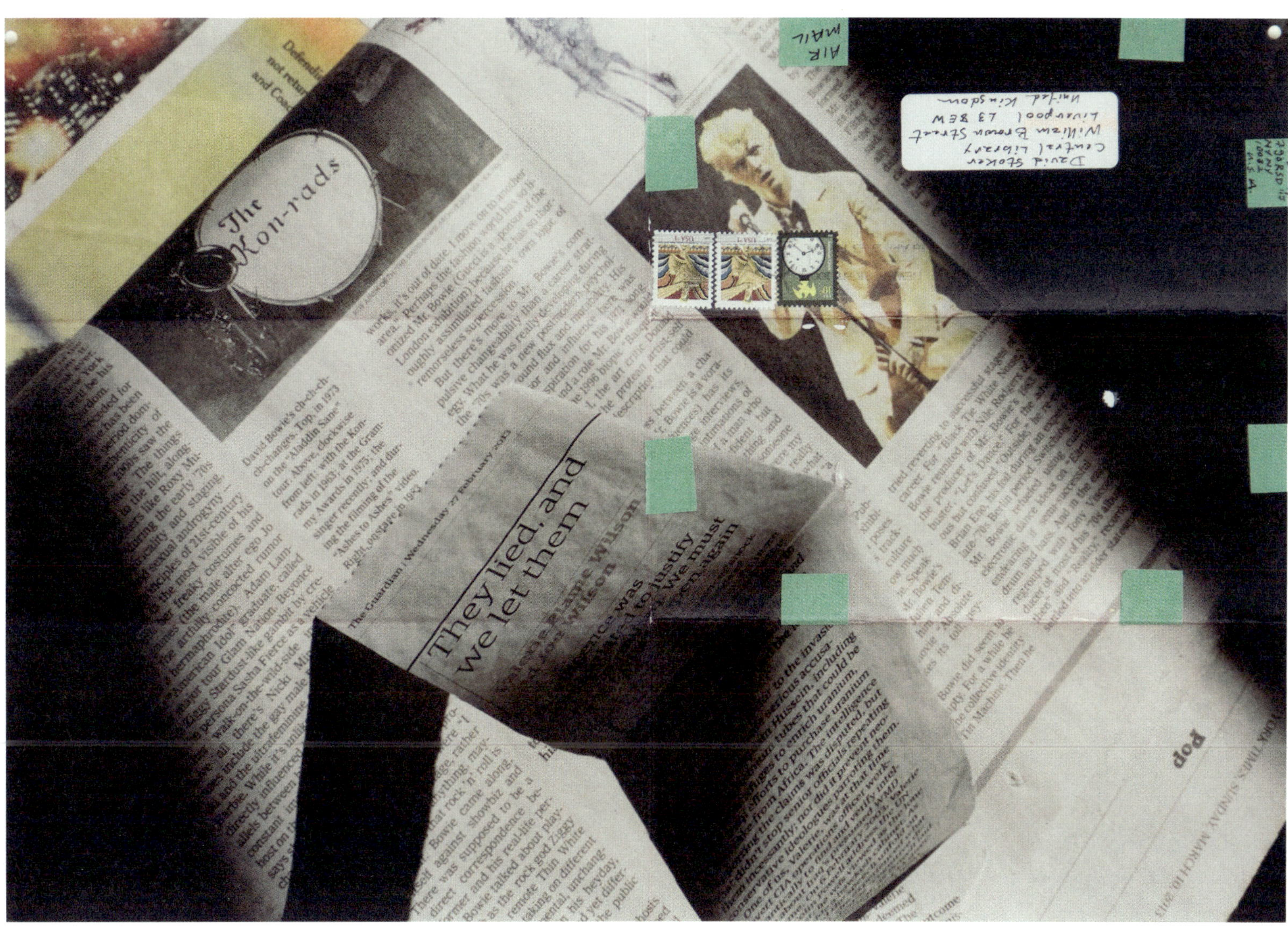

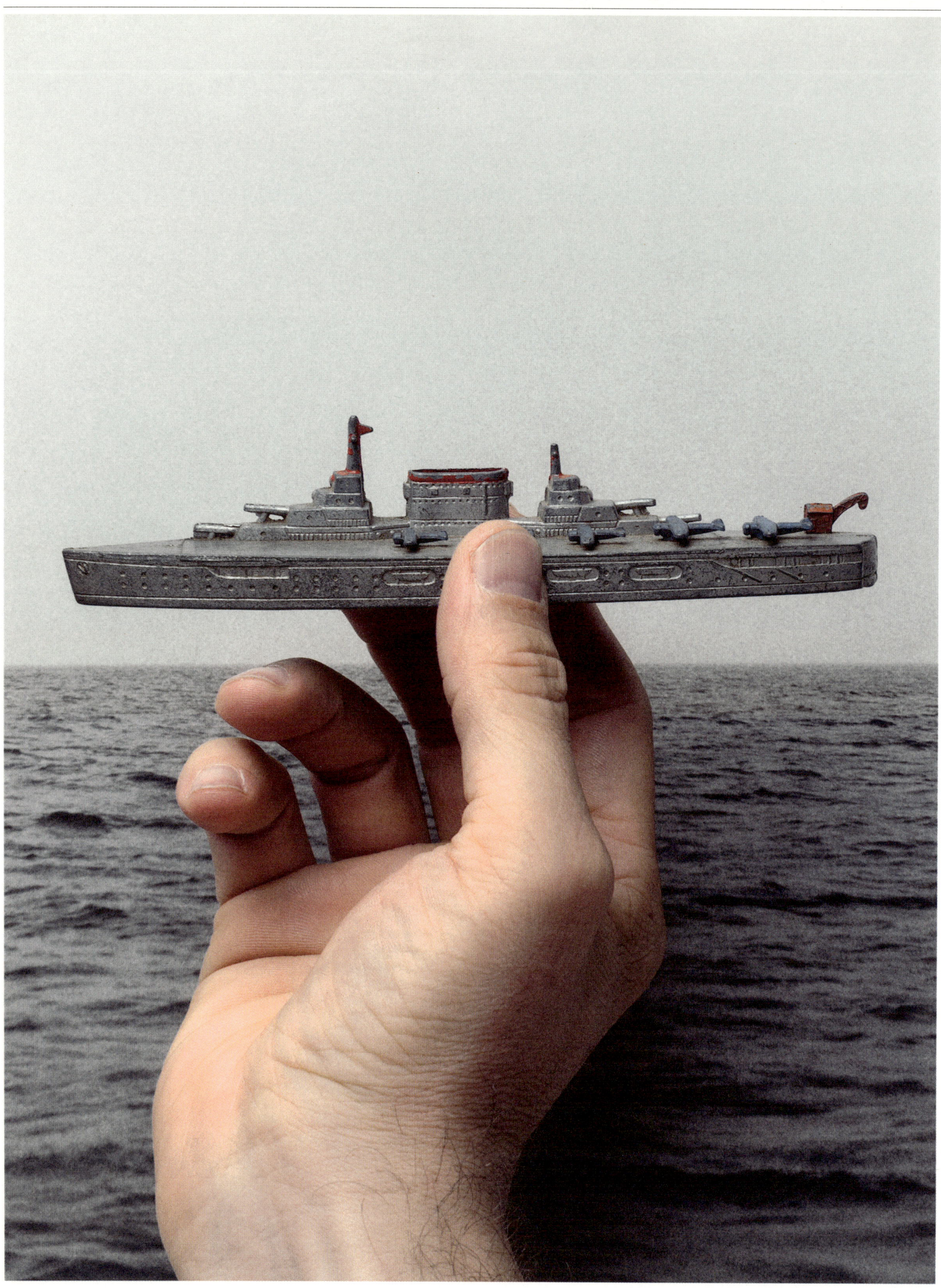

Geoff Dyer
&
Janet Malcolm

On Photography, Writing, and Aircraft Carriers

Of the influential British art critic and novelist John Berger, writer Geoff Dyer deems most striking Berger's "ability to keep looking, staring at a picture until it yields its secrets." Dyer's comment appears during the following exchange with critic Janet Malcolm. Dyer and Malcolm, two distinguished writers on photography, were drawn to the medium for different reasons. Although Malcolm suggests that they may even reside within different rooms in photography's many mansions, both agree that good writing on images begins with an urge to "keep looking."

Malcolm is a longtime staff writer for the *New Yorker* and a force in American writing and journalism. She is the author of more than ten books, which include *Diana & Nikon: Essays on the Aesthetic of Photography* (1980); *The Journalist and the Murderer* (1990); *The Silent Woman: Sylvia Plath and Ted Hughes* (1994); *Two Lives: Gertrude and Alice* (2007); and *Iphigenia in Forest Hills: Anatomy of a Murder Trial* (2011). Her recent collection *Forty-One False Starts: Essays on Artists and Writers* (2013) includes, among other pieces, writings on Diane Arbus and Thomas Struth and a brilliant 1986 portrait of *Artforum* then-editor Ingrid Sischy, and demonstrates that, no matter the subject, Malcolm's approach is analytical and precise, almost photographically so.

Geoff Dyer is equally catholic in his selection of topics, usually approached in a pleasurably digressive style entirely his own. His book about photography, *The Ongoing Moment* (2005), is organized around various photographers' handling of subjects, from blind individuals to hats to benches. Dyer warns his readers in the book's introduction: "I suspect that this book will be a source of irritation to many people, especially those who know more about photography than I do." Surely even the most informed readers benefited from his unique approach. Dyer's other books include *Out of Sheer Rage* (1997), an achingly funny book about not writing a book about D.H. Lawrence; an essay collection titled *Otherwise Known as the Human Condition* (2011, winner of a National Book Critics Circle Award for Criticism); *Zona* (2012), about Andrei Tarkovsky's film *Stalker*; and most recently, *Another Great Day at Sea: Life Aboard the USS* George H.W. Bush (2014).

When *Aperture* asked Dyer and Malcolm this past summer to correspond about their respective practices as writers who share an abiding interest in photography, the ensuing email exchange took place over a number of weeks, with Dyer corresponding from his temporary residence in Venice, California, and Malcolm from her summer home in rural Massachusetts. The conversation is fittingly interrupted at one point by a summer storm; an impasse is overcome, improbably, by a surprisingly relevant discussion of aircraft carriers. Dyer and Malcolm may not reveal any secrets as to how they both so precisely bring their subjects into sharp focus. Indeed, there may be none to reveal— aside from a preternatural talent for translating close looking into shrewd writing. **—The Editors**

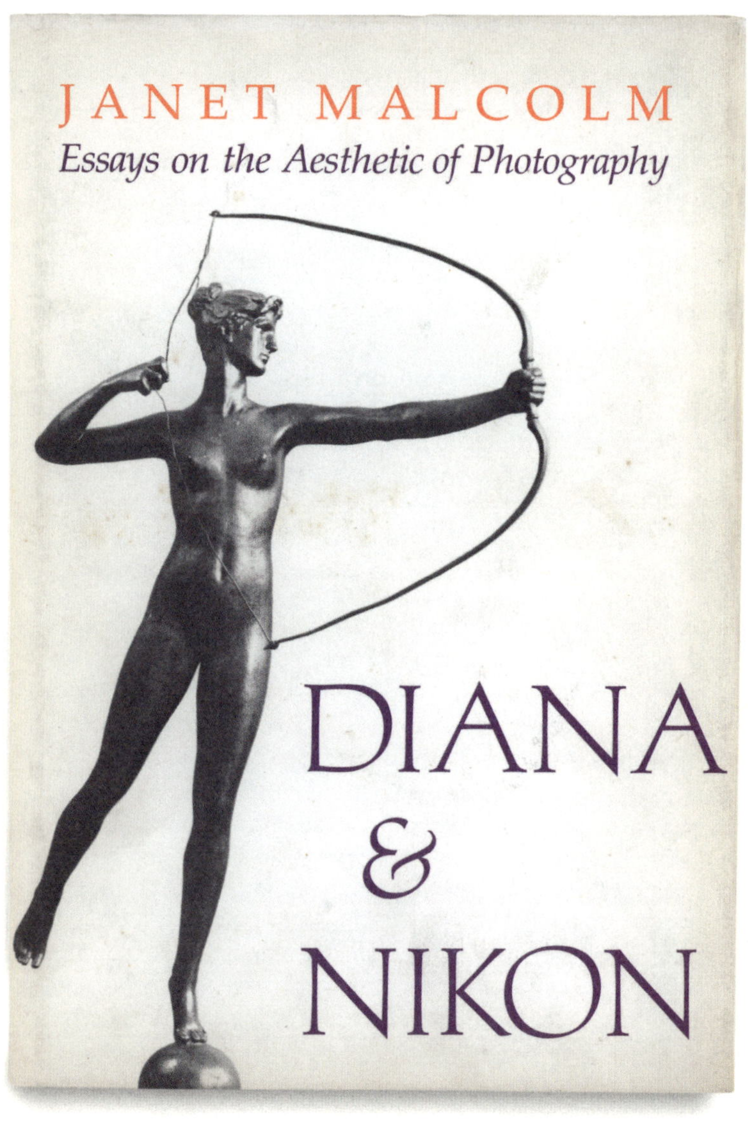

Geoff Dyer: **How did you first become interested in photography? Did this interest precede your writing about it or did the two things occur more or less simultaneously? At the risk of preempting your answer, at what point did an interest in photographs or photographers become an interest in photography?**

Janet Malcolm: Like Julia Margaret Cameron, I became interested in photography when a relative gave me a camera. Unlike Mrs. Cameron, I did not become a great photographer, or even a good one. I learned no technique. Most of the pictures I took were either under- or overexposed. Chance dictated that some images emerged clearly. But I loved taking pictures and would take the camera—a Leica M3—on all trips.

I had read that Cartier-Bresson thought of his Leica as an extension of his eye, considering it a great improvement over the large, heavy cameras that were its predecessors. It permitted him to run around Paris having his decisive moments. It has taken me years to realize that (1) traveling with a camera and seeing everything through its eye rather than through one's own may not be the best way to see the world, and (2) the Leica is not a lightweight object but a heavy, cumbersome thing when compared to the deliciously lightweight point-and-shoot and cellphone cameras of today.

I began writing about photography with the spurious authority of the young. I probably thought that my experience as an amateur photographer was some sort of qualification. Above all, I was inspired by John Szarkowski's brilliant directorship of the Museum of Modern Art's photography department and by his book *Looking at Pictures*. What about you? How did you come to write about photography? What drew you to it?

GD: **Almost entirely it was reading about it (rather than actually looking at pictures). The big three: you know, two *B*s and an *S*—Barthes, Berger, and Sontag—and a bit of a third *B*: Benjamin. I wrote a few small things on photographers for British papers and then I became very interested in photographs of jazz musicians when I was writing *But Beautiful* in 1989, particularly in the question of whether, or how, to convey sound visually. But I was using the pictures mainly as a source for fiction so was far more concerned with the people in the pictures than I was with the people who took them, something I became interested in only later. (That happened when I realized that a picture of D.H. Lawrence was also a picture by Edward Weston.) I still think jazz is an art form that's been very well served by photography. Do you know Roy DeCarava's amazing picture of Ben Webster and John Coltrane?**

JM: No, I don't.

GD: **I didn't know it at the time I was writing *But Beautiful* but wish I had, especially since DeCarava, in *The Sound I Saw*, had very consciously explored the question that interested me. Webster is cuddling him—Coltrane!—with such rough tenderness. There it is: tradition in jazz condensed into a single picture. I still love it—it's so intimate and telling—even though DeCarava turned out to be impossible about having his pictures reproduced in *The Ongoing Moment*. That's a subject—the right to reproduce images—I'm sure we'll want to come back to. Anyway, my knowledge of photography was still very scanty in the early 1990s. I remember going to dinner at John Berger's place in the Paris suburbs in 1991. Cartier-Bresson was there. The name rang some kind of bell but**

I wasn't sure if he was a film director or a maker of watches. In 1997 I was invited to the Center for Documentary Studies in Durham, North Carolina, to help work on a book of photographs by William Gedney that Margaret Sartor was putting together. That's when I became aware of how incredibly ignorant I was about the history of photography and began to study it in a far more thorough way. Perhaps appropriately that's when and where I first read your book *Diana & Nikon*. I only read Szarkowski much later, by which time I had a sense of what a huge figure he was. I read and reviewed his Atget book—the one with a picture on one page and a few paragraphs of text on the facing page—which I think is one of the great books about photography and a beautiful work of art. (Incidentally, I hope I won't go to my grave without having done a similar kind of book—picture on verso page, text on recto or vice versa—myself.) He saw the review and sent me a signed copy of his book *Mr. Bristol's Barn*. Obviously that's something I treasure. Anyway, going back to what I said at the beginning, I'd be very interested to hear what Berger, Barthes, and Sontag—each of them—meant to you.

JM: I had to smile when I read your reply to my question. *Aperture* could not have brought together two people who are more apart in their relationship to photography than we are. Berger's, Barthes's, and Sontag's writings on photography have meant almost nothing to me. I struggled and failed to grasp Barthes's and Berger's thought, and while I could understand Sontag's, with a few exceptions (the Leni Riefenstahl piece, for example), I found her interests remote from mine.

The house of photography has many mansions, and you and I live in different parts of the building. You are on a high floor with a large view while I am in the garden apartment. The first publisher of *Diana & Nikon* gave the collection the rather clumsy subtitle "Essays on the Aesthetic of Photography." But what he had in mind was to distinguish my approach from Sontag's. These are conceptual writers, while I am—I don't know—someone who is better equipped to look at pictures than to think about what photography is.

So what are we going to talk about—aircraft carriers perhaps? I read your piece in the *New Yorker* about your experiences aboard one of those amazing vessels with the most enormous pleasure and admiration. I have been interested in aircraft carriers ever since I read a book called *We Captured a U-Boat* by Rear Admiral Daniel V. Gallery, in which an aircraft carrier called the *Guadalcanal* subdues a German submarine and tows it 1,700 miles back to America. The submarine is now in a museum in Chicago. Did you read this book in preparation for your project? I'm not sure why, but I think aircraft carriers will help get us over our impasse re: photography.

GD: As it happens I was on the carrier with a rather distinguished photographer, Chris Steele-Perkins, who was not at all happy, when he was sent proofs of the book, to find himself referred to throughout as "the snapper." And I've just written the introduction for a book of photographs of the U.S. Navy by An-My Lê, many of which were taken during her time aboard a carrier, so, yes, it's possible that the two subjects—photography and carriers—are not so remote. I haven't read *We Captured a U-Boat*, though it sounds exactly like the kind of thing I do like to read. But let's go back a bit. I'm not convinced that our apartments are quite as far apart as you claim, because *The Ongoing Moment* is actually made up of a whole lot of quite close readings of individual photographs,

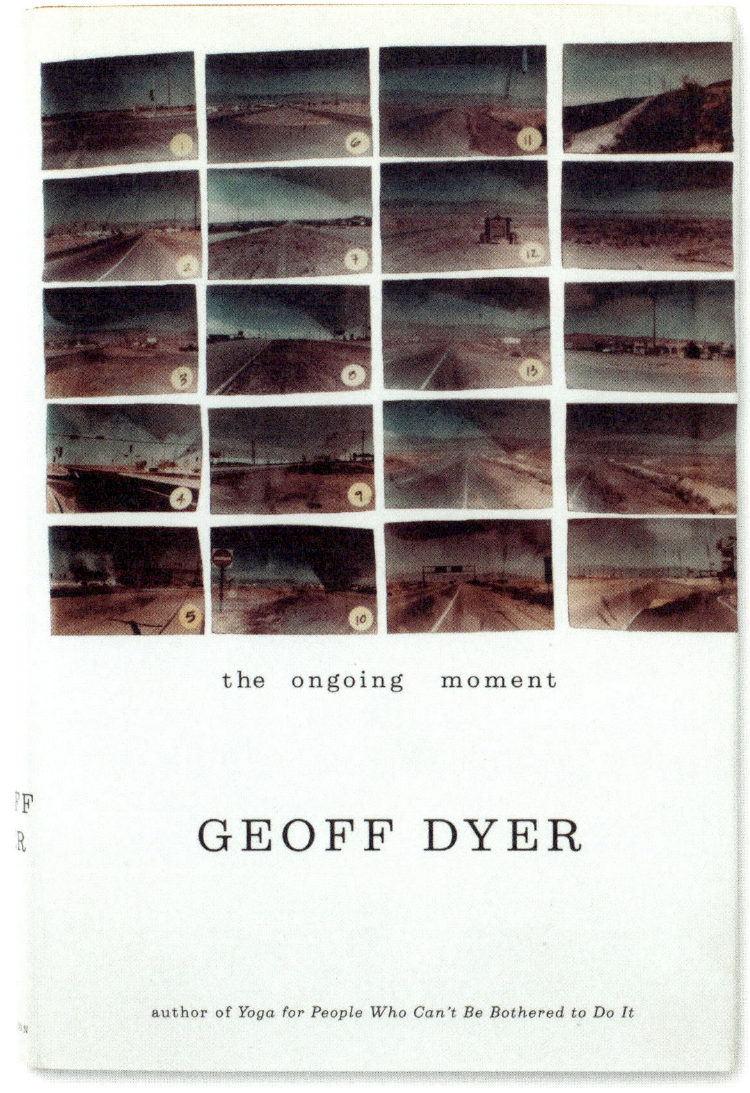

Geoff Dyer,
The Ongoing Moment,
(New York: Pantheon,
2005)

I began writing about photography with the spurious authority of the young. I probably thought that my experience as an amateur photographer was some sort of qualification.
— Janet Malcolm

The house of photography has many mansions, and you and I live in different parts of the building. You are on a high floor with a large view while I am in the garden apartment.

—Janet Malcolm

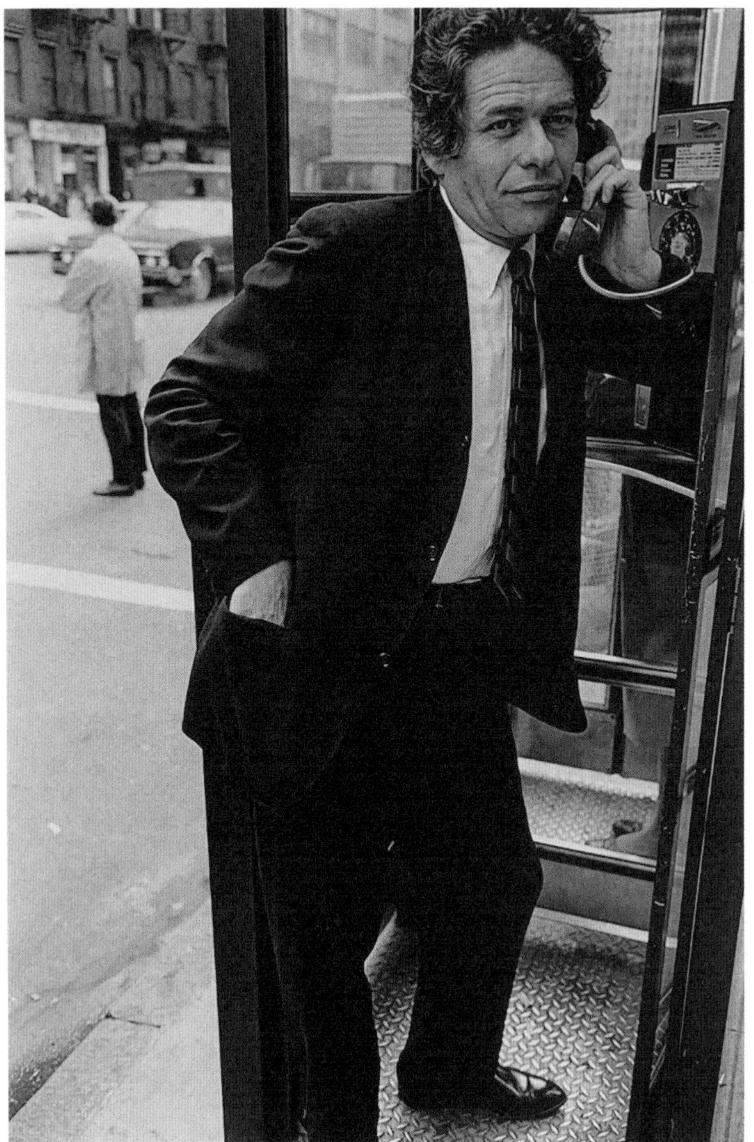

something I became interested in through … Berger! I think, for example, of his reading of the Kertész picture of *A Red Hussar Leaving Budapest* in *Another Way of Telling*, but there are loads of others. Berger's most distinctive quality, in my opinion, is his ability to keep looking, staring at a picture until it yields its secrets (which are often also its obviousnesses). There's an irony in what you say as well. Tod Papageorge, in his book *Passing Through Eden*, writes, "Garry Winogrand never read Roland Barthes, and found whatever he'd seen of Malcolm's and Sontag's original articles about photography in the *New Yorker* and the *New York Review of Books* grimly laughable." But from what you say here it turns out that you were of Winogrand's party after all! Except, it turns out, Papageorge is not being entirely reliable as a witness: in the catalog to the big SFMOMA show, curator Sarah Greenough points out that Winogrand's discovery of Sontag's writing was quite a big thing for him. He recommended her essays—admittedly not the ones directly on photography—to students at Rochester as a way of understanding his own work. I know you wrote about Winogrand briefly in *Diana & Nikon* but wonder if you are going to write about the Winogrand show now that it's at the Metropolitan Museum in New York? Frustratingly, I've missed it everywhere it's been so far, in Washington, D.C., by only about two days (but wrote about it anyway—looking very closely at a couple of pictures—in the *London Review of Books*, see lrb.co.uk). It seems to me, given what you said about the importance for you of Szarkowski, that quite a lot of stuff converges on Winogrand.

JM: Thanks for sending the link to your *London Review* piece on Winogrand, which gives us a text to engage with. You write that in Winogrand's late work:

> *A much smaller number of successful pictures resulted from a larger reservoir of images. And our response remains fundamentally unaltered too: we wanna see 'em anyway! More from the early years, more from the mature period, more from the last years even if much of it's not worth seeing.*

Even if much of it's not worth seeing! You are indeed smitten. I have to confess that over the years, I have changed my mind about Winogrand's photographs. I no longer "wanna see 'em." I find them consistently and uniformly uninteresting. I think I was wrong about them in my book. You write about "the mind-blowing amount of information [Winogrand] provided about the social landscape of America in the 1960s and 1970s." I don't see this information as anything special, anything you wouldn't find in any snapshot taken with a point-and-shoot (pointless-and-shoot?) camera.

The enormous, powerfully structured photographs of Thomas Struth and Andreas Gursky give us the valuable information I find lacking in Winogrand, information not available elsewhere. I suppose this kind of information (it would require many pages and much analysis to characterize it) can be found in all the best photographs. August Sander's portraits have it in spades.

I am in a remote country house in Massachusetts and we are having violent storms here that disrupt Internet access. So I had better send this off while I can, and take up some of the other points in your article when the weather calms down.

• • •

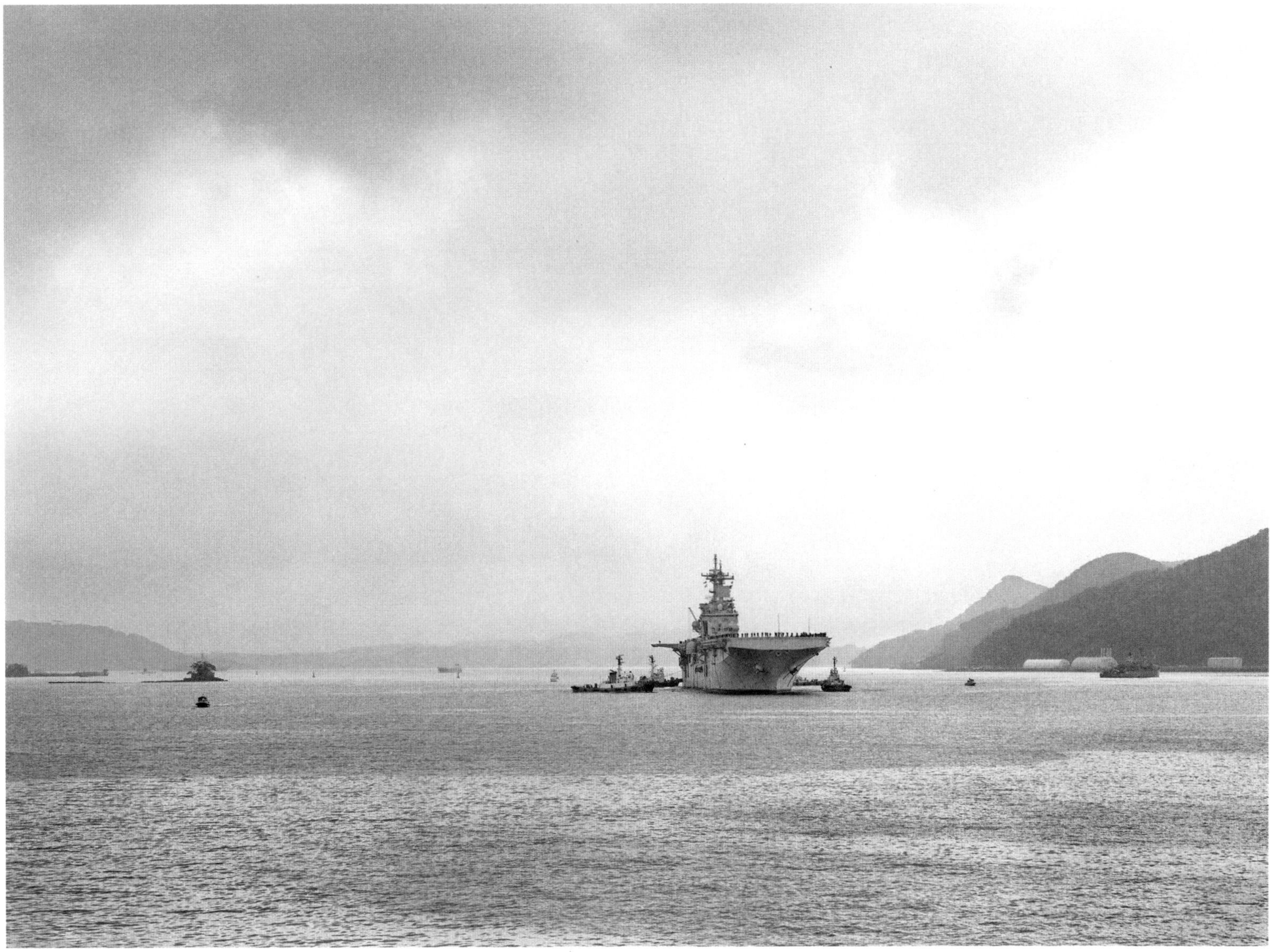

The sun has come out and the Internet has dried itself off
and returned, so I can get back to your Winogrand article and
to the "twinned pictures" by Winogrand and Tod Papageorge
with which you end it. These pictures are essentially the same
picture. You tell us that Winogrand and his disciple Papageorge
"were out photographing together." They evidently came upon
the mystifying sight of the couple leaning against a tree kissing,
with a woman leaning against the other side of the tree who
is dressed like and exactly resembles the woman being kissed.
Both photographers took the picture, though we don't know
whether they did so simultaneously or if one took the picture
first and the other followed. In either case, the question of
authorship comes up. Whose picture is it? Are pictures there
for anyone to "take"? Or are they made by the photographer?
You discuss the slight differences between the two pictures
and conclude that Winogrand's version is better. But would
you agree that there is something complicated going on here
that neither of us have put our finger on?

GD: **Well, I was sort of joking about wanting to see the
stuff that's not worth seeing, or at least that was meant to
be a jokey way of summing up the Winogrand conundrum.
Regarding facts/information, I think Szarkowski put it
best when he said Winogrand's most impressive pictures
contained "new knowledge." And because that knowledge
came in a form that was unique to photography—the
content was not unique; as you say, we could get it from
other sources—it also doubles as new knowledge about**

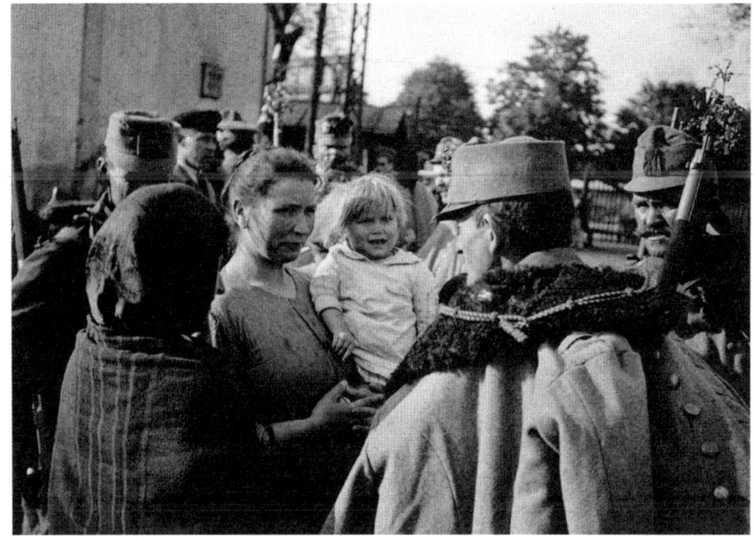

Top: An-My Lê, *USS
Kitty Hawk, U.S. Fleet
Activities, Yokosuka,
Japan,* 2007
© An-My Lê and courtesy
Murray Guy, New York

Bottom: André Kertész,
*A Red Hussar Leaving
Budapest,* 1919
© Estate of André Kertész
and Higher Pictures,
New York

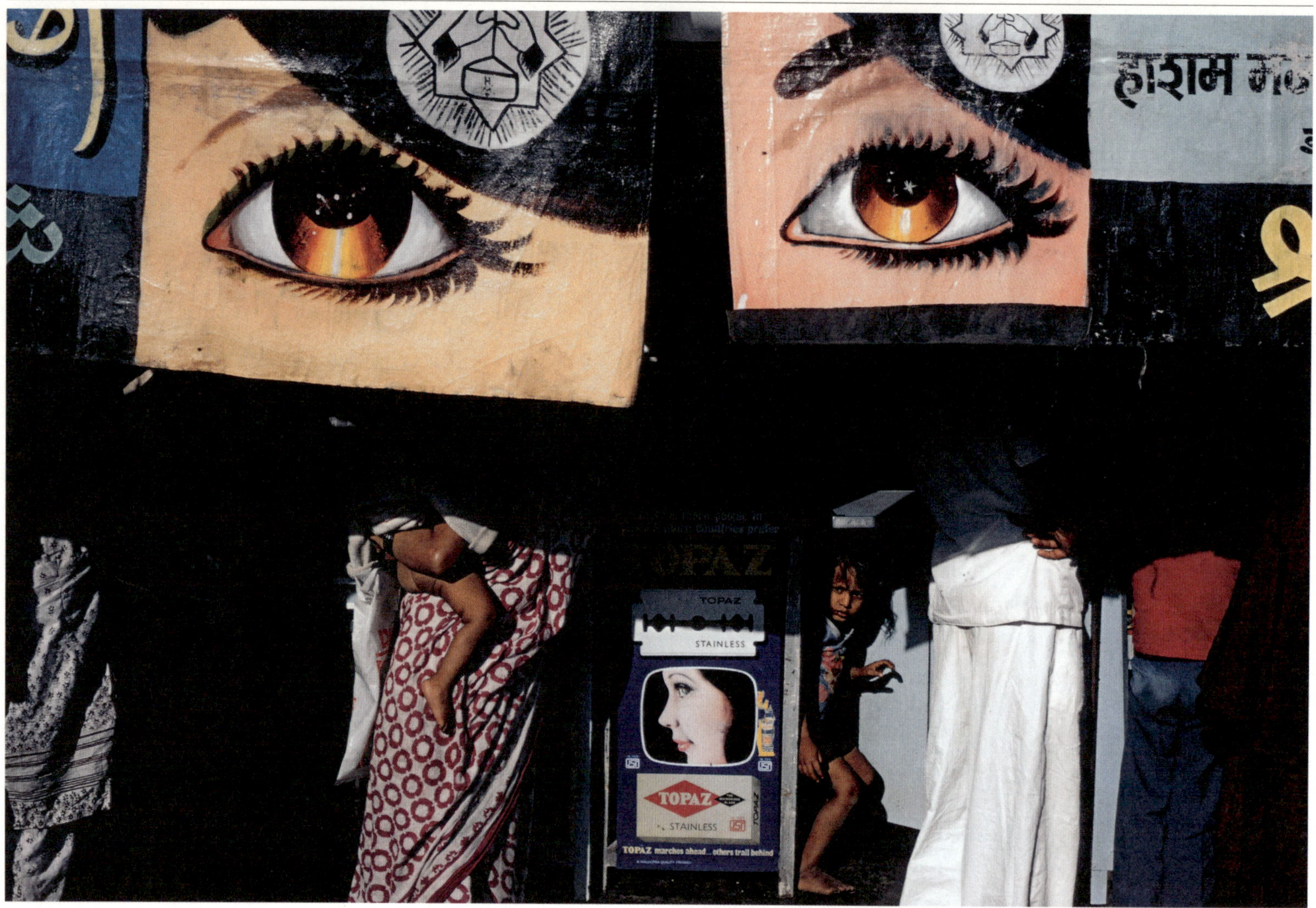

Alex Webb,
Bombay, India, 1981
© Alex Webb/Magnum
Photos

> **This is the eternal question about photography, isn't it: the old who by/what of? Is a photograph defined by what's in it or by who took it? Well, a bit of both, obviously.**
> — Geoff Dyer

photography. For me that knowledge has stayed new in spite of all the changes in hairstyle and lapel widths in the photographs and in photography.

To take up your point about the Winogrand pictures, this is the eternal question about photography, isn't it: the old who by/what of? Is a photograph defined by what's in it or by who took it? Well, a bit of both, obviously. And it can never be settled for good: it depends on the picture and the photographer. I often think of the sliding scale of options offered by Wallace Stevens in "An Ordinary Evening in New Haven," from "simple seeing, without reflection" to "Reality as a thing seen by the mind,/Not that which is but that which is apprehended …"

As it happens, and at the risk of seeming like a Winogrand nerd, I recently saw a show in Portland, Oregon, of pictures by Winogrand and Jonathan Brand. They often photographed together and Brand took lots of pictures of Winogrand on the phone. Apparently he checked his answering service obsessively. So Brand, to me, has provided a great bit of new knowledge about Winogrand. The world is out there and some photographers transform it more thoroughly than others. In the process of recording the world, Alex Webb—who despite his considerable reputation, I think is actually *under*rated— reconfigures the world in a way that is consistently jaw- dropping: "Everything as unreal as real can be," to continue the Stevens theme.

Moving on, I'd like to ask if, as a writer, you've approached photography differently than other subjects you've covered? Does anything about the medium of photography seem not exactly to insist but to encourage that?

JM: Since we are conducting this exchange in a journal of photography, I wish I could agree that photography has some special, mysterious, maybe even mystical quality that causes writers to write differently about it than about other subjects. But I'm afraid that I have never felt the force of this quality. For me the task of writing about photography is the same as the task of writing about anything else. Your question suggests that your experience is different—that your writing on photography is inflected by the medium itself. Would you talk about this experience?

GD: I think the difference might be between writing essays or pieces that are then collected into a book with something conceived at the outset as a book. With books I've always felt a compulsion to try to make the form of what I was writing share some of the qualities of the thing I was writing about (something one can't do so readily in pieces for publications which have their own formal requirements and imposed limitations). So, for example, the book on jazz, *But Beautiful*, is a series of improvisations. But that form and style would not be appropriate to photography. The form of *The Ongoing Moment* takes on some of the experiences of looking at photographs—rummaging in a drawer or box of pictures with all the adjacencies and echoes that that throws up. So it's not that there's anything especially special about photography, as it were: nothing more special about it than jazz or anything else, but something distinctive, certainly, which I have tried to bring out in words. That might be why musicians have tended to like the jazz book and photographers the photography book even though I was in some ways ill-equipped to write either since I neither play an instrument nor take pictures.

Let's go back now to that question of the right to reproduce photographs in critical discussions of them. You are merciless, in your recent collection of profiles on artists, *Forty-One False Starts*, about Doon Arbus and her claim that she wanted to protect her mum's pictures from interpretation. I had to send the relevant bits from *The Ongoing Moment* to the Arbus people in order for them to consider whether they would grant permission to reproduce pictures in the book (which was already a retreat from my principled position that I wasn't going to let anyone I'd written about see what I'd written, but, well, I knew the book would be better with the pictures). They wrote back saying that they couldn't grant permission because of the factual errors in the book. I started to write back immediately thanking them, was about to ask them which facts these were so that I could correct them.... Then I paused and realized, um, there were no facts—except Arbus's birthday and I'd got that right. There were just my thoughts about the pictures. So the words appeared in the book unchanged, without the pictures. (Incidentally, I've gotten to know Doon a bit since then and have come to like her, as I always like anyone with a sense of humor.) There were two other major problems with permissions: I mentioned DeCarava earlier; the other was Robert Frank or at least his gallery. At one point, after numerous delays and much pleading from me, this person wrote to tell me that Mr. Frank was having surgery on his knees and so ... etc., etc. I wrote back that I was going to need surgery on my knees if I had to keep crawling on them like this. But the general point or question is this: don't you think there should be the same freedom to reproduce pictures in the context of commentary about them that there is in using quotes in literary criticism?

So that, say, if you wanted to write something about what a crock of shit *The Ongoing Moment* was, you could quote bits to support your argument and I'd—rightly—be powerless to stop you.

JM: I couldn't agree with you more—that the "fair use" doctrine should apply to photography criticism no less than it does to literary criticism. Of course, photography critics should be able to "quote" the same way literary critics do. When I was preparing *Diana & Nikon* for publication, I experienced the same shock and disbelief you did when you were refused illustrations for *The Ongoing Moment*. There were three photographers who refused permission to reproduce any of their photographs. One of them, Chauncey Hare, was particularly adamant. He wrote a letter to the publisher saying he would never allow a picture of his to appear in a book written by an effete East Coast writer like me. That I had highly praised his pictures cut no ice.

An argument that the Doon Arbuses and Chauncey Hares might put forward is that literary critics quote excerpts while photography critics reproduce (perforce) whole pictures. I'm not sure I know how to answer that—except, perhaps, by citing the tradition in art criticism and art historical writing whereby whole pictures are reproduced as a matter of course.

I love your line about needing knee surgery yourself. And I admire your forbearance toward Doon Arbus after all the trouble she caused you. Your comment about new knowledge coming from the form of Winogrand's best pictures has given me something to think about. It almost makes me want to see the Winogrand show at the Metropolitan Museum.

GD: Not to see it would be an act of lunacy!

JM: Then I had better go see it. In turn, I hope you will have a chance to read *We Captured a U-Boat*. There is an incredible moment in it on a moonless night when the commander has to decide whether to turn on the lights of his aircraft carrier so that a group of returning airplanes can land on it—thus risking the lives of everyone on board because of patrolling packs of German submarines—or to maintain the blackout and doom the pilots of the airplanes. Talk about decisive and ongoing moments!

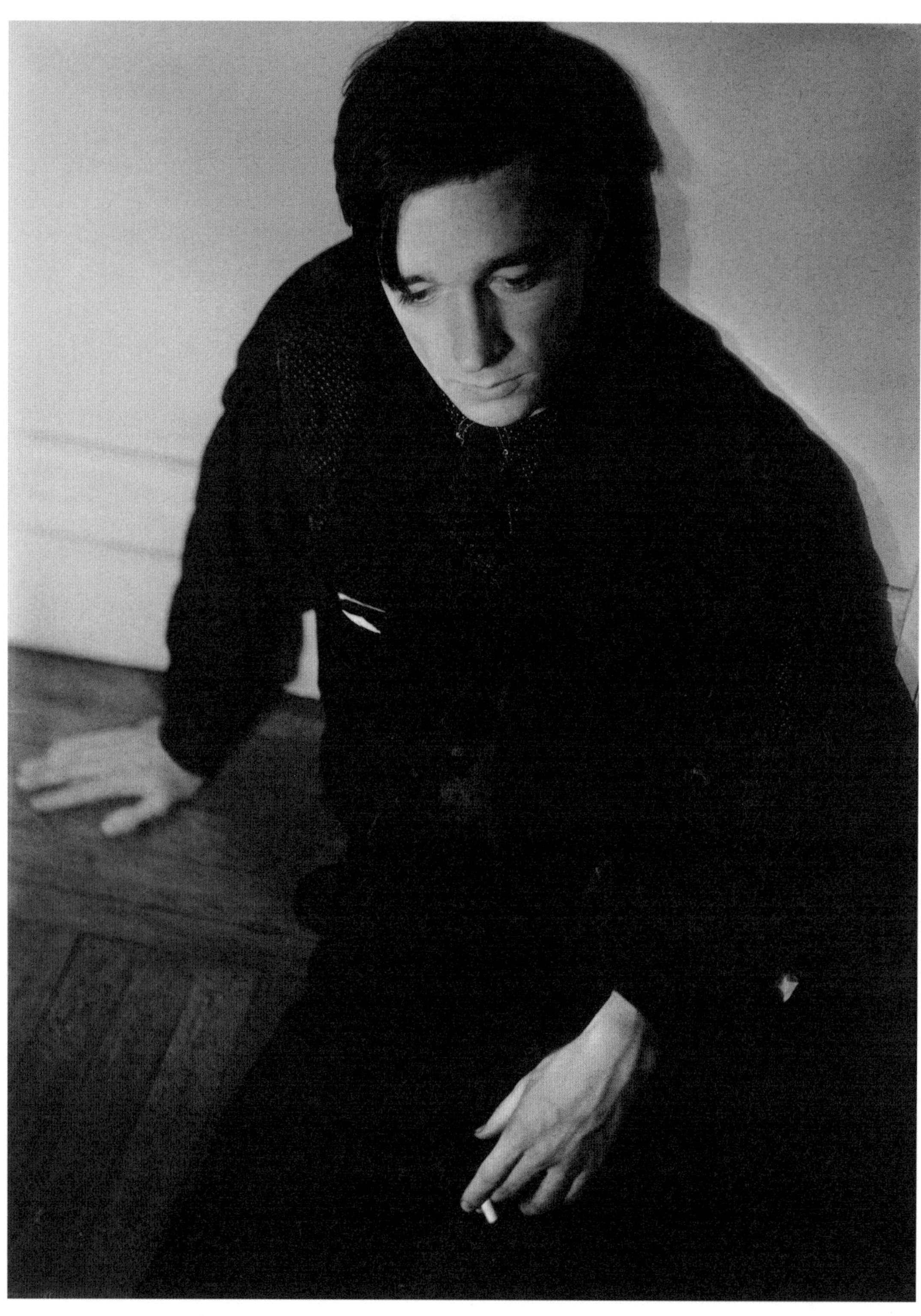

How did Flaubert, Baudelaire, Proust, and other writers inform the creator of "documentary-style" photography?

Walker Evans & the Written Word

David Campany

Of all the various practices of photography—advertising, industrial imaging, family albums, and the rest—it is perhaps photojournalism that brings together word and image most often and most necessarily. Usually it involves two people—a photographer and a writer—collaborating, ideally. Sometimes the photographer writes, but this is less common than the writer who photographs. In an economic climate that is challenging for photojournalism (to put it mildly) it seems easier to get a writer to photograph than it is to get a photographer to write. But there have been a handful of individuals who wanted and were able to do both. One of the most remarkable was Walker Evans.

Evans's first calling was the written word. At college he studied French literature and was an avid reader of the cutting-edge literary journals of the 1920s, when fussy Victorian prose was giving way to the lucid and fragmentary language of modern life, and James Joyce and T.S. Eliot were idolized. During a year in Paris (1926–27) Evans also read Flaubert, Baudelaire, Proust, and others. He attempted to write, in the form of short and intense prose pieces, but the ambition was crushing: "I wanted so much to write that I couldn't write a word," he recalled at the end of his career. Returning to New York in 1927, he sensed the camera might offer the descriptive and expressive power that had eluded him in words, but he never lost the desire to write.

In August 1929, at the age of twenty-five, Evans was first published. A new magazine titled *Alhambra* carried two unrelated contributions: a typically modernist photograph of soaring cranes constructing the Lincoln Building on Manhattan's East 42nd Street, and an accomplished translation from the French of an extract of *Moravagine* (1926), Blaise Cendrars's delirious novel about a psychotic killer. Evans's image was too deferential to the city's spectacle but Cendrars's language came close to the frank but equivocal description that would come to define Evans's photography.

While perfecting what he came to call "documentary-style" photography, Evans produced sequences of images to sit alongside texts by other writers: Carleton Beals's political exposé *The Crime of Cuba* (1933), the experimental journalism of James Agee's *Let Us Now Praise Famous Men: Three Tenant Families* (1941), and Karl Bickel's documentary travel book *The Mangrove Coast: The Story of the West Coast of Florida* (1942). Rather than being smoothly integrated in the manner of populist books and mainstream magazines, in each case Evans's images sat apart from the text, obliging the reader–viewers to actively negotiate their own response.

Opening page from
"The Pitch Direct,"
Fortune, October 1958

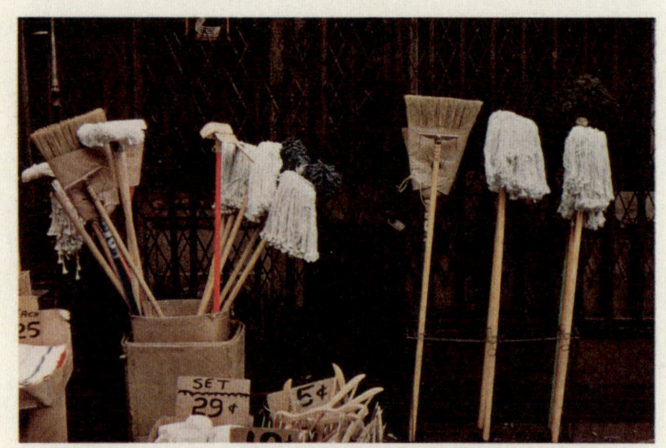

THE PITCH DIRECT

The sidewalk is the last stand of unsophisticated display

A man needn't travel to the Andes, strapped to his color camera, to relish the sights of outdoor markets. There are American sidewalks, like these in New York, that spill with them. They can look and smell much like market places anywhere, from Naples to Tehuantepec to Nairobi. The stay-at-home tourist, if his eye is properly and purely to be served, should approach the street fair without any reasonable intention, such as that of actually buying something. The cut-rate whistling kettle must sit where it is, along with the mops, the sneakers, the crockery, and the petticoats.

Does this nation overproduce? If so, one can get a lot of pleasure and rich sensual enjoyment out of contemplating great bins of slightly defective tap wrenches, coils upon coils of glinty wire, and parabolas of hemp line honest and fragrant. A man of perfectly good sense may decide after due meditation that a well-placed eggplant (2 for 27 cents) is pigmented with the most voluptuous and assuredly wicked color in the world. There are other delights. Why is it that there is always something comic about a sash weight? What is as dependably entertaining as a really enthusiastic arrangement of plumbers' tools?

—W. E.

Photographs by Walker Evans — FORTUNE October 1958 139

Evans did take commissions from magazines, and sometimes this led to interesting work. In 1937 *Fortune* magazine published "Six Days at Sea," Evans and James Agee's sly observation of a tourist cruise to Havana (an assignment conducted entirely incognito). Evans worked with the journalist Katherine Hamill to produce a report on slum clearance and social housing in 1939 for *Harper's Bazaar*. In 1943 he landed a job as a writer at *Time*, reviewing films, books, and exhibitions. Agee was on the staff, as were James Stern and Saul Bellow. With a little help from Agee, Evans soon mastered *Time*'s concise, urbane, and witty house style. He drew readers' attention to gems of popular culture and obscure treasures: the Krazy Kat cartoon strip, children's art, the little-known sculptures of Edgar Degas, Winston Churchill's paintings, anatomical drawings, and self-portraits.

Two years later Evans became the only staff photographer at *Fortune*. This offered the chance to get more involved in the form his work might take on the page. But the real breakthrough came in 1948 when he was made *Fortune*'s special photographic editor. Part of his task was to advise on the magazine's visual style, but in answering directly to the managing editor rather than the art director, Evans was able to set his own assignments. With a degree of autonomy unheard of in magazines before or since, he would shoot, edit, write, and design his pages.

To accompany his photographs Evans cultivated a style of writing that was rich in rhetorical flourish, vernacular expressions, literary quotations, obscure historical references, pithy facts, and adjectives of baroque splendor. There were also moments of high polemic. Although these texts were rarely longer than a few hundred words, he crafted them tirelessly. He also kept a close eye on the typesetting, with a poet's sensitivity to the placement of line breaks. In a 1971 interview, he recalled: "The writing wasn't easy for me to master. But I was determined to be my own editor, so I worked hard on it. Any test met is part of one's development." He understood the deep connections between photography and literature. "Photography seems to be the most literary of the graphic arts," he reflected in his chapter written for Louis Kronenberger's anthology *Quality: Its Image in the Arts* (1969). "It will have—on occasion, and in effect— qualities of eloquence, wit, grace, and economy; style, of course; structure and coherence; paradox, play and oxymoron." Indeed, the cool sobriety of his great literary heroes had far less effect on his prose than on his photography:

> *I wasn't very conscious of it then, but I know that Flaubert's esthetic is absolutely mine. Flaubert's method I think I incorporated almost unconsciously, but anyway used in two ways: his realism and naturalism both, and his objectivity of treatment; the non-appearance of author, the non-subjectivity. That is literally applicable to the way I want to use a camera and do. But spiritually, however, it is Baudelaire who is the influence on me.*

Evans's lifelong interest in the commonplace things that modern progress deems trivial or forgettable was thoroughly Baudelairean. In society's rejects and refuse we may find its truth. *Fortune*'s ethos was to champion the new, but Evans looked to the outmoded or the enduring. *Fortune* celebrated the world of work; Evans reflected on unemployment or idle pleasures such as wandering. *Fortune* heralded steel-and-glass construction; Evans cherished endangered vernacular buildings of wood and stone that improved with age and patina. While *Fortune* announced the new modular office, Evans looked at reliable establishments, such as local insurance firms, run by "men who cannot possibly put in a honest day's work while clad in a razor-sharp two hundred dollar suit of clothes." ("Vintage Office Furniture," *Fortune*,

August 1953). *Fortune* celebrated department stores; Evans looked to the sidewalk displays of small shops.

His images of everyday objects and life in the slower lane anticipated by decades the American color photographers of the 1970s (William Eggleston, Stephen Shore), while his words were ironic but affectionate. Take, for example, this from "The Pitch Direct" (*Fortune*, October 1958):

> *The stay-at-home tourist, if his eye is properly and purely to be served, should approach the street fair without any reasonable intention, such as that of actually buying something […] Does this nation overproduce? If so, one can get a lot of pleasure and rich sensual enjoyment out of contemplating great bins of slightly defective tap wrenches, coils upon coils of glinty wire, and parabolas of hemp line honest and fragrant. A man of perfectly good sense may decide after due meditation that a well-placed eggplant (2 for 27 cents) is pigmented with the most voluptuous and assuredly wicked color in the world.*

At times Evans's captions would deliberately change the meaning of, or undermine, his pictures. His article "Imperial Washington" (*Fortune*, February 1952) resembles a simple tourist's survey of the capital's stately architecture—which is really showbiz:

> *The last, large burst of classicism struck Washington as a direct result of the Chicago World's Fair of 1893. So successful was the midwestern creation in plaster that its chief architects and planners moved on to the capital almost to a man and forever froze the face of the city into its Roman Renaissance expression.*

Across the 1950s and '60s Evans's photography grew increasingly Flaubertian—simple, direct, and incisive, while his words grew poetic and arch. To do it the other way around, with plain text introducing florid images, would risk pretention, like a gallery of grandstanding pictures. The last thing Evans wanted for his magazine pages was Art. He was making resistant *journalism*,

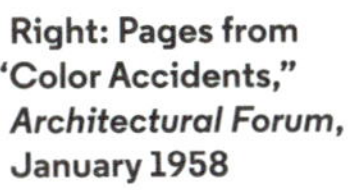

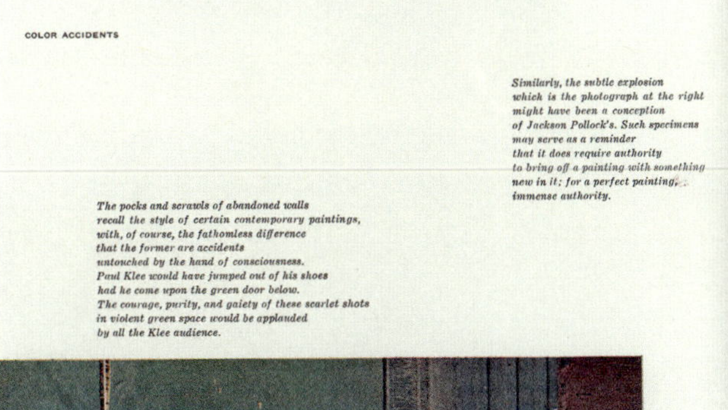

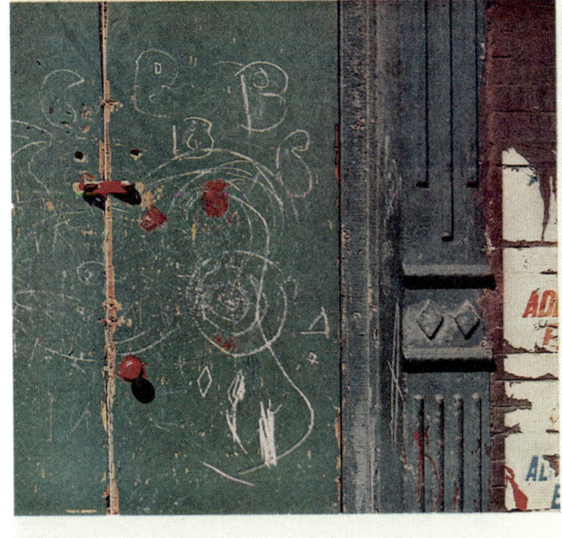

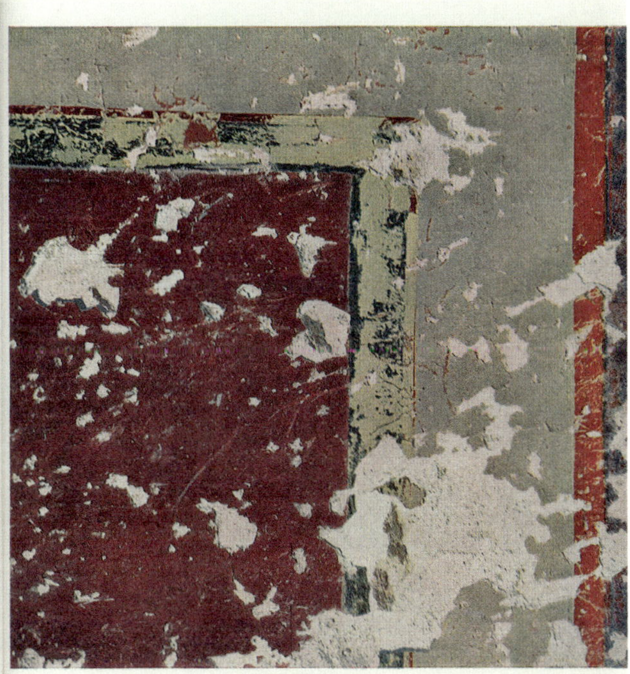

countering the values and conventions of the mainstream. He produced more than forty photo-essays for *Fortune* and several for other titles. "Color Accidents" (*Architectural Forum*, January 1958) was a suite of square compositions picked out from weathered walls of a New York street. The writing compares but distances them from abstract painting, then at its popular height:

> *The pocks and scrawls of abandoned walls recall the style of certain contemporary paintings, with, of course, the fathomless difference that the former are accidents untouched by the hand of consciousness. Paul Klee would have jumped out of his shoes had he come upon the green door below.*

Evans's photographs of these colors and marks are consummate formal exercises. However, the text suggests that what's important are the walls themselves and that his photographs are, in the first instance, documents of things worth noticing in the world. These were not pictures for exhibition: they were elegant reports fashioned for the page.

At times Evans's love of literature became explicit. In 1948 he was commissioned by *Vogue* to photograph the Southern landscape depicted in the novels of William Faulkner. He admired the writer, who was about to break six years' silence with the publication of *Intruder in the Dust*. Faulkner's novels were set in the fictional Yoknapatawpha County, so, strictly speaking, it could not be photographed. Evans's languid and haunting six-page response is almost devoid of people. A cemetery, rail tracks, wood-frame houses, shacks, and fading mansions—these are spaces where something has or could happen, as if each photograph might preface a chapter.

Evans does something similar with "The U.S. Depot" (*Fortune*, February 1953), in which a survey of single-building railroad stations seems more like a set of locales for short stories once we read the introductory paragraph. "And what is on that green-paper note handed up on its looped stick to the engineer

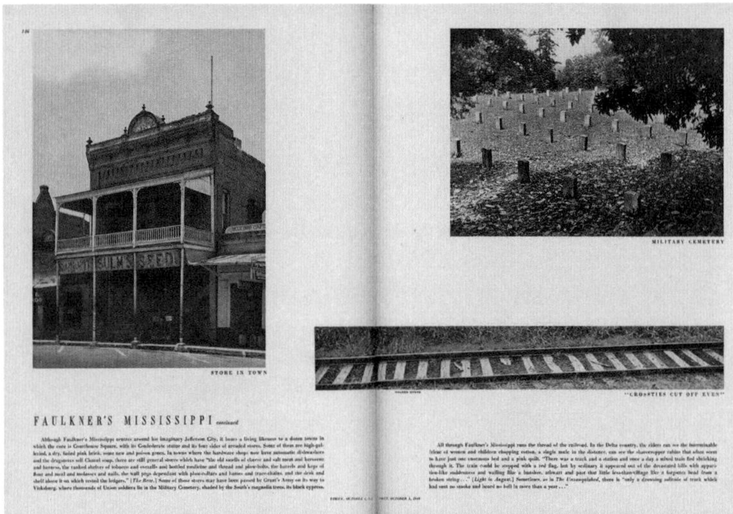

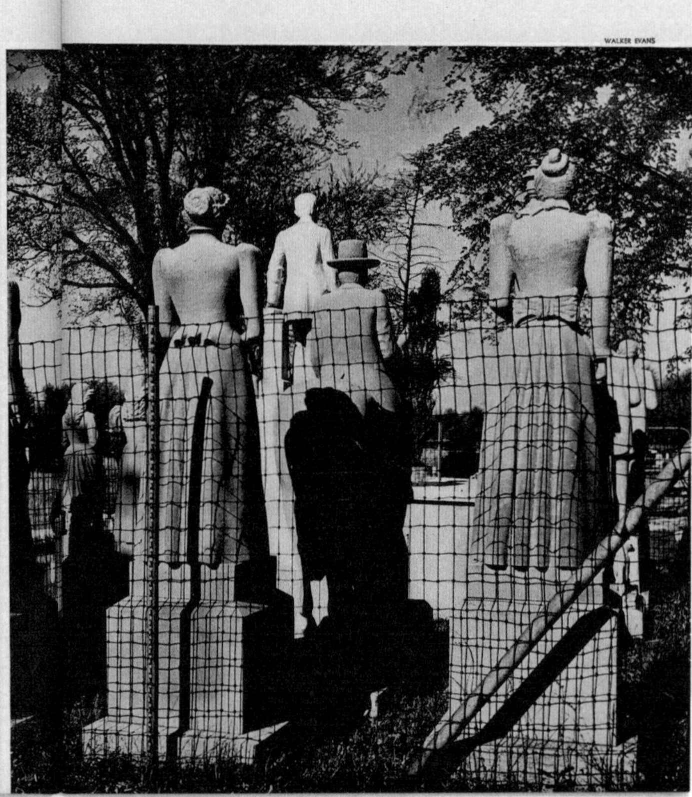

The magazine spread reproduction:

Along the Right-of-Way

In Roomette 6, Car 287, the light has not yet been switched on. For an hour the train has swayed and rattled across the land. This rented steel cubicle, with its solemn and absorbing printed directions of how to work those basic gadgets, is the harassed man's haven of detachment. The captains and the kings depart. Now if ever, in this place and in this mood, the traveler can abandon himself to the rich pastime of window-gazing.

Along the paths of railroads, the country is in semi-undress. You can see some of the anatomy of its living: a back yard with its citizen poking into a rumble seat for a trusted toolbox; an intent group of boys locked in a sandlot ball game; a fading factory wall; a lone child with a cart. Out on the plains, the classic barns and the battalions of cabbages ...

To some, these sights gain meaning because men like Mark Twain and Sherwood Anderson and Thomas Wolfe have, in a sense, laid hands on them. For others, one fleeting landscape can flush the mind with images of the enchantment a child feels with train trips: waking at dawn to see a cool cornfield cut by a rutted road; a farmer in his wagon drawn up at the crossing; the *TING TING TING TING TING TING TING* of the warning bell–that heart-rending tinny decrescendo which is an early lesson in relativity of the senses. *W.E.*

Seven photographs by Walker Evans of middle-western and eastern landscapes seen through train windows

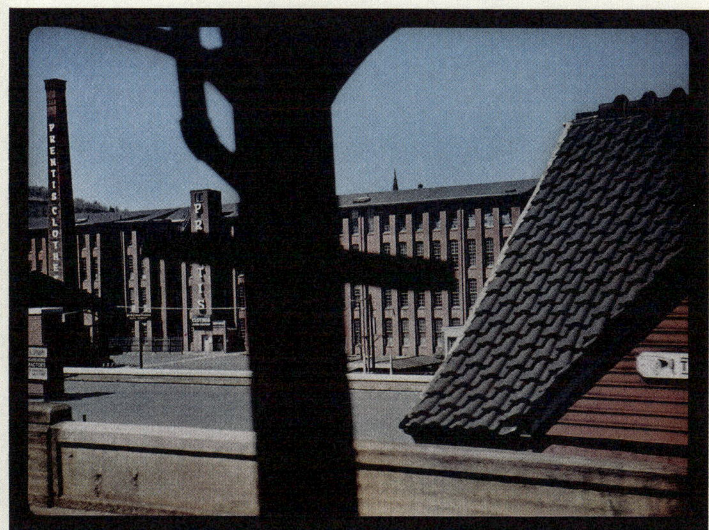

From the Sunday A.M. local, winding through the New Jersey factory towns

106

107

as the 3:52 brakes to a stop? Does it say 'Train five Engine eight four nine six delayed at Millerton hot journal box,' or does it say 'Tell Jeanie I'll get pork chops'?"

The following year, 1954, Faulkner saw a photograph by Evans of a cemetery plot (*Woodbridge Family Monument, Mansfield, Kentucky*, 1945), inspiring him to write the short story "Sepulture South: Gaslight." It was published in *Harper's Bazaar* alongside the imposing image. It's a Proustian remembrance, part fact, part fiction, of the funeral of Faulkner's grandfather. The narrator returns to the gravestones, "stained now, a little darkened by time and weather and endurance, but still serene, impervious, remote, gazing at nothing, not like sentinels, not defending the living from the dead by means of their vast ton-measured weight and mass, but rather the dead from the living …." Seen from the rear, Evans's stone family now appears to be turning away from time itself.

Evans's enduring reputation, endorsed by museums worldwide, is that of an artist operating in the guise of a documentarian. His magazine work complicates this casting. It is clear he was interested in making independent and resistant photojournalism that really only worked when image, text, and design came together on the page. A photojournalist can, of course, be informed by art and literature. Such influences certainly made Evans's work better. The finest illustration is perhaps "Along the Right-of-Way," an eight-page piece from 1950 on the simple pleasures of gazing from train windows. The opening photograph is as good as any painting by Edward Hopper or Charles Sheeler. And his text is a minor miracle of reported fact, remembrance, suggestion, allusion, flight of fancy, and even physics. All in three short, sublime paragraphs.

Across the 1950s and '60s Evans's photography grew increasingly Flaubertian—simple, direct, and incisive, while his words grew poetic and arch.

David Campany is a writer and curator. He teaches at the University of Westminster, London, and recently published *Walker Evans: The Magazine Work* with Steidl.

Campany's *The Open Road: Photography and the American Road Trip* was published by Aperture this fall.

What kind of pressure does photography place on the written word today? *Aperture* recently spoke with contemporary fiction writers Teju Cole, Mary Gaitskill, Rivka Galchen, Tom McCarthy, and Lynne Tillman about photography and the role of the image in their writing process.

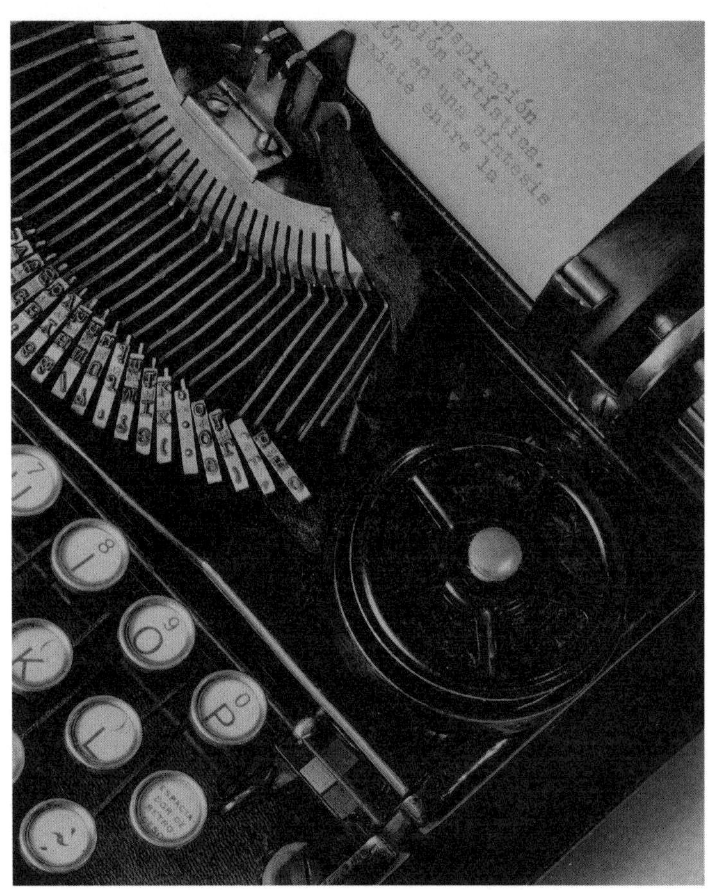

Words vs. Images

Tina Modotti,
*Mella's Typewriter or
La Técnica*, 1928
© The Museum of Modern
Art/Licensed by SCALA/
Art Resource, New York

Maxime du Camp,
*The Great Sphinx
and the Pyramids of Giza,
Egypt*, 1852
© HIP/Art Resource,
New York

Tom McCarthy

I've become very interested recently in the idea of the negative and how this photographic concept is relevant to fiction. Almost the very first image in my next novel, *Satin Island*, is of a picture looming into view from noxious liquid in a darkroom, like some kind of fish approaching through murky water; I use it as a metaphor for thinking or remembering. So the mechanism of photography stands for me as a kind of analogue for what it is to bring data, memories, or whatever into a coherent image—and ultimately, for what it is to write.

In my novel *Remainder*, which is all about trying to reproduce an ideal, if mundane, scenario (walking down a staircase, exchanging words with a neighbor, etc.), the hero is, in a sense, making a print of a negative of something that was never based on reality. The negative really is a negative. It's a memory of something that never existed. So, like a photographer, he's trying to bring this reality of the image out of the darkroom. He's trying to actualize this picture, or world, from the darkroom of his mind—and it never quite goes right.

Like many writers, I take lots of photographs and work from them. When I was writing *Remainder*, I walked around Brixton in South London (this was back in 2000) with a camera and a Dictaphone. I photographed the texture of the sidewalk, the reflections in puddles, the letters from the gas and electricity holes, and other markings in the street. But I was also recording running commentary, because ultimately, as a writer, you're dealing with words. Even if those words carry or generate images, words are still your currency. So I was using the Dictaphone to say, "Here in the street is this, and you can see the *a* and *r* of *airports* reversed in this puddle." I typed it all up, word for word, even the "umms" and "ahs" and repetitions, and pinned it all to my wall—the photographs as well. More recently, with *C*, my last novel, which is set a hundred years ago, I looked at lots of old photographs—of Alexandria, Egypt, and London in the 1920s—and again transcribed them, turned them into words. I was reading Flaubert's accounts of going up the river in Egypt with the photographer Maxime du Camp, an amazing piece of writing. Flaubert says, "this is all fake; we're just in some panorama." There's one passage detailing the bright sunlight falling on the black skin of their servants against this silvery rock. It's an incredibly photographic description.

Perhaps in the end the difference between image and word isn't relevant. Because ultimately it's all scriptural: things such as light or ink mark and are recorded on surfaces, and that's an event of writing. I also don't think there's a massive categorical distinction between digital and analog photography, or digital writing on a laptop and writing on a typewriter or by hand. We live in what Michel de Certeau calls the "scriptorium." Everything is written. We're within a set of networks of archiving, recording, transmitting, and making visible, or hiding and eavesdropping. This is totally anticipated in Greek literature and *Hamlet*. The advent of the NSA or of the Internet doesn't change that. It just builds on a situation that's already there. I recognize this is a very writerly vision, because everything else ultimately becomes inscription. So yes, maybe for me, photography is a branch of writing.

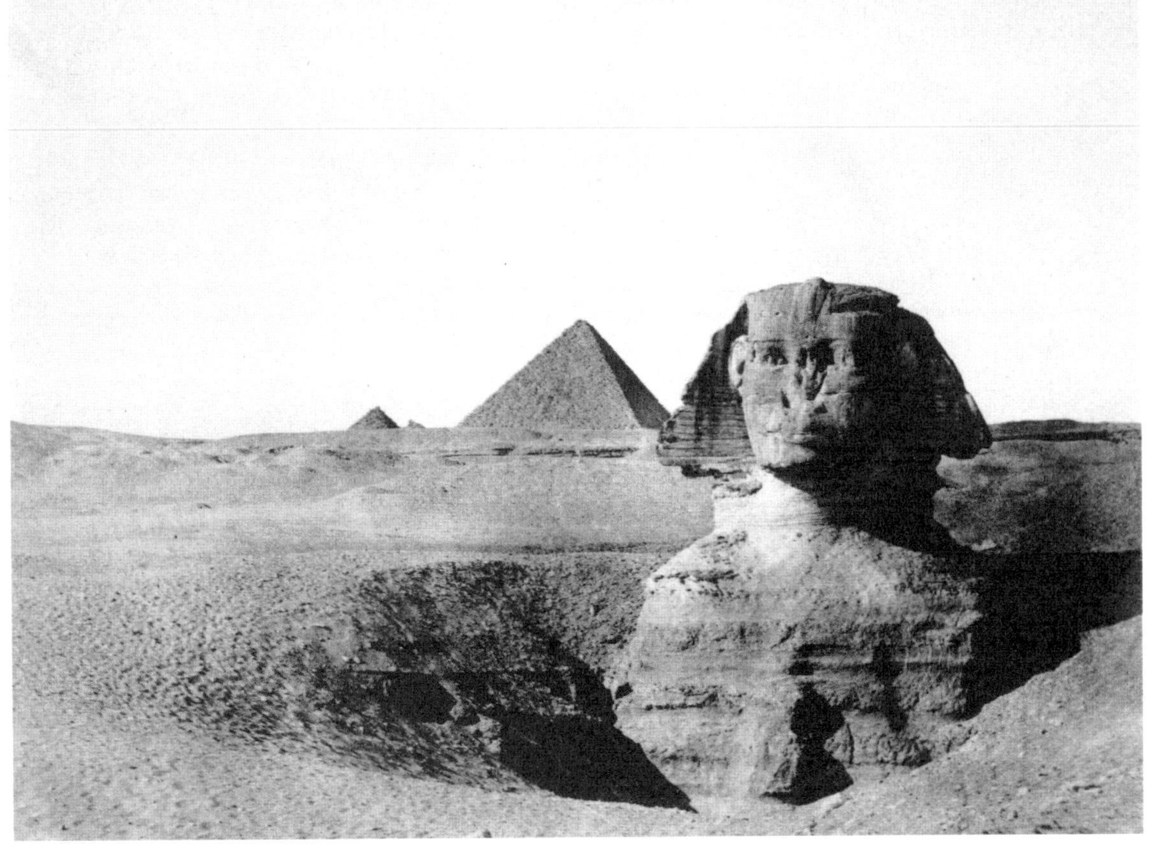

Tom McCarthy's novels include *Remainder* (2006), *Men in Space* (2007), and *C* (2010), which was shortlisted for the Man Booker Prize. His next novel, *Satin Island*, is forthcoming from Knopf in February 2015. McCarthy writes on literature and art for the *New York Times*, the *London Review of Books*, and *Artforum*, among other publications.

Mary Gaitskill

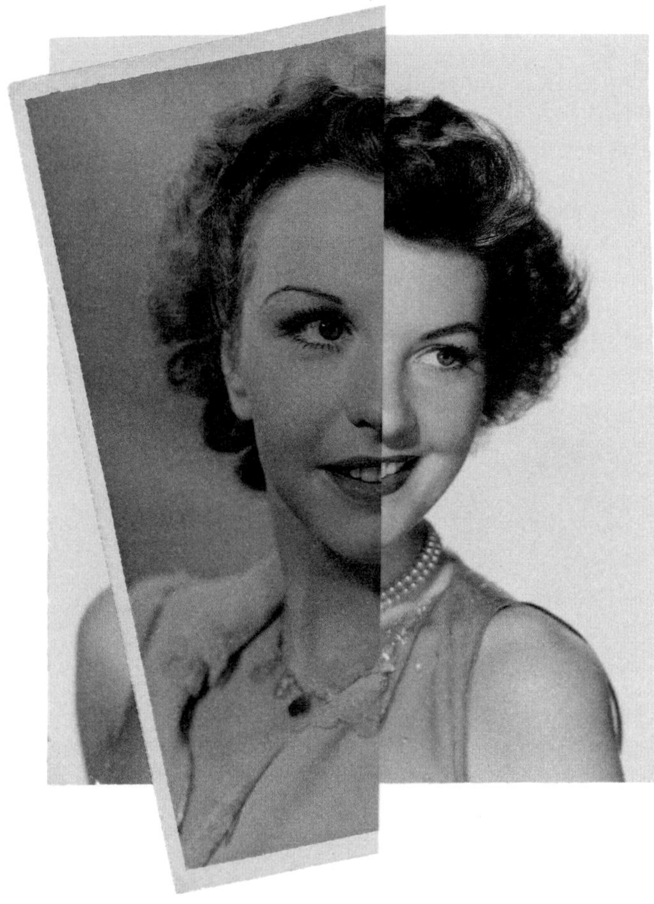

John Stezaker,
She (Film Portrait Collage)
II, **2008**
Courtesy the artist
and Petzel, New York

I take pictures with my phone if it's something beautiful
and I want to remember it, or if it's something interesting.
Recently I was having a very emotionally fraught conversation
with someone—we were quarreling, actually—and then the
quarrel sort of ended and I went for a walk down the road to
clear my mind while he took a shower. We were staying at
someone's house in the country and there were these incredibly
beautiful animals, which I thought were cows. One of them
was staring at me and when I stared back it trotted up to the
fence. It was a bull, a very young bull. There were two of them.
They were beautiful, bulls with the eyes of Bambi, blue eyes.
And there was also a little miniature donkey in the field,
which came up to check me out too, and I was so excited by
this. I went back to the house, and I said, "You've got to come
out; there's these beautiful animals." So we completely forgot
about the quarrel, and I took pictures of the animals, which
were sweet but also primal. Something like that I like to keep
on my phone.

I have some books of photography, mostly books that
people gave to me. One of them is a book of photographs of
Nabokov and his family that I like very much. I get pleasure out
of looking at pictures of him and of his wife and relatives. I like
looking at pictures of women, actually. What I like to do most
with photographs of people is to cover one half of the face with
my hand and look at it, and then do the same with the other half.
Most of the time one side of the face wears a different expression
than the other. The face is usually bifurcated. It's rare that you
have somebody who looks the same on both sides of their face—
I think Hitler actually does look the same, or maybe it was Stalin;
it was some psychopathic leader. In some people the difference
is really extreme; it looks like two different personalities. If I look
at photographs of myself, there is some version of this going
on. One side of my face looks quite young, wholesome, like a
cheerleader, and then the other half looks positively lunar, like
someone who is not part of the world. Many people are like that.
They have a strong personality show up in one half of their face
and another personality show up in the other half. It's weird. But
it's weirder or at least more unusual when there is no difference—
at least in my casual explorations of photographs.

For my novel *Veronica*, I made a puzzling underuse of
photographs. I don't know why. Considering the narrator is a
model, I don't think there are any descriptions of what she looks
like in pictures. I think there's one instance in which she describes
herself in a picture with another woman, but she mostly describes
the other woman. It seems like she might have a picture of
herself, framed and up on a wall, and I kept thinking I should put
that in there, but it just intuitively never interested me. It's kind
of odd. For research on being photographed, I went on stories
I heard from women who had been models, but the better stories
were from stylists and assistants who would describe things
more bluntly. I also had the experience of *being* photographed
by a fashion photographer; it was a book-jacket photograph
taken by a former fashion photographer—he was the most
bullying person I've ever had my picture taken by, just incredibly
aggressive. He wanted to constantly keep me off balance.
It's a very good picture, though, so it works. He did a good job.
Maybe he was looking for tension and drama in the picture,
and I do look frightened and horrified—what's funny is that
people who don't know what happened think I look frightening
or intimidating! I guess fear can be frightening. But I would
never work with him again.

I don't especially feel pressured as a writer by the presence
of images. I guess this is because I'm a very visual person and
tend to express ideas and feelings with images, sometimes
kooky images. The thing I dislike about a lot of images, say,
online or otherwise present in culture, is that they tend to be
flat and unimaginative, yet they have a strong visceral impact—
and because they're so omnipresent, people expect to be
"talked to" in that language and it seems like they aren't as open
to a more individual vision. It even seems scary and weird to
them maybe. But maybe that's always been true. I don't know.

Mary Gaitskill is the author of the novels
Two Girls, Fat and Thin (1991) and
Veronica (2005), which was nominated
for the 2005 National Book Award.
She is also the author of the story
collections *Bad Behavior* (1988);
Because They Wanted To (1997), which
was nominated for the PEN/Faulkner Award
in 1998; and *Don't Cry* (2009).

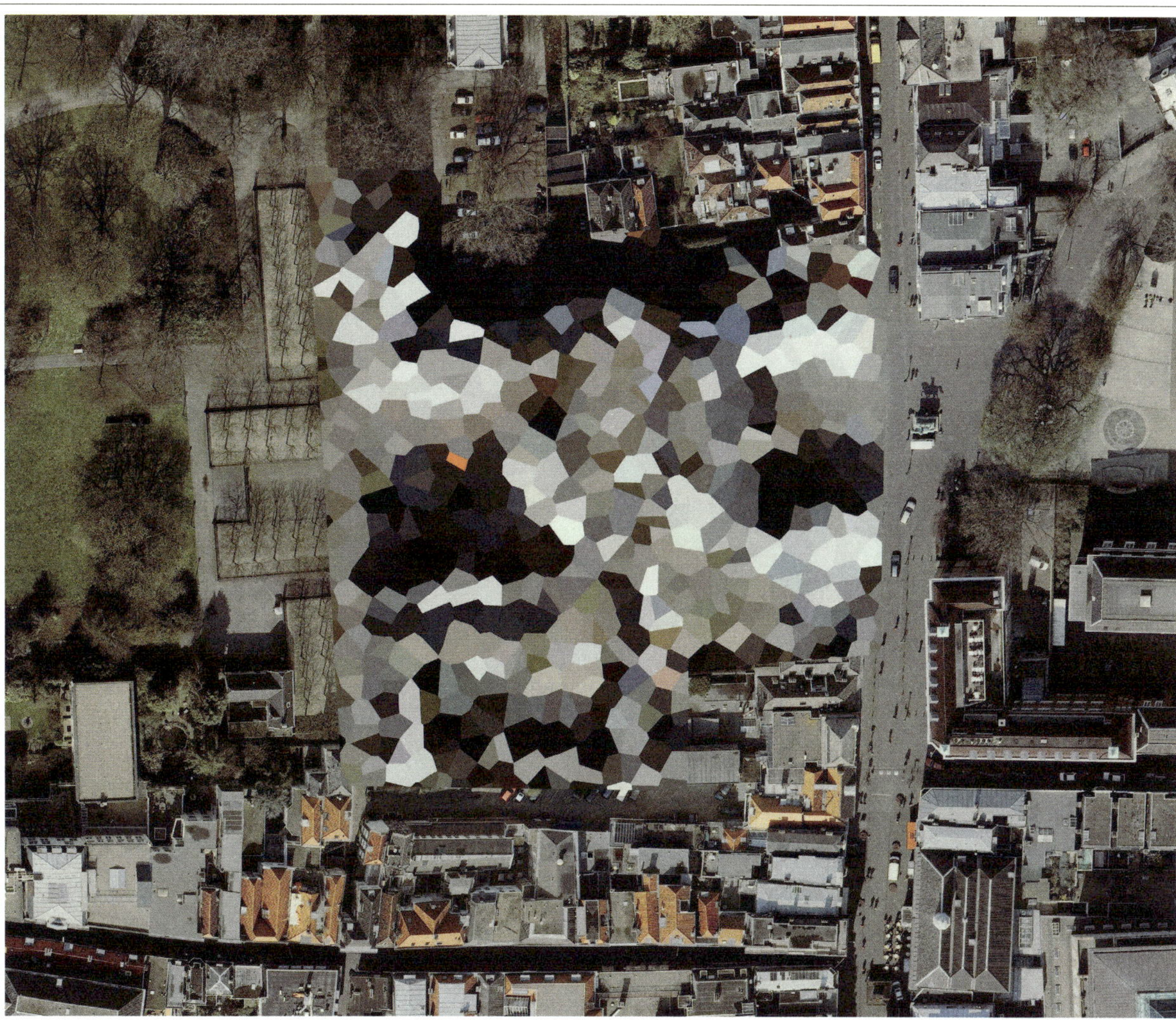

Teju Cole

In a response to a recent article on "seeing machines" by a contemporary photographer I really like (Trevor Paglen), another contemporary photographer I really like (Mishka Henner) wrote something intriguing. Paglen's piece was about the expanded reality of photography in the present time. So much of this photography, Paglen argued, was about a given machine following a certain script to do a particular kind of seeing. In his thoughtful response, which agreed with and tried to think through the implications of Paglen's arguments, Henner described the result as follows: "a world with no auteurs, one where style and the single viewpoint are irrelevant, and where poetry and lyricism are mere follies."

This caught my attention. I am ready to let the auteurs go, and in the age of Instagram and drone photography, the single viewpoint has indeed been taken off its pedestal. But: are "poetry and lyricism" truly "mere follies"? I hope I'm not misreading Henner here. I do feel that his work with Google Maps, like Paglen's on secret sites and the American security apparatus, are part of the great work being done that help us visualize the New World Order. My question, then, is: what about the *old* world order? This still lives on in quite a powerful way inside all of us. It's not all motherboards and circuits and optical recognition software. We may be on our way to becoming androids, but we are not there yet: we still have a hunger for poetry and lyricism, an intense hunger that is difficult to satisfy. I think this, in part, is why Paglen and Henner and other photographers don't limit their works to the theoretical. Yes, they have great ideas. But they turn these ideas into prints, editions, shows, books. Many of them still center their work on the tactile elements of paper, ink, and binding. The stuff could be really far out conceptually, but much of it still ends up in a frame on the wall of a gallery. And I think that's great.

So that's what I think of when I take or look at photographs: I want images that address the predicaments of the present moment, in a political sense, but that also allow for poetry and lyricism. In any case, those things may not be necessarily divorced from each other: paper has to come from somewhere; the equipment used to make a camera is made from materials that are traded on the world market, including materials that come from conflict zones. Machines have lyricism (once we learn to see it) and poetry comes at a cost (if we are willing to admit it). The connection this has to my writing? I try to apply those same goals (of politics and poetry) to the written word, too. So, we may be awash in images and words these days, but poetry still matters. It is still as elusive as it ever was, and, just as ever, it is still worth chasing down.

Paglen's text and Henner's response can be read here: blog.fotomuseum.ch/2014/03/ii-seeing-machines/

Teju Cole is a photographer and the author of two works of fiction, *Every Day Is for the Thief* (2014) and *Open City* (2011), for which he won the PEN/Hemingway Award.

Cole wrote the introductory essays for *On Street Photography and the Poetic Image*, by Alex Webb and Rebecca Norris Webb, and *Touching Strangers*, by Richard Renaldi, both published by Aperture.

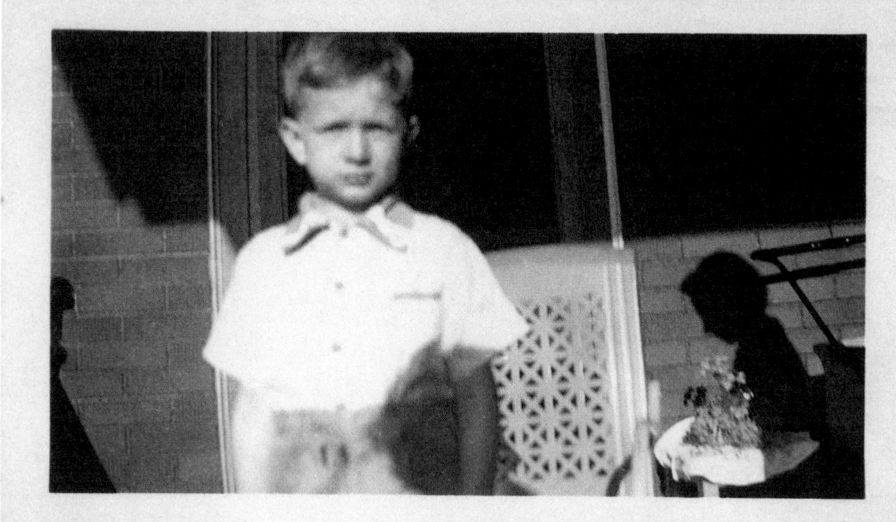

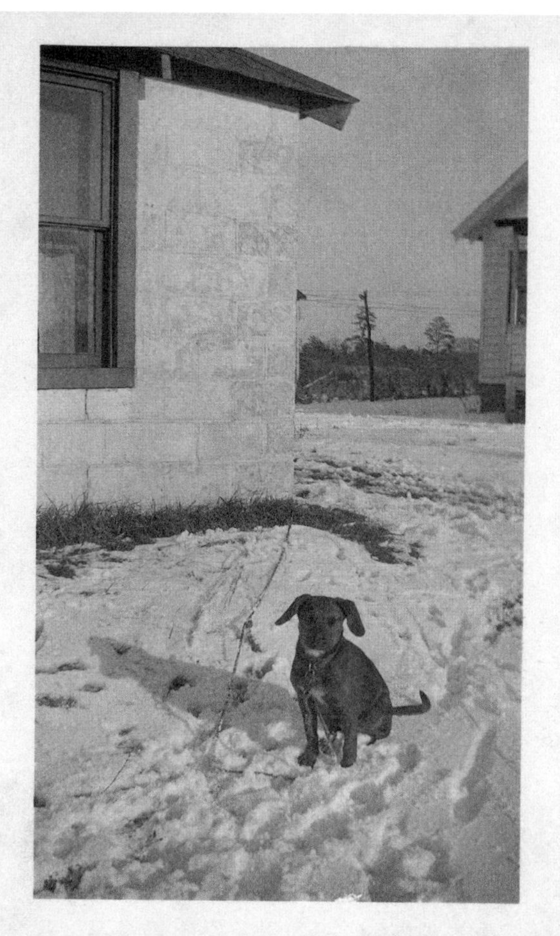

Lynne Tillman

I started writing my new novel, *Men and Apparitions*, because it's said we live in "a glut of images" and also because of the belief that there's a crisis in art photography, with cellphones and everyone taking pictures all the time. I began to think: What does that mean? How would you narrate that story? How do you make characters who are based in images, in some sense, or whose lives seem to be based on images?

My protagonist in the novel, Zeke, is a cultural anthropologist, an ethnographer, not a photographer himself. His field is photography, family photography in particular. As a child I was very interested in our family photographs. My father shot a lot of 8mm films, too, before I was born, and I would take out the projector when I was eight or nine, very young, and all by myself watch these home movies, which, as I think about it now, seems funny. In part it was because I was the baby of the family and quite a bit younger than my sisters, so there was an already established family I'd entered. Seeing these films, I guess, gave me some sense of family history. I am not using these for the book, but I've found some family albums at flea markets and borrowed friends' found photographs. In the novel, I do want to do some analyses of photographs.

Zeke, my character, goes off theoretically in some wild directions—the novel form allows me to do everything I can think of. It allows me to be unaccountable, also—unaccountable to so-called "facts." Some of what Zeke thinks about photography and cultural anthropology is credible, and, I think, there's some interesting theory about images, but some of what he comes up with is wack. If I were writing a straight essay, I couldn't do that, and it wouldn't be as much fun to write.

I don't usually take photographs for what I'm writing. But if I go to an art exhibition and I think that I'll want to remember something, I'll take a picture of the work if I can, or of the way the work has been installed, if the security guards let me (though never with a flash), as an aide-memoire. But I don't do that for writing. I still might write notes, use words to remember, because I'm working with words. They're my medium. Mostly I rely on my memory—it's a memory game I play with myself, and sometimes lose.

To photograph is to step out of the moment. When we photograph, we are objectifying. We look at something, shoot, and it becomes a kind of object. It may be a picture of an event, a tree, a person. But in the end you have a representation, just that. It is an abstraction. I think photography, like writing, is a translation, from the impossible Real to the page. I think of translation and representation as being close kin. Taking a photograph, like a selfie, is a way to record a moment, and to proclaim Being, which writing also does, in a sense. People think writing, especially fiction, has been subsumed, even vanquished, by picture making. But fiction is another form of image making. Words are images too. I'm hoping to finish the novel at the end of this fall. If not, I'll shoot myself. I will use a camera.

Lynne Tillman is a novelist, short-story writer, and critic, whose most recent book, her second collection of essays, *What Would Lynne Tillman Do?*, was published last spring. She is currently working on a novel titled *Men and Apparitions*.

Rivka Galchen

I don't particularly think of photography as an inspiration or as a constraint. And yet photography is so enormously powerful and pervasive, to think it has no effect would be like thinking the shape of a guitar doesn't affect the sounds made with it. Even though I love both personal and professional photographs, I don't use them as part of my writing process. It's as if they obliterate something for me. I did once take some video footage for a piece that I was writing about an annual festival in Germany around the work of Karl May, who wrote many adventure tales in the late nineteenth century about a German among Native Americans in the American West, even though he had lied about having ever visited America. But I didn't use the video footage, or the snapshots. My notes had done the essential culling, a kind of thinking, and the images just flooded that thinking away.

Photographs, though, are better at communicating some things that I once would have tried to put into words. When I want to communicate with my family, say, in a postcard kind of I'm-thinking-of-you way, I just send a smartphone photo of, probably, my daughter. Words now gravitate to where they're most ideal, in a certain way, and this has pushed language toward two different, not very related places: the contract and the joke. There are no pictogram contracts. Of course words are still good at ordinary communication, but they are *irreplaceably* good, at least for now, in the contract and, well, maybe joke is not quite the right label, but in a very particular kind of entertainment. For example, think of how often headlines in the *Onion* rely on a kind of half-rhyme with some clichéd phrase, like, "Loved Ones Recall Local Man's Cowardly Battle with Cancer"—the effect here can only be produced by the way we process language.

Where does all this leave the novel? The novel must remain ideal for something, right? Though I don't think we know what, yet. It seems best to keep our noses down and let the abstractions reveal themselves in time. Prognostications can be fun, but are best understood as fictions. If I were going to guess where the novel will go, and what it will become uniquely capable of, it seems to me that it may drift toward more genuinely private spaces and, at the same time, more political spaces. Private in the sense of inner dialogue; political in the sense of legal language, or nation naming… it's telling how a bill on, say, small dairy farms, requires four hundred pages not just of pork but also fine specification. Novels can play with the way language has moved into these realms, or they can rebel, but, either way, language is their medium, and where the medium has moved matters. The form will surely continue to document the external world, as it always has, but that aspect may become less essential. Though maybe the pressure the image has placed on literature, compressing the field into a smaller country, will paradoxically allow for an opening up into something unforeseen, an unexpected vastness. It'll feel like those dreams of terraforming Mars.

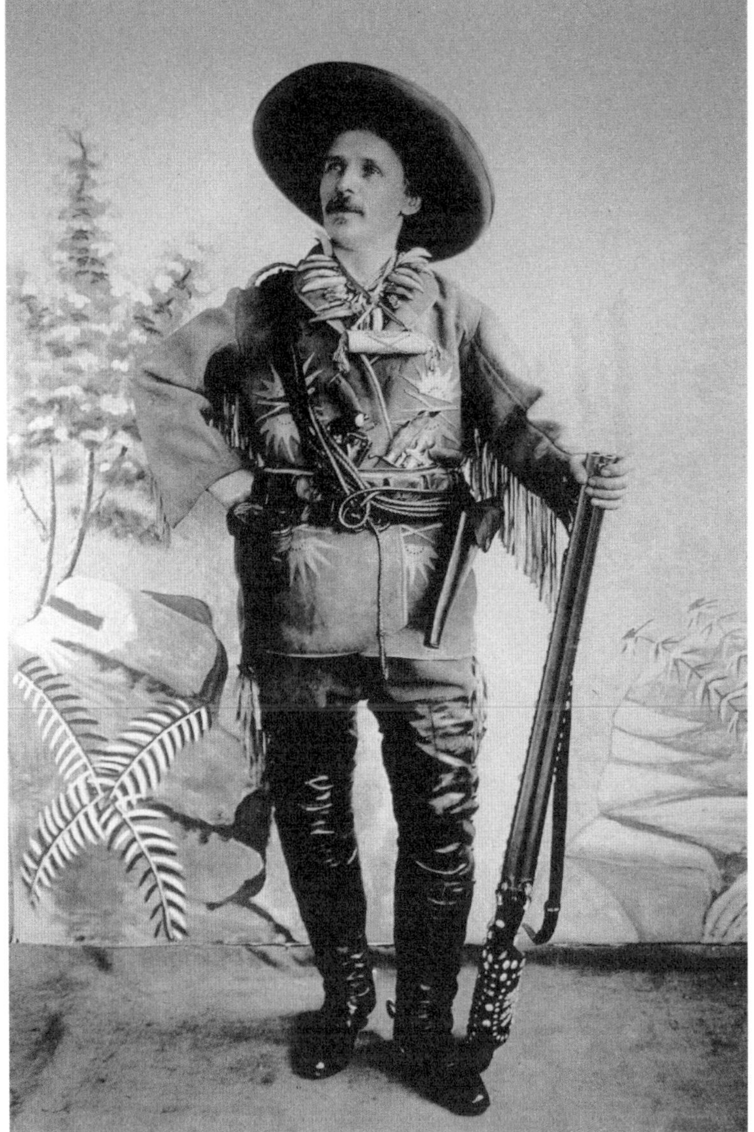

Rivka Galchen is the author of the novel *Atmospheric Disturbances* (2008), and a collection of short stories, *American Innovations* (2014).

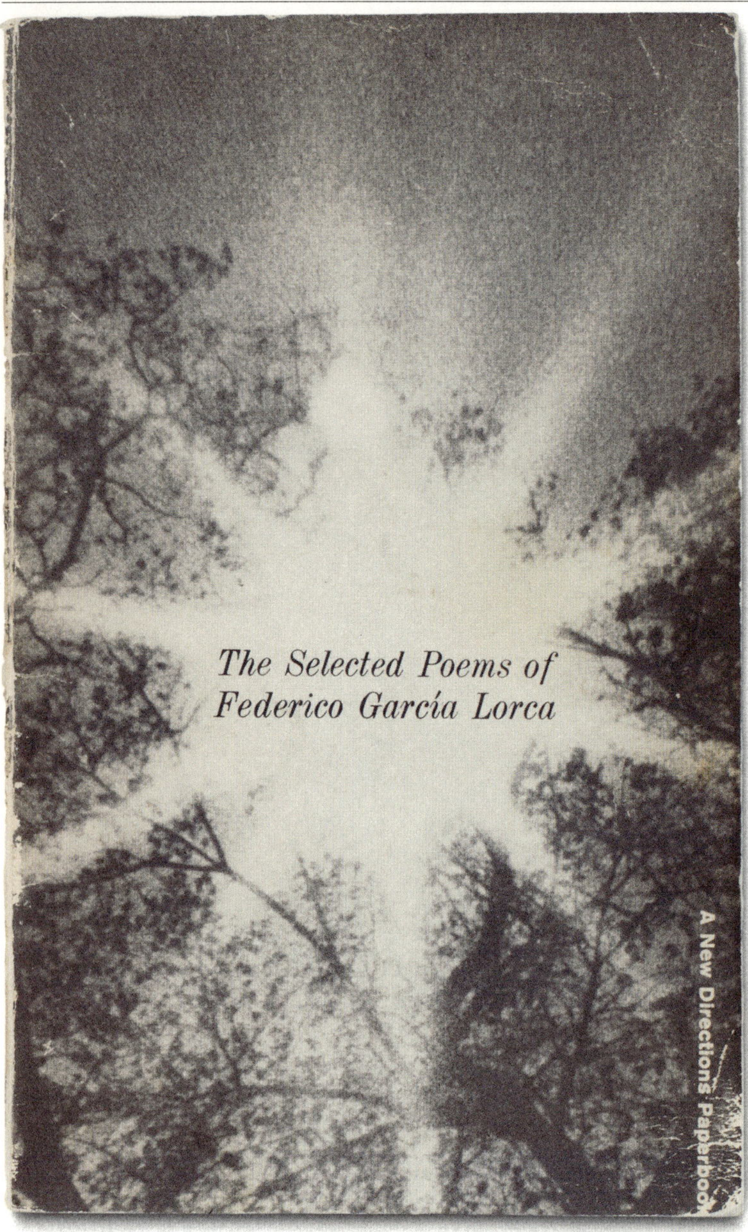

Above: *The Selected Poems of Frederico García Lorca*, 1968

Right: Franz Kafka, *Amerika*, 1946

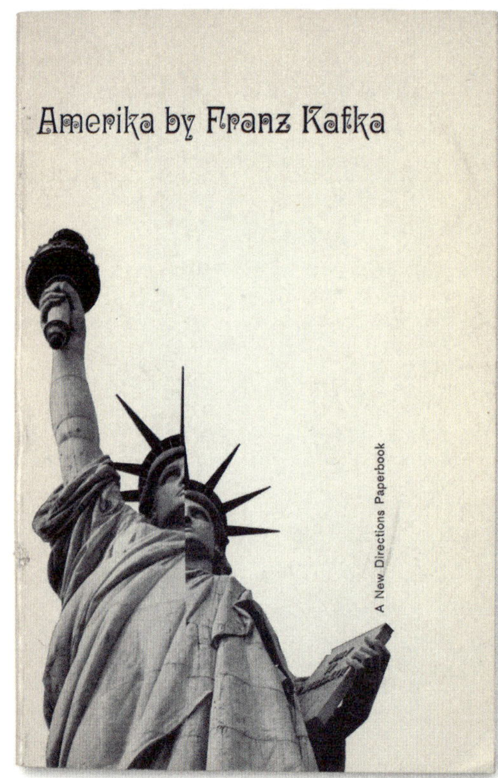

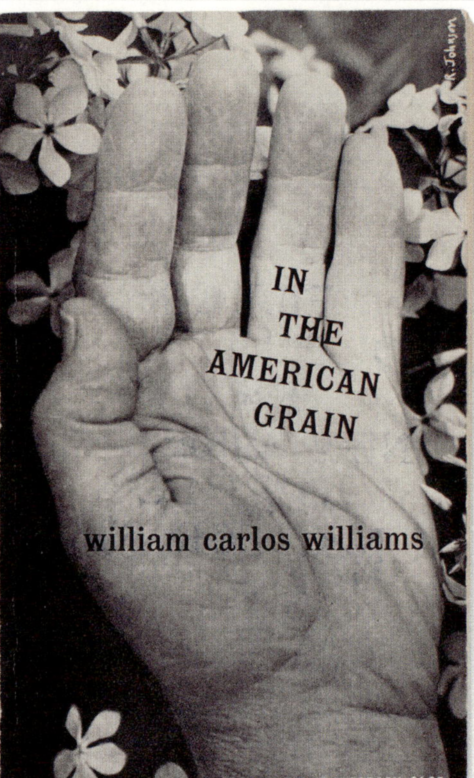

Left: William Carlos Williams, *In the American Grain*, 1956

Below: Yukio Mishima, *Confessions of a Mask*, 1968

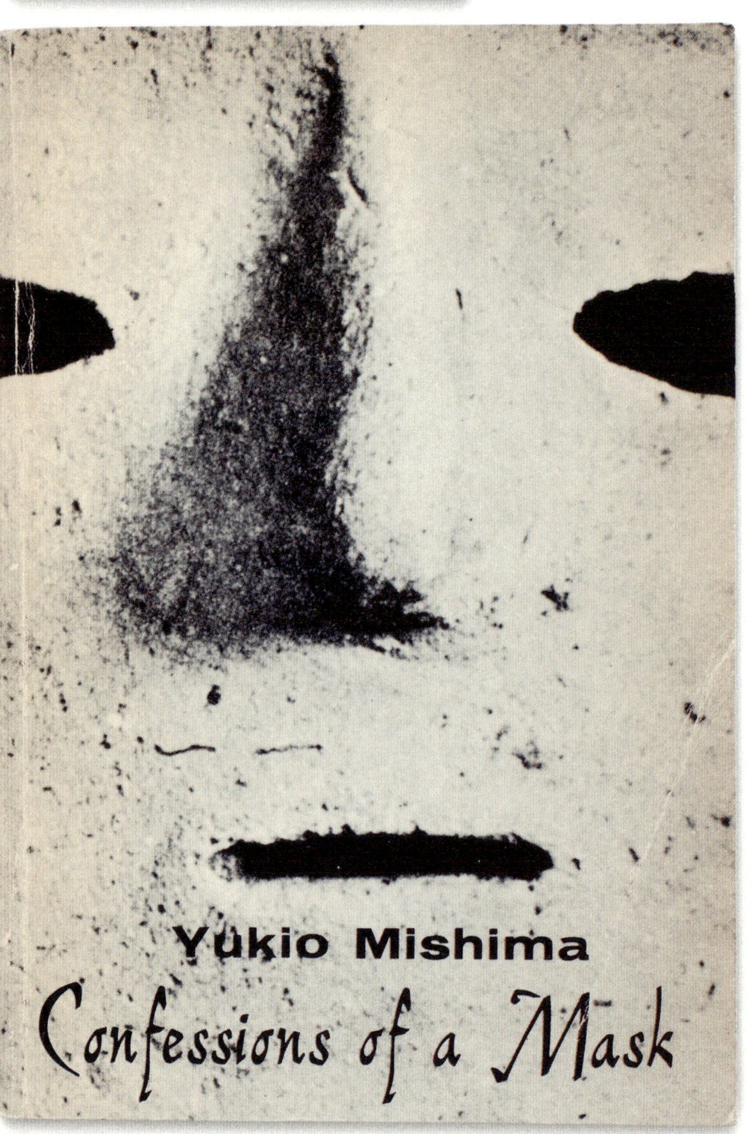

At midcentury, New Directions press published an unparalleled group of writers, packaging challenging literary works in austere and often experimental photographic covers that matched the freshness of the writing inside.

The Publisher's Eye

Carmen Winant

New Directions, one of the most significant publishers of modernist literature, was founded on a failure. In 1933, James Laughlin, a twenty-year-old Harvard freshman and aspiring poet, traveled to Italy to study with Ezra Pound at his so-called "Ezuversity." After assessing the younger man's work, Pound deemed him hopeless and suggested Laughlin "do something useful.... Go back [to school] and be a publisher." Three years later Laughlin took his advice, which surely would have demoralized most young writers, founding New Directions in his college dorm room. Using a hundred-thousand-dollar familial gift—Laughlin was a Pittsburgh-steel heir—his first publication was titled *New Directions in Prose and Poetry*. An anthology, it featured William Carlos Williams, Elizabeth Bishop, Marianne Moore, e.e. cummings, Henry Miller, and Pound himself.

Laughlin would go on to publish a coterie of twentieth-century writers, including T.S. Eliot, Djuna Barnes, Tennessee Williams, Edith Sitwell, Nathanael West, John Hawkes, Kenneth Rexroth, Octavio Paz, Robert Duncan, Gary Snyder, Gregory Corso, Lawrence Ferlinghetti, Gertrude Stein, and Robert Creeley. Unlike some other American presses, Laughlin was interested in publishing foreign writers, and New Directions reprinted Herman Hesse, Rainer Maria Rilke, Franz Kafka, and Guillaume Apollinaire; Laughlin was Nabokov's first American publisher. This whole article could be about those books and how they came to shape an essential cultural ethos. Instead it is about their significant, if less examined, covers and how they came to do the same. Ironically, given how influential the New Directions look came to be, Laughlin morally objected to the idea of people "buying books by eye." In the preface to a 1947 collection of New Directions book jackets, he wrote, "It's a very bad thing. People should buy books for their literary merit. But since I have never published a book which I didn't consider a serious literary work—and never intend to—I have had no bad conscience about using [designers] to increase sales."

New Directions covers are easy to spot but difficult to describe. They are black-and-white. They are stark, contemplative, inky, and dreamlike. They often feature cropped images—usually taken by the designers themselves and rarely credited—printed full bleed, appearing to strain against the margins that hold them. From the 1940s through the mid-1960s, the covers were designed by a small handful of art directors and freelancers, most notably Gilda Hannah, David Ford, Rudolph de Harak, and Gertrude Huston (Laughlin's wife). In some cases, they are simple and straightforward, illustrating the title (*Stand Still Like a Hummingbird* by Henry Miller, which features...a hummingbird arrested in

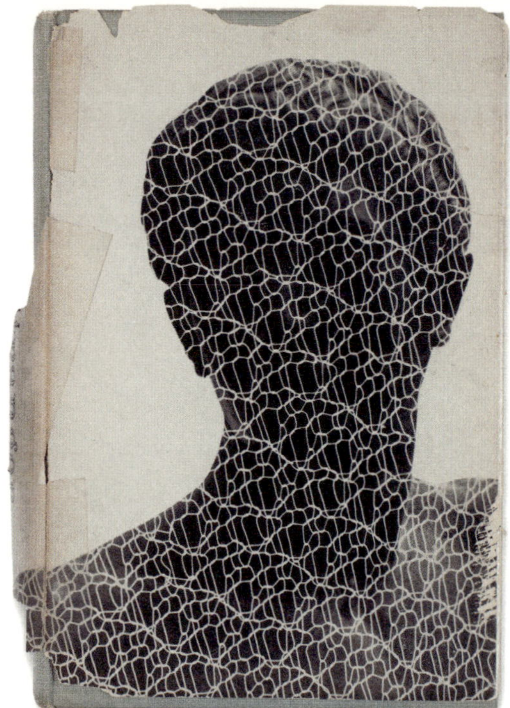

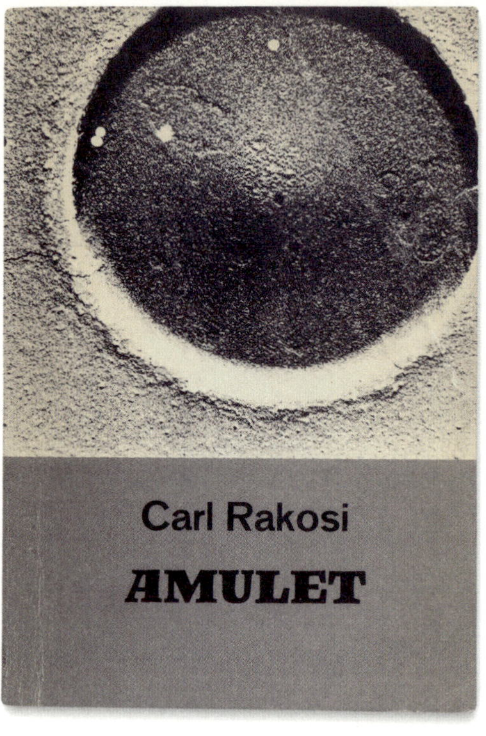

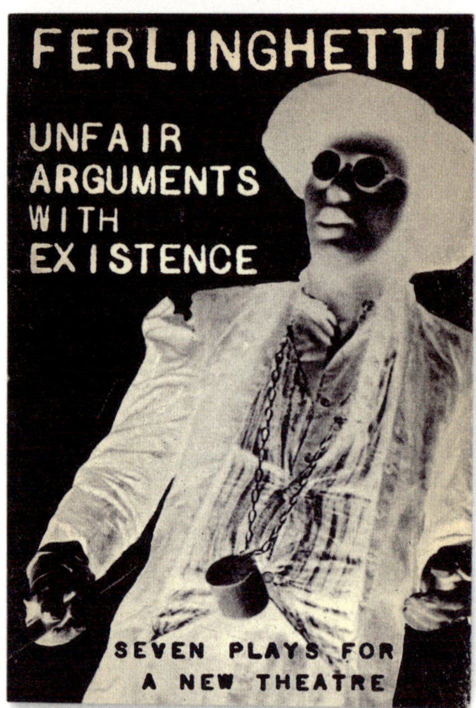

flight), or picturing the author (*Selected Cantos* by Ezra Pound). In other cases, they flirt with abstraction: double exposures (*Nausea* by Jean-Paul Sartre), extreme close-ups (*Confessions of a Mask* by Yukio Mishima), long exposures (*A Season in Hell* by Arthur Rimbaud), negative images (*Unfair Arguments with Existence* by Lawrence Ferlinghetti), reticulated negatives (*Confessions of Zeno* by Italo Svevo), blur (*The Lime Twig* by John Hawkes), photogram and photo-collage (*A Dark Stranger* by Julien Gracq), and heavily contrasted images (*The Happy Birthday of Death* by Gregory Corso) proliferate within their ranks. In rare cases, the covers feature pure photographic abstraction (*New Poems* by Eugenio Montale). Titles and author names are at times marginalized, pushed to the edges of the frame or otherwise worked into the composition of the image. These early photographic covers are arrestingly original—before this point in publishing, book covers tended to feature billboard-esque typography on a plain background—and influential in their experimentation with the plasticity of the printed image and use of photography as integral to the cover design.

Perhaps due to Laughlin's lack of interest in visual appeal, New Directions never had an institutionalized creative mandate. Instead, its earliest book covers reflect the vision that emerged from one man's sensibility, Alvin Lustig. Laughlin met Lustig in 1940 while visiting Tennessee Williams in Los Angeles. At the time of their meeting, the young designer was working as a freelance printer and typographer, doing jobs on a letterpress that he kept in the back room of a drugstore. (Their mutual friend, the noted writer, intellectual, and bookseller Jacob Zeitlin introduced the men.) Less than a year later, Lustig designed his first New Directions cover. In an interview for this article, Lustig's widow, Elaine Lustig Cohen—who also worked at New Directions and photographed for, designed, and collaborated on a handful of covers herself—explained that her husband had full creative reign. "There was no such thing as an art director," said Lustig Cohen. "James did it all. Every time there was a new book, he told Alvin to do the jacket. James either liked the result or he didn't." This lack of interference was in keeping with Laughlin's treatment of manuscripts, which were barely edited before being sent off to print; perhaps Laughlin's response to Pound reflected a tendency to trust other people's instincts with his life project.

Lustig is not especially known for his photographic covers—he worked with largely abstract collage strategies that referenced, and sometimes used, type metal from a print shop—but he did set the tone for New Directions (and indeed, the book design industry) by moving away from purely text-based covers and utilizing pared-down, graphic images that referenced the printing process. When he died at the age of forty in 1955, Gilda Hannah (then Kuhlman) succeeded him as the in-house designer. During her tenure, New Directions covers became almost entirely photographic. It was an all-in-one, streamlined job: Hannah took the majority of the photographs, occasionally commissioning an image or buying from stock, made the design and type decisions, and chose the book's paper. She produced the cover image for *The Selected Poems of Federico García Lorca* using "a defective Leica" in order to achieve lens flare, went uptown in Manhattan to photograph a "relatively non-responsive" Jorge Luis Borges in his hotel room for an early edition of *Labyrinths*, and collaged her photograph of the Statue of Liberty for Kafka's vertiginous *Amerika* cover. By the time she parted ways with the publisher in the early 1960s, citing Laughlin's

notorious lack of prompt payment, New Directions had
established a recognizable and effective formula for its covers,
begun by Lustig and propagated by Hannah and a small handful
of freelancers (including the early Pop artist Ray Johnson): a
graphic black-and-white photograph matched with modest text.

In addition to New Directions, there were other pioneering,
modernist publishers during and after this era. Knopf, and
their imprint Pantheon Books, published significant fiction
and poetry, including Ezra Pound; Grove Press published
Samuel Beckett, Harold Pinter, and the majority of the Beat
writers (including Henry Miller's *Tropic of Cancer*, which
New Directions had turned down for being too sexually explicit).
Meridian Books printed writers like Grace Paley, Thomas
Pynchon, and Ralph Ellison before going out of business.
Independents such as the Jargon Society, Capra Press, Black
Sparrow Books, Graywolf Press, and North Print Press, founded
between 1951 and '74, each modeled themselves in some way on
New Directions. While these other publishers also tried out new
design strategies—Grove Press was particularly innovative—
they did so inconsistently, shifting back and forth between
black-and-white and color, abstract design, photographic images,
and text-only covers. New Directions managed to experiment
with design without losing uniformity; they articulated a
recognizable visual treatise that also boosted sales. As avant-garde
poet Eliot Weinberger wrote in his 1997 obituary for Laughlin
in *Jacket* magazine, "In my adolescence, the black-and-white
photographic covers of ND books were unmistakable on the
bookstore shelves, and I would buy any of them at random,
knowing that if ND had published it, it was something that had to
be read." This holds true decades later for any reader of modernist
literature; an early- to midcentury New Directions book is
instantly identifiable on a crowded shelf.

Today, Laughlin's theory that a cover is just an advertisement
for its book, the "serious" content, would be considered
diminishing and unimaginative. Covers matter beyond the
stores where books are purchased or passed over; readers return
to them hundreds of times over as they tunnel through a book.
Cover design (especially involving photographic images) has
become inexorably entangled with the experience of encountering,
and traveling through, literature.

These several decades of New Directions' photographic
book covers, often the most original when they were simplest,
did something truly modern: by using pictures to describe
words rather than the other way around, they jettisoned the
artificial boundaries between the two. They remind us that both
text and image require a kind of literacy; we often speak of
"reading images," for instance, and poets challenge us to "see"
words on the page. Both text and images have the potential to
objectify and document our lives in a different way from, say,
painting or sculpture (which are rarely utilized in a "nonartistic"
sense). Denise Levertov, who published more than thirty books
of poetry with New Directions, put it best in her early-1970s essay
"Looking at Photographs," written in response to a request from
this magazine: "I have come to see that the art of photography
shares with poetry a factor more fundamental: it makes its
images by means anybody and everybody uses for the most banal
purposes, just as poetry makes its structures, its indivisibility
of music and meaning, out of the same language for utilitarian
purposes, for idle chatter, for uninspired lying … photographs
teach the poet to see better." Levertov could have illustrated
her essay with the cover of *The Cosmological Eye*, the first book
of Henry Miller's published in the United States—by New
Directions—in 1939. Superimposed atop a full-bleed, black-and-
white photograph of clouds is a single, open eye. It belongs to
James Laughlin.

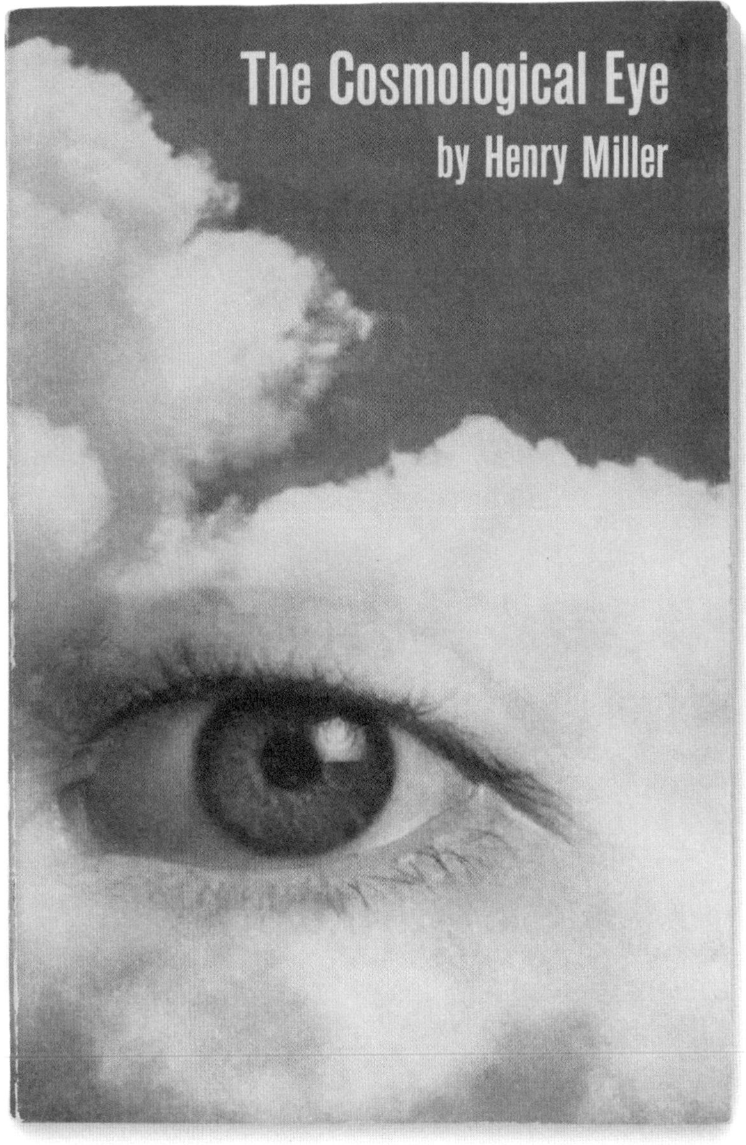

Henry Miller,
The Cosmological Eye,
1939
Courtesy New Directions
Press, New York

Carmen Winant is an artist and writer.
She is a professor of visual studies and
contemporary art history at Columbus
College of Art and Design.

With additional research from Luke Stettner

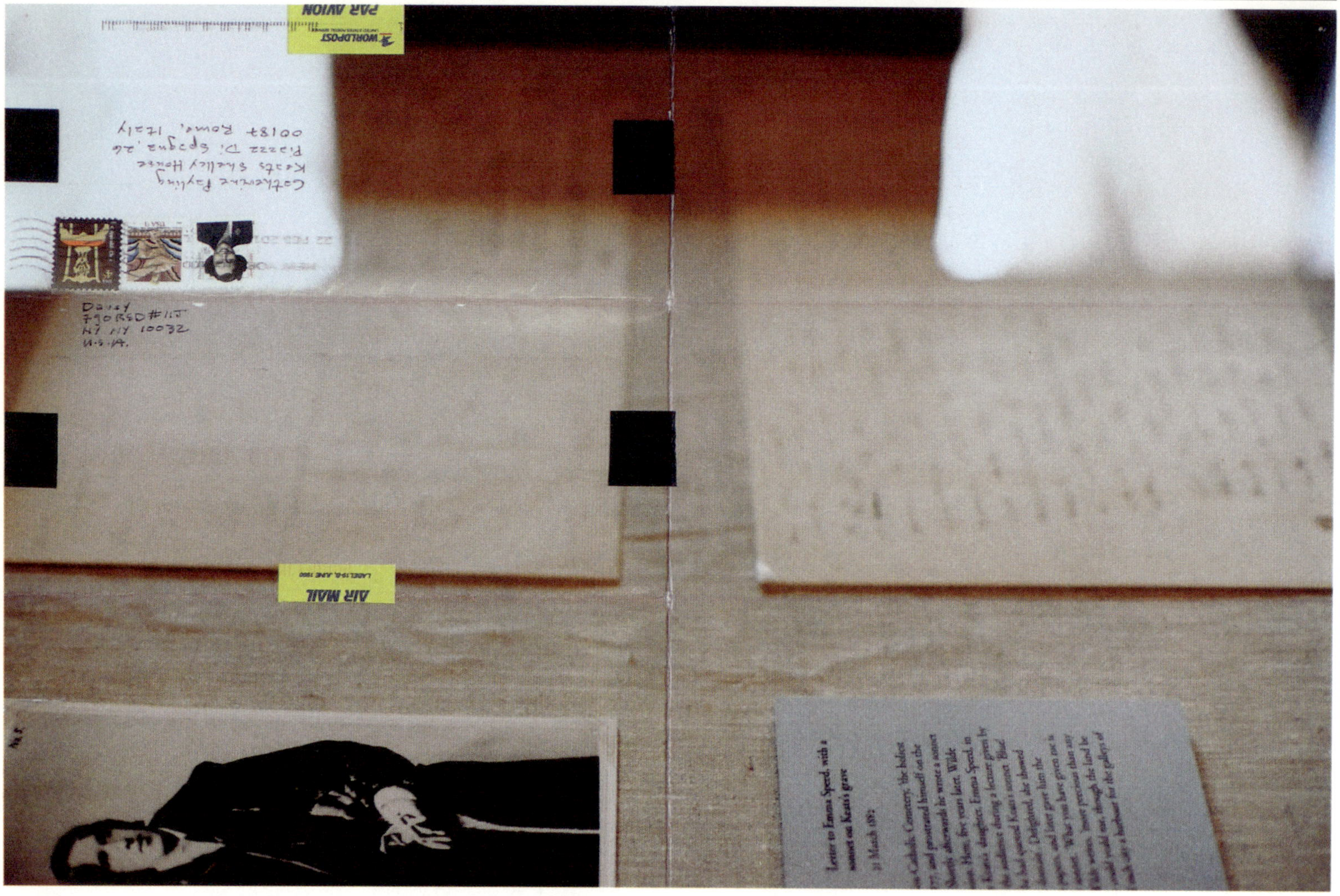
Daisy
790 RSD #15
NY NY 10032
U.S.A.

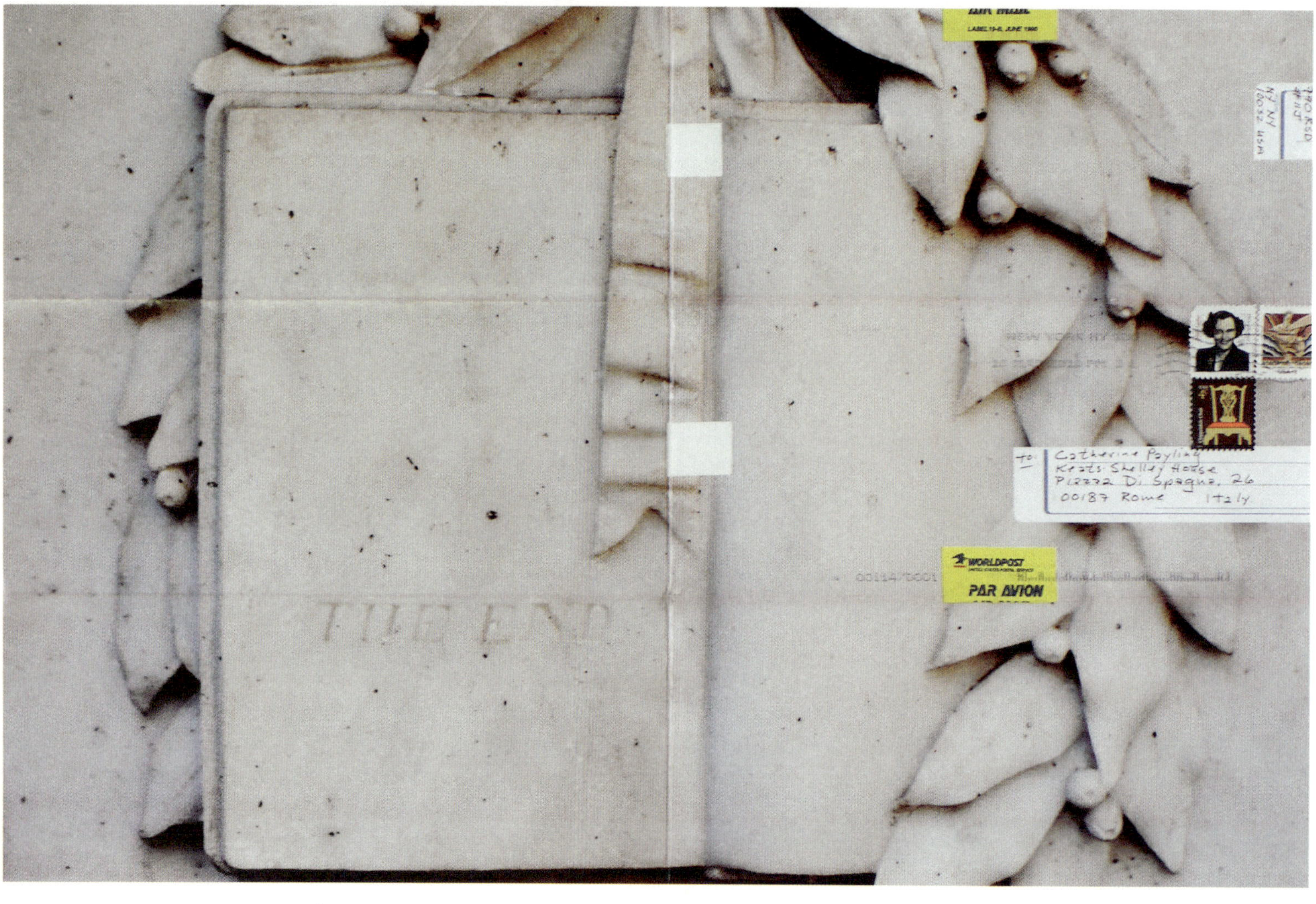
LABEL 19-B, JUNE 1990
to:
Catherine Payling
Keats Shelley House
Piazza Di Spagna, 26
00187 Rome Italy
WORLDPOST
PAR AVION
THE END

Rescripted

After a conversation between Moyra Davey and Matthew S. Witkovsky

Literary and personal histories coalesce in Moyra Davey's elegant works in photography and video. For her ongoing "mailer" projects, begun in 2006 and included in the 2012 Whitney Biennial, Davey folds photographs made with a point-and-shoot camera and printed on durable paper and mails them to various recipients, including family and colleagues; when unfolded and displayed in grid formation on gallery walls, the images, photo-letters marked with sections of colorful tape and postage stamps, bear the traces of transit. Her video works invoke writers, from the transgressive Jean Genet to the nineteenth-century proto-feminist Mary Wollstonecraft, as in *Les Goddesses* (2011), a piece Davey describes as "a love letter to my family," and at other moments depict readers' reactions to passages of writing. In the following conversation, loosely structured as a play, the artist speaks with Matthew S. Witkovsky, curator at the Art Institute of Chicago, about her practice of interlacing photography with literary touchstones, the Norwegian literary phenomenon Karl Ove Knausgaard, with whom Davey shares an affinity for the quotidian, and her work as a writer, which ranges from reflections on photography to personal essays. —**The Editors**

An eleventh-floor apartment on Riverside Drive in northern Manhattan. Stately multistory buildings, sloping streets, longtime tenants. "How the Upper West Side used to be." Sunny rooms, improbably bare in feel despite the jumble of books and framed artworks coating the simple plaster walls: posters by Sister Corita Kent, photographs by Bruce Davidson, Zoe Leonard, Danny Lyon. Furniture has a spartan or improvised quality (which is it? Moyra says both). In the kitchen at rear, a lovingly restored midcentury stove with a griddle and four small ovens sits in an elongated space that evokes rusticity. None of her own photographs, but of course plenty of what appears in them, such as shelves of records topped by old stereo equipment. A sense of being on set, even, for viewers of Moyra Davey's Les Goddesses, *particularly strong when one sees in the back bedroom two bikes and a low mattress, on which Davey leafed through her early photographs in that book-length video.*

MW: **While it is true that artists in every domain make books, there is a long history of the photobook in particular as a main form of expression, rather than a side project or a record of other works of art. As a photographer, did you come to writing through an interest in making books? What was your first book of writings?**

MD: *Long Life Cool White* (2008). But what got me hooked on writing as part of my working method was editing *Mother Reader* (2001). I spent a couple of years reading all those texts, shaping the book, and then wrote an introduction. After that, reading and writing became so much more central to what I do.

Habits of writing give you certain license, I think, that for better or worse you don't get in the visual arts.

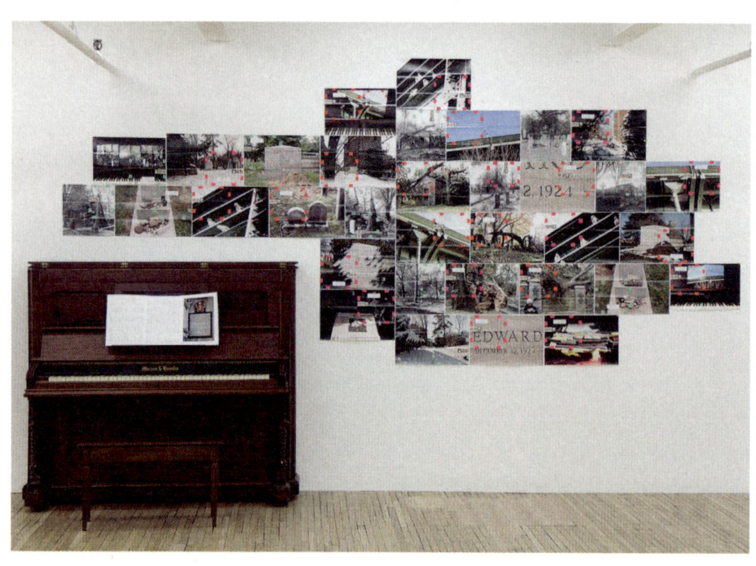

Ornament and Reproach,
2012–13 (installation view)

MW: **Were you not reading as much before putting that book together?**

MD: I was reading while studying for my MFA, so, targeted theoretical stuff, and then in the Whitney program, also targeted reading. After that I stopped that kind of reading and started to read literature.

MW: **Funny: I stopped reading literature, which had given me all my ideas, once I was through with my undergraduate major in literary theory and had shifted fully into art history. The malformation of the art historian, no doubt: you get impatient with plot and drop the book once you think you've understood its underlying structure.**

MD: I don't read so much fiction, but like everyone lately I have been reading Karl Ove Knausgaard (*My Struggle*, 2012 [English translation]). It took me a hundred pages to get into it, and I frankly didn't think I would continue—but then halfway through there's a major dramatic event and I was hooked. He's like candy now.

MW: **What's his style?**

MD: Endless description. You have to imagine that the guy has a photographic memory. Run-on pages of mundane but fascinating details of his life, conversations recorded, and, here and there, digressions on figures like the poet Friedrich Hölderlin, or jabs at post-Structuralist theory. It's amazing.

MW: **Is it the sort of thing where he tries to keep an impersonal voice, so that meaning comes out of an endless accumulation of facts?**

MD: He has a slightly caustic voice, a bit misanthropic, ever so slightly, and maybe that's what keeps it impersonal. Although he does express a lot of emotion, a lot of grief. I want to think more about how he does it, because it interests me.

MW: **You're building your craft as a writer …**

MD: I am, yeah, slowly. I've never taken a writing class, though, in my entire life. I've always been a very reluctant student, in photography as well. Impatient. Always thought of myself as a bad student. If Eileen Myles were teaching a poetry class, though, I would jump on that. I know she has done that, back in the day.

Getting back to structure: I know it's important. For someone to want to read something, there has to be some glue, a raison d'être, but yet I resist it. To read any piece of writing or see a movie that does the full circle thing is very satisfying—the closure, the return—but for some perverse, stubborn reason, I avoid it.

MW: **And yet your video *Les Goddesses* is beautiful, like a nineteenth-century novel. Expansive yet incredibly tightly composed. It does have closure of a sort, and it employs many novelistic attributes: lengthy narration, the introduction and development of characters. It also has the symmetry of a return at the end to what comes in the beginning.**

MD: I guess it does. It starts and ends with still photographs. But I did that almost unconsciously.

MW: **Yes, we begin the film by looking at your photograph of your sisters in the early 1980s, standing, as you say, like caryatids, and then at another that shows two of them, Jane and Kate, lying on the grass—but in voice-over you are talking**

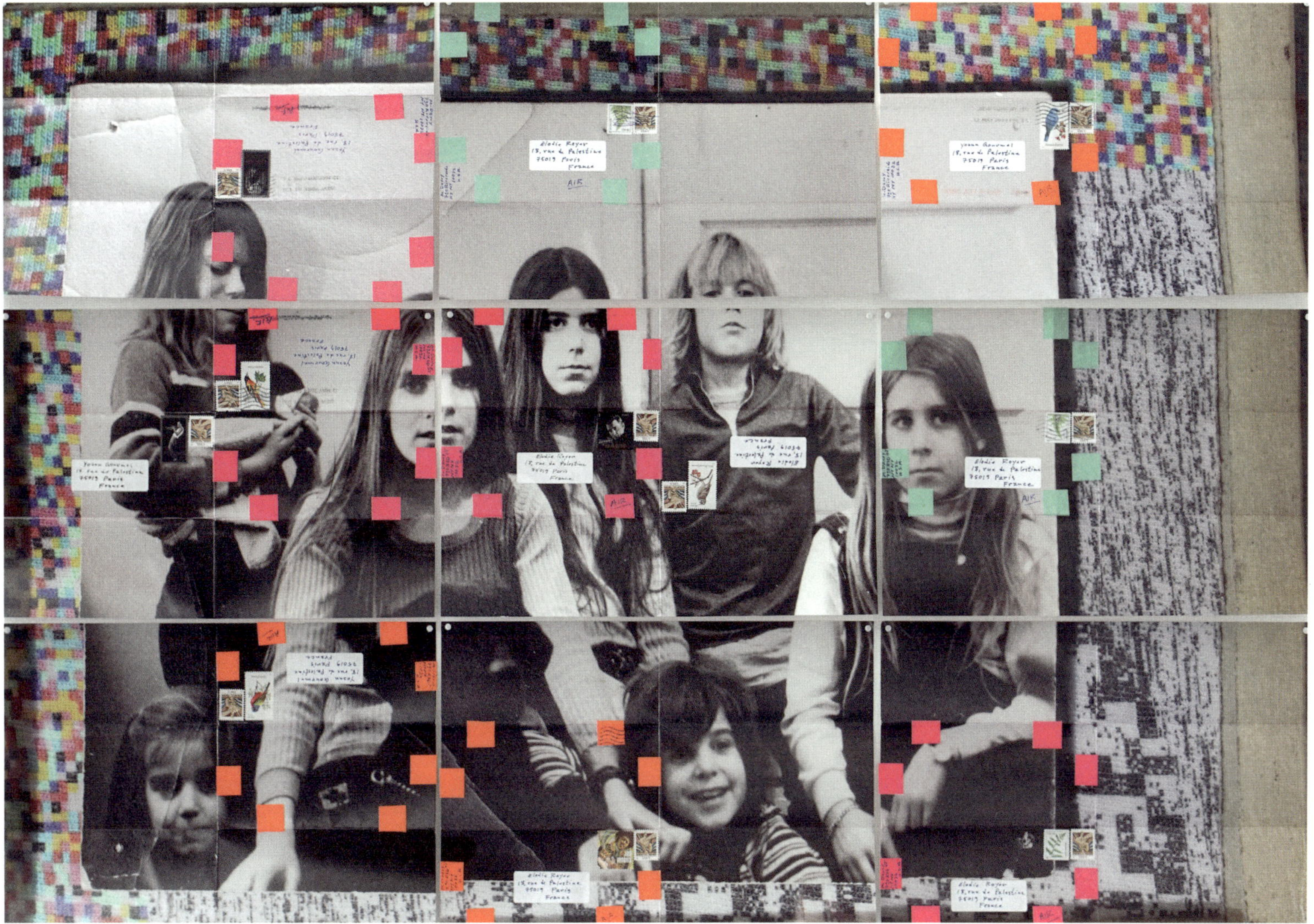

about the Wollstonecraft family. Literature and photography are held up for comparison and further analogized to the relation of still and moving images.

MD: And to mise-en-scène versus documentary photography.

MW: These comparisons are not parallels, not sets of lines that never touch. Instead, you've polluted relations, crossed the lines. Nor is the content exactly pure: sex, drugs, debauchery!

MD: Yeah, I think I'm going to do a part two. Things have happened in my family since I made that video. Jane's youngest daughter, Hannah, overdosed on fentanyl, a synthetic opiate. Very potent. She was nineteen. She's in the last video I made, *My Saints* (2014).

MW responds with surprise and momentary upset at the revelation. MD's voice remains steady.

Hannah hid it so well. When you see her in *My Saints*, she's chatting, ebullient; you would never suspect she was on downers. There were signs, but a lot of people missed the signs. That and other things make me want to—[*emphatic*] Matt, I could revisit that entire video and remake it totally differently.

MW: A rewrite then. Habits of writing give you certain license, I think, that for better or worse you don't get in the visual arts. Published revisions are a normal part of the writing process. A fictional story—or an art history essay—

can start its public life at a reading, then become a magazine **article, a contribution to a multi-author anthology, and after, a chapter in a book. What would you revisit if you did remake the video?**

MD: *Les Goddesses* was kind of a love letter to my family. I think I idealized them. Everything in it is true, of course. But a lot is left out, which is one reason I term those videos "auto-fiction." Remaking the work, I could do something much grittier. I didn't show the family as they are now, for instance—

MW: Would you then be putting people back in the work? In *Les Goddesses* you treat the living human figure literally, but not pictorially. The video shows photographs of your family only from your earliest years—pictures that you showed no more than one or two times before "giving up" taking photographs of people around 1985.

MD: I actually videotaped my sister Jane walking, talking, smoking cigarettes in the park. But I don't know if I'd have the guts to pursue that kind of thing. The remove and control you have working with still photographs is pretty great. Although, *My Saints* is made up of interviews with friends and family. So maybe I'm a step closer to filming my siblings in the flesh.

MW: You do have remarkable formal means to bridge the gap between photography and writing. The mailers, for example: these are recent photographic grids of yours, the prints for which you have printed on heavier, coated paper, then folded and sent by post to friends and colleagues. The individual

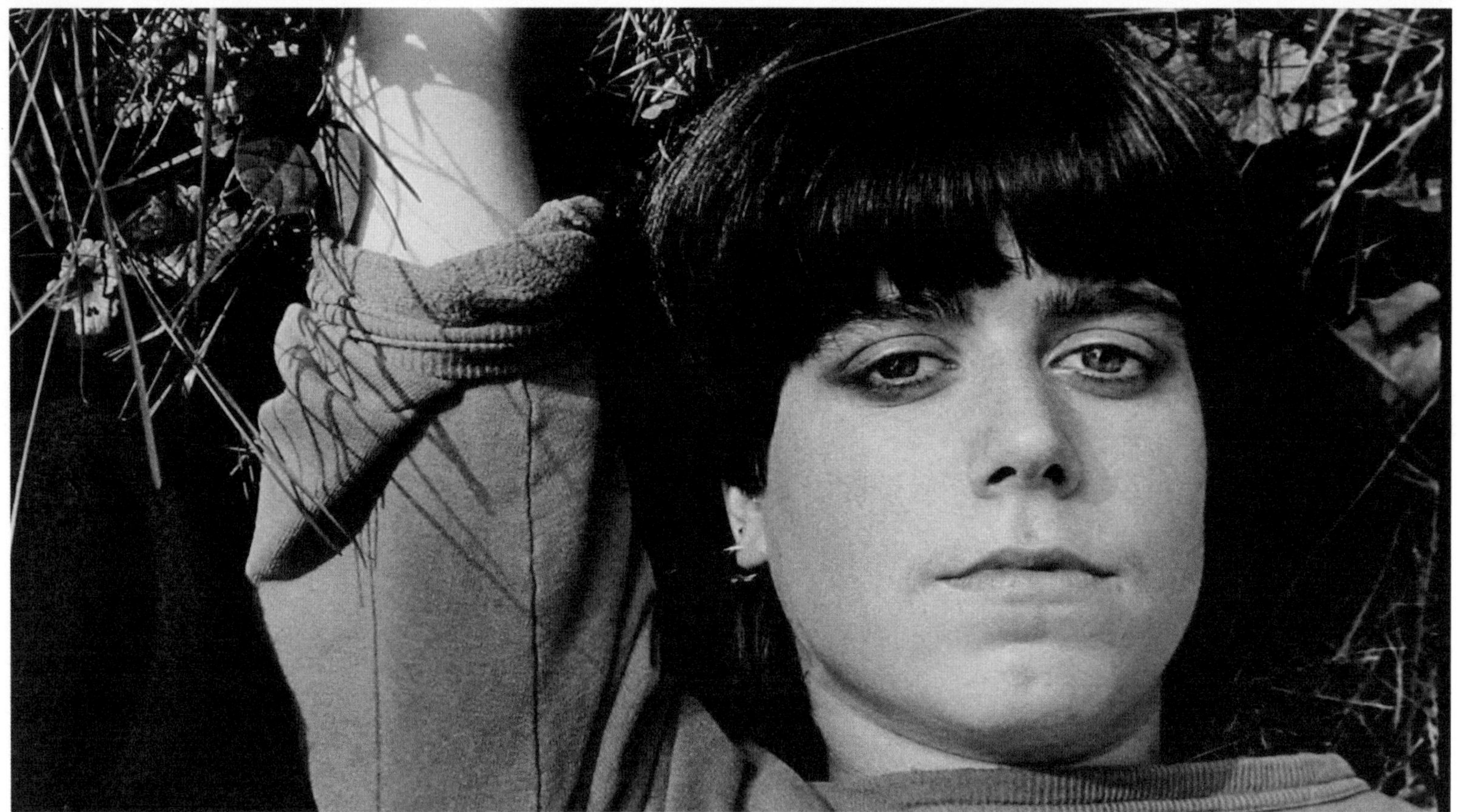

images (ranging from a handful to several dozen) are gathered together for display as a composite wall work. Their address and your own are plain to see, covering the images, along with adhesive tabs that were used to hold the folded photograph flat in the mail. They, too, are love letters, sent only to those you know.

MD: Here is one I made showing my sisters, derived from a group photo taken around 1971. We all have that hippie look. It's called *Seven* (2014), based on a J.D. Salinger character who is one of seven siblings. It's funny because, other than *Catcher in the Rye* I don't really like Salinger…. After I made the photo piece, I dug up this clever, sniping letter from one of my sisters, sent to me when I was in Paris in 1977, describing all the shenanigans going down with my siblings in my absence. And it was exactly seven pages long, a perfect match. I photographed each page separately and concealed her name to protect her privacy, though I doubt she'd care.

MW: **Fragments of writing, on the one hand, and fragments of a picture on the other hand. It should be pointed out that the pictorial fragments don't divide neatly—we see parts of one or more sisters in each of the (nine) parts of the family photo mailer—whereas your mailer of the one sister's letter does appear as a single sheet per picture.**

MD: Except that parts of the writing are covered with stamps and labels and tape, so you can't read everything. You can read passages but not all of the writing.

MW: **It's another way of revising: covering over. Hiding and revealing simultaneously seems to be your way of coming to terms with a sort of confessional self-expression.**

MD: It is confessional, but I've found distance through a certain dispassionate, dissociative stance. I feel simultaneously that it's me and not me writing and performing this material. It would

be a good challenge now to make a video where the faces are no longer pretty.

MW: **You've quoted a line from Jean Genet, saying I'm fifty and I look like sixty, and I think that's fabulous …**

MD: He says, I'm not ashamed.

MW: **Right, and he's writing to this young man, Java.**

MD: His former lover. And he adds, "I even find it rather restful."

MW: **Yes, I'm amazed I forgot that bit of the quote, because it is beautiful. *Restful*: what a perfect word. A whole lot of youthful energy is expended in making oneself presentable.**

MD: And middle-age energy too. In a section of *My Saints* titled "Vanity," I start with a line about the "bleaching white light of vanity," and then enter the frame, my face sun-bleached out. Later I go to "Vanitas," a view of one of my nieces, who has a tattoo of her skeleton on her back—all the bones—wait, I have to get you the picture to show you…

Walks away. A half-minute of silence while she searches.

MW: **This is an incredible picture, your niece, her skeletal structure imprinted on her skin. Like wearing your own X-ray—more questions of how to articulate structure and content. I was about to ask how you structure the making of your videos, whether you follow conventions of scripting or storyboarding.**

MD: I don't storyboard, but I always write something. I wrote this text (*Burn the Diaries*) and thought it was going to be the video (*My Saints*). Then I started to perform it and realized that I need to get others in front of the camera to make this work. I do appear in the one scene, and I'm heard off-camera pretty regularly. There's a lot of talking but also text—rolling and static. That was a device I set out to use from the onset as a way to modulate the spoken word.

MW: You ask viewers to look at language and read it as well. Unlike many career writers but like a lot of visual artists interested in language, you seem fascinated by the material objects and paraphernalia of writing.

MD: I love paper, and I have fountain pens, and I love soft pencils; but the only way I can seriously compose anything is on the computer. Actually, I really began writing only when I met Jason [Simon, a filmmaker], in 1986, and he had a little Mac. It was so much more accessible to me to type on that.

MW: When I read your books now, I hear your voice, not my own. You read more slowly aloud than I do when reading to myself, so I slow down to accommodate what I remember as your cadences and pauses. It's an odd feeling, having another voice in my head.

MD: When I sit down to write something, my instinct is "start with the most pressing thing." Then I go to the notebooks, read through them systematically and pull out anything of interest. And then build on those extracts. You know what I would like to do: write without intertitles. That would be a good challenge, because using intertitles is a very easy way for me to write, in short fragments. Having the intertitles gives my writing a de facto structure.

MW: I just assumed you used intertitles out of a persistent love for Walter Benjamin.

MD: Yes, and Roland Barthes. But it is a bit of a crutch.

MD and MW each get up to fetch something for the other. MW returns with a small book of pictures and quotations from Japanese photographer Shomei Tomatsu.

MW: There were just a few copies printed of this book after a show that we did last fall, which in its concept was intended as a book on a wall. The installation had writings interspersed with photographs, in quotations printed at the size of a standard 11-by-14-inch photograph; text as image and also as the equal of images. He was a brilliant writer, I think. It was an especially meaningful show for me, largely because of the importance of his dual practice as writer and photographer.

MD: Thank you for this!

Speaks as she leafs slowly through the book.

I have his book [*Chewing Gum and Chocolate*, Aperture, 2014] and have just started reading it. You can tell right away he had the knack, a natural scribe. It's so unpretentious, so unassuming, but so observant of what is going on around him, and of himself, his own position in that postwar world. Writing that's a little bit elliptical, running on a parallel track to the photographs yet intersecting at points with them.

MW: When you think about it, for all the emphasis on book-making in photography—and that is where we started this afternoon—there seem to be relatively few photographers who give themselves seriously to writing. Tomatsu is unusual in that sense. Maybe it's a further sign of his promiscuity, a word you've used lately as well. Tomatsu moves in and

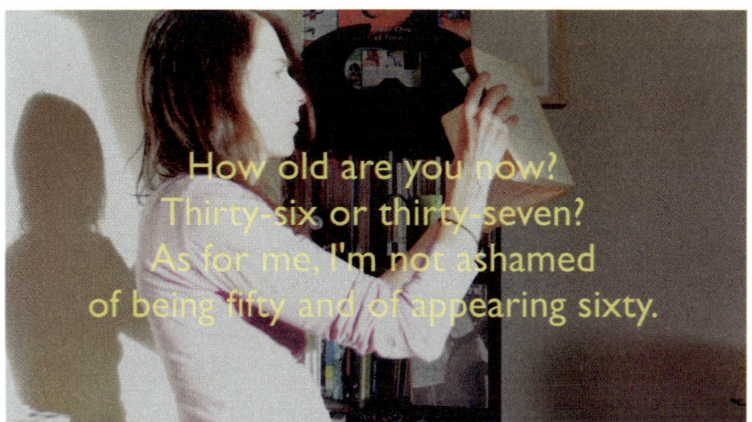

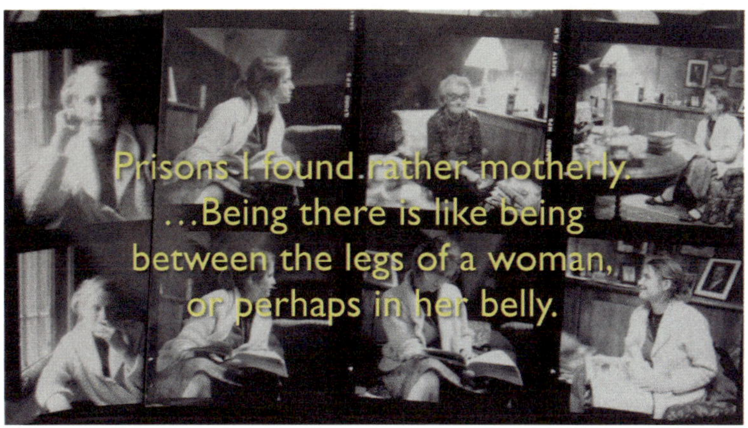

Above:
Video stills from *My Saints*, 2014

To read any piece of writing or see a movie that does the full circle thing is very satisfying— the closure, the return—but for some perverse, stubborn reason, I avoid it.

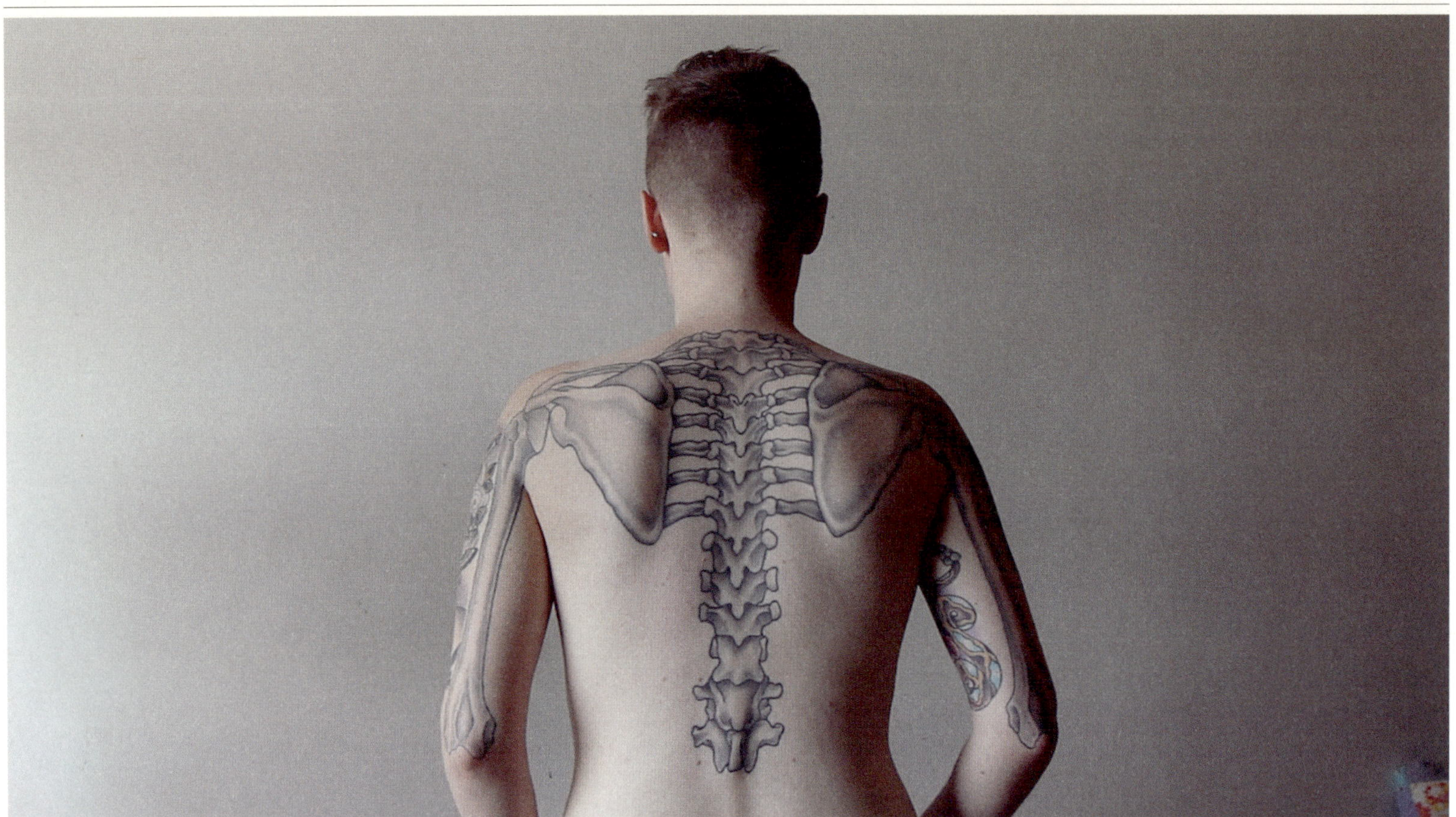

out of straight documentary photography, but he also likes montage, he likes abstraction, he likes mixing color and black and white … and he likes to write, and even to test different voices, from the statistical to the emotional, the novelistic to the epistolary. His great midcareer retrospective book *I Am a King* (1972) has at its center a section on the height of the student protests, in 1969–70, and in this section he pairs photographs with a month's worth of diary entries. In short, Tomatsu does not mind being literary. That's true right from his start in magazines at the tail end of the 1950s and early 1960s. This is very unlike his near-contemporary Robert Frank, whose book *The Americans* (1958–59) depended for its words on Jack Kerouac. It's even further from the classic photobooks of the 1920s and '30s, in which photographers' efforts were often framed with essays or statements by hired critics. Although there are many more examples of photographer-writers in recent decades, an extensive literary commitment such as yours remains unusual.

Of course there is still the question of whether anyone reads.

MD: Living with a seventeen-year-old boy who only wants to leave the house with his phone (permanently outlined on his thigh) and his wallet—won't carry a book—it's a question we ask here every day. He listens to music, and he reads challenging stuff for school, but he stopped reading for pleasure once electronics entered his life. I, on the other hand, should devote more time to listening to music.

[*Conversation continues.*]

Matthew S. Witkovsky is Richard and Ellen Sandor Chair and Curator, department of photography, the Art Institute of Chicago. Photography is now celebrating its fortieth anniversary as a curatorial department with a series of presentations from the permanent collection, including a room devoted to work by Moyra Davey.

Pictures

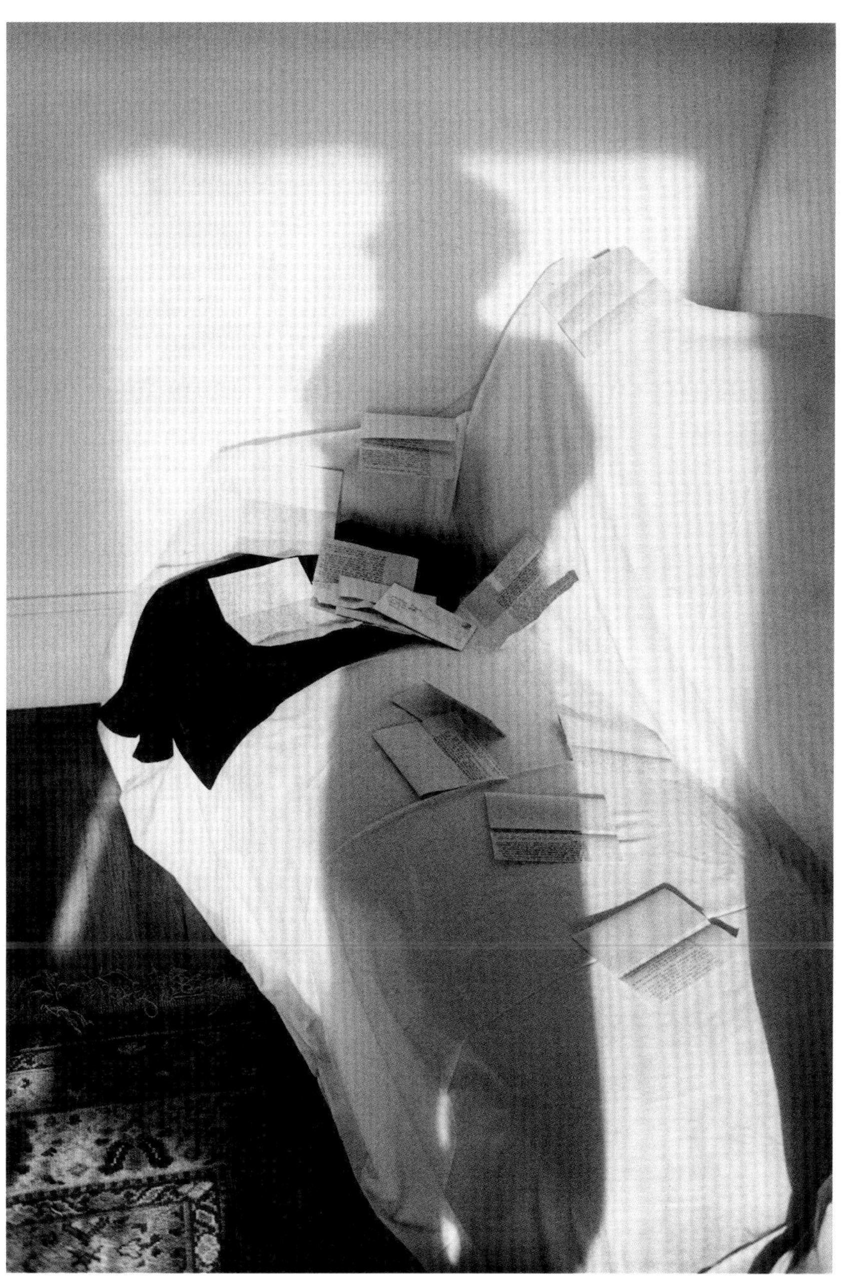

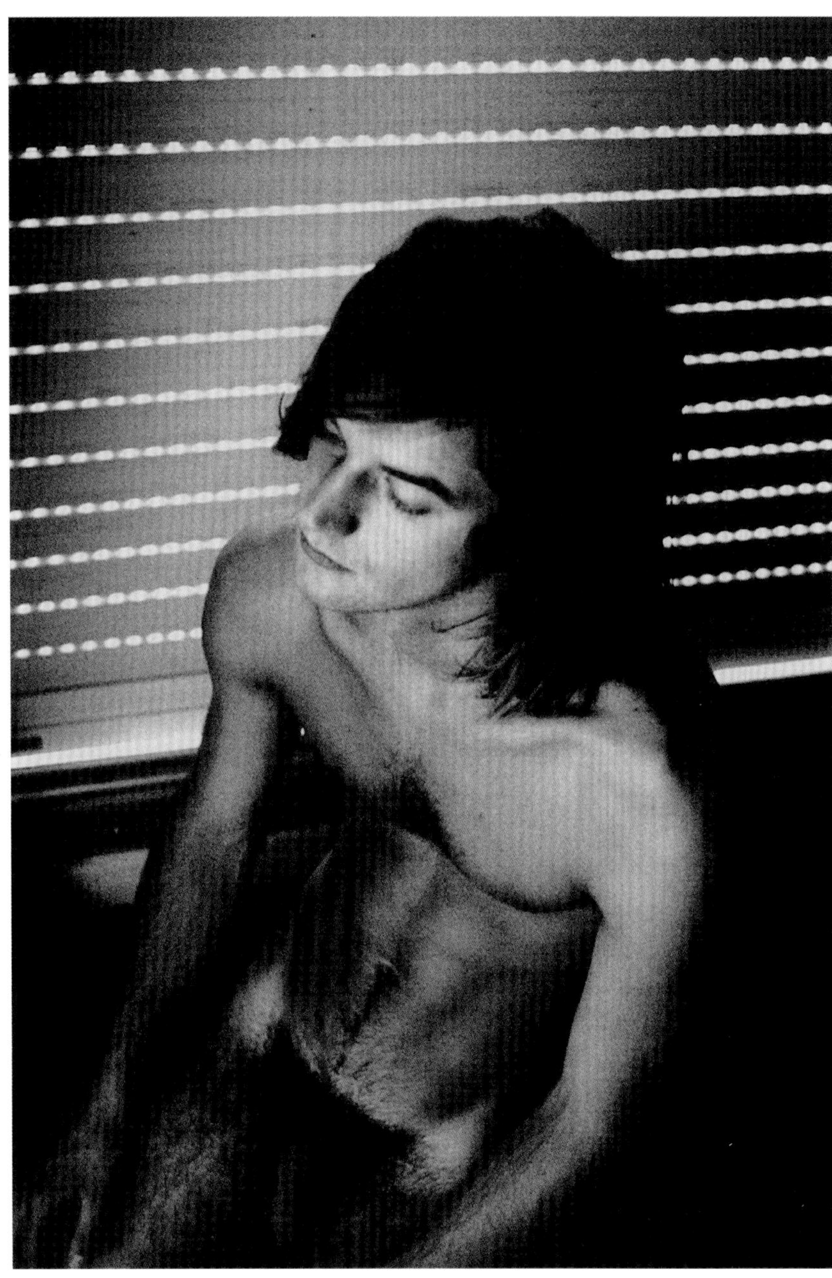

I shall always refuse to be a photographer: this attraction frightens me, it seems to me that it can quickly turn to madness, because everything is photographable, everything is interesting to photograph, and out of one day of one's life one could cut out thousands of instants, thousands of little surfaces, and if one begins why stop?
—Hervé Guibert, The Mausoleum of Lovers, Journals 1976–1991

When Hervé Guibert died in 1991, he had just turned thirty-six. A year before, the writer, journalist, and photographer had opened his autobiographical novel, *To the Friend Who Did Not Save My Life*, with the declaration that he had AIDS, but went on to insist that he "would become, by an extraordinary stroke of luck, one of the first people on earth to survive this deadly malady." When the book caused a sensation (magnified by the fact that one of its characters was a thinly disguised Michel Foucault, whose HIV-positive status contributed to his death in 1984), Guibert became the strikingly handsome, articulate, and very public face of AIDS in France. He didn't avoid the spotlight, but it made him famous in a way he never wanted to be, and the attention exhausted him even before the disease left him frail and nearly blind. That extraordinary stroke of luck eluded him. Two weeks before he succumbed, he tried to commit suicide with an overdose of pills but failed.

Wildly prolific, Guibert was driven, compulsive, and rarely satisfied. He wrote twenty-three other books, nearly all of them in the ten years before his death (only a handful have been translated into English). In *The Mausoleum of Lovers*, a collection of journal entries published posthumously in 2011 and just translated, he often sounds melancholic, if not desperate, but then much of it was written as an open letter to an inconstant lover who was allowed to read the journals as they were written. Melodramatic moments—furious, passionate, delusional—alternate with cooler observations, often about photography, which was, along with writing, a highly personal form of expression for Guibert. "The photo that someone other than I could take, that isn't bound to the particular relation I have to this or that, I don't want to take it," he writes.

Very little of his photographic work has been published or exhibited in the United States, so the larger body of work remains rather elusive. Still, much of what has appeared is striking: emotionally warm, even a bit sentimental at times, but stylistically cool and confident. His images range from artful interiors and landscapes to pictures of friends, family, and lovers. The mood is usually hushed and intimate. Working in a distinctive black and white that tends toward soft platinum grays, he made what feel like visual diary entries, quick but thoughtful notes, often recording his immediate surroundings—his desk, his mantel, his bookcase—with the same descriptive intensity he brought to photographs of boys in his bed. Even in his most seductive self-portraits, Guibert never seems show-offy. The work is restrained and subtle—as if it were made not with a public in mind but for himself and a small circle of friends. We often feel we're peeking into a private and somewhat privileged world, where much is revealed and just as much withheld.

In *Ghost Image*, a 1982 collection of Guibert's brief essays on photography, reissued this year by University of Chicago Press, he writes about photographers he admires. They're an idiosyncratic pantheon that includes Diane Arbus, Pierre Molinier, F. Holland Day, George Hoyningen-Huene, and Duane Michals, the last of whom seems especially influential on the selection of images included here. Clearly, he looked long and hard at his precursors and his contemporaries, but some of his most telling essays are dialogues with his critical self, an accusatory voice that he never allows to have the last word. When that voice points out that much of his work "oozes homosexuality," he shoots back,

How could it be otherwise? It's not that I want to hide it, or that I want to boast about it arrogantly. But it's the least I can do to be sincere. How can you speak about photography without speaking of desire? If I mask my desire, if I deprive it of its gender, if I leave it vague … I would feel as if I were weakening my stories, or writing carelessly …. The image is the essence of desire and if you desexualize the image, you reduce it to theory.

Guibert's criticism can stray into knotty intellectual territory, but he steers clear of dry, deadening theory. What's most engaging about his work in writing and photography is its frankness and sincerity—qualities the contemporary avant-garde has little use for. Even his restraint feels passionate—an elegance at once instinctive and hard-won.

Hervé Guibert

Vince Aletti

Vince Aletti writes about photography exhibitions for the *New Yorker*'s Goings on About Town section and on photography books in a regular column for *Photograph*. He is also a regular contributor to *W*, *Artforum*, and *Camera*.

This page:
Autoportrait (Self-portrait),
1976

Opposite, top:
La sacristie (The sacristy),
1980

Opposite, bottom:
Sienne (Siena), 1979

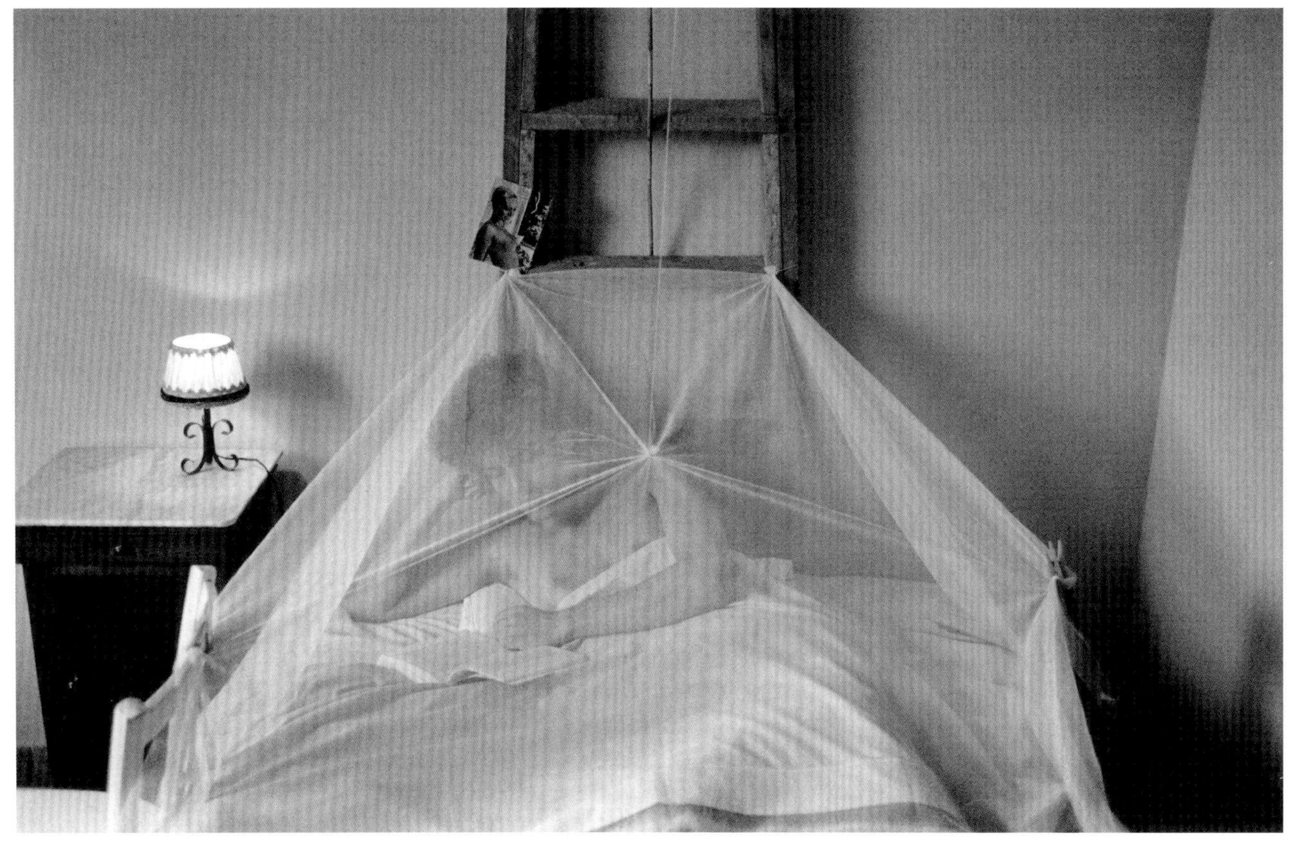

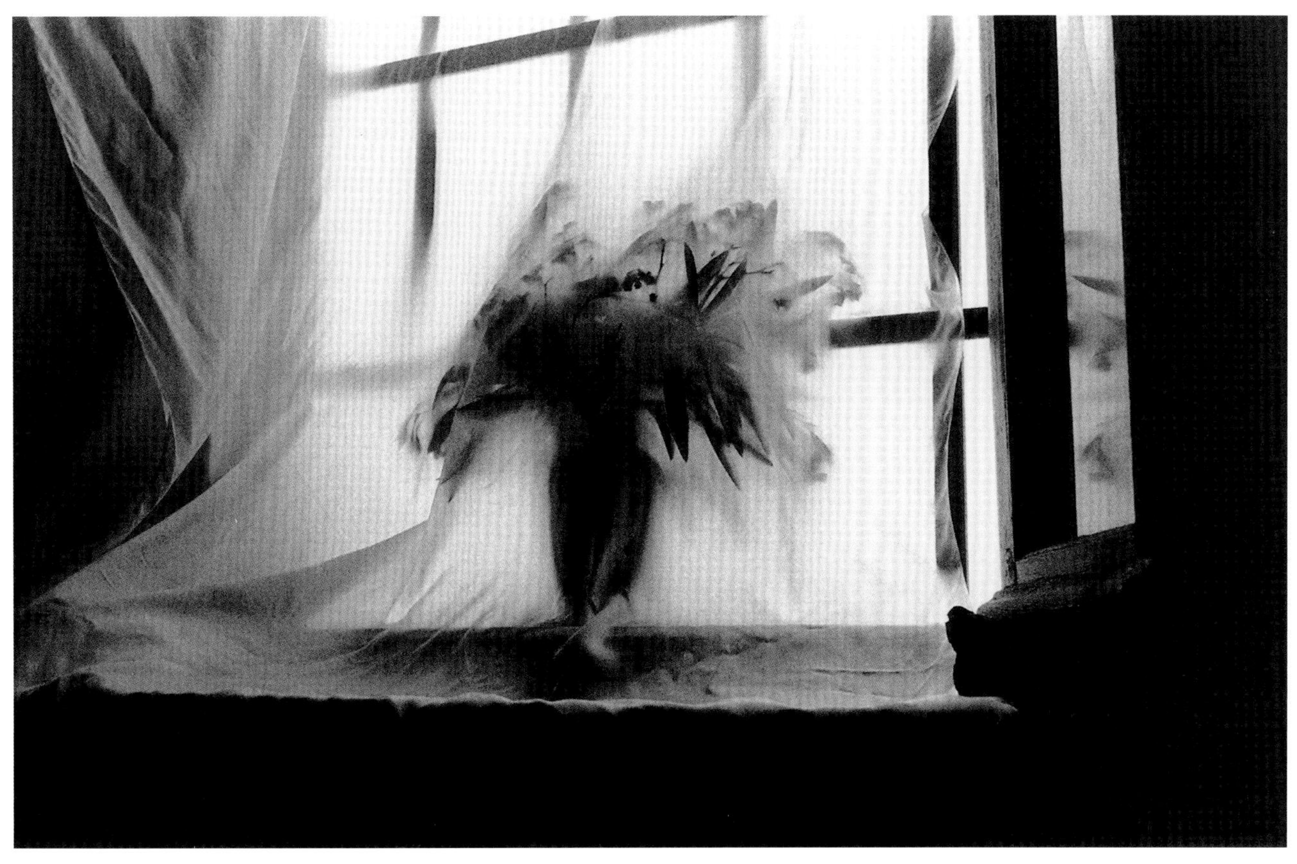

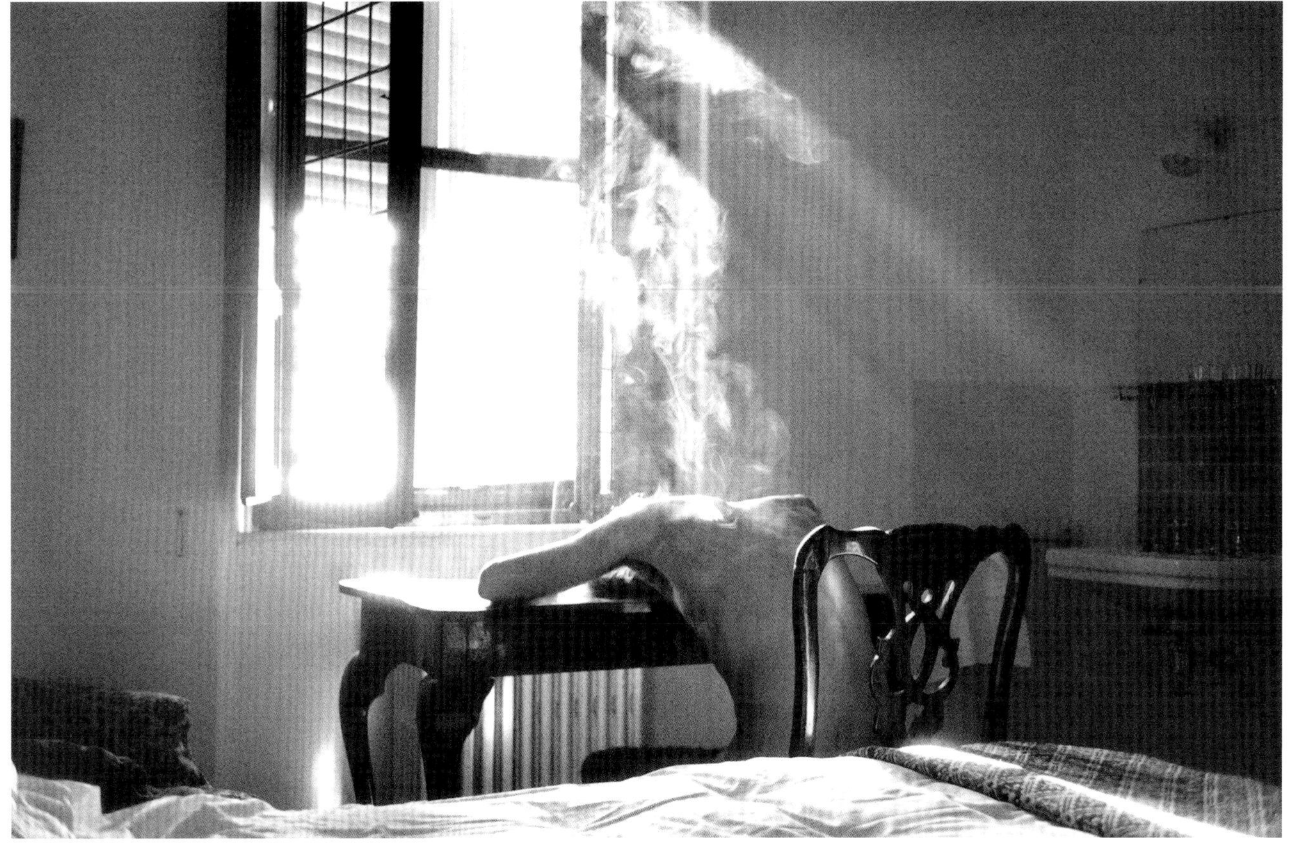

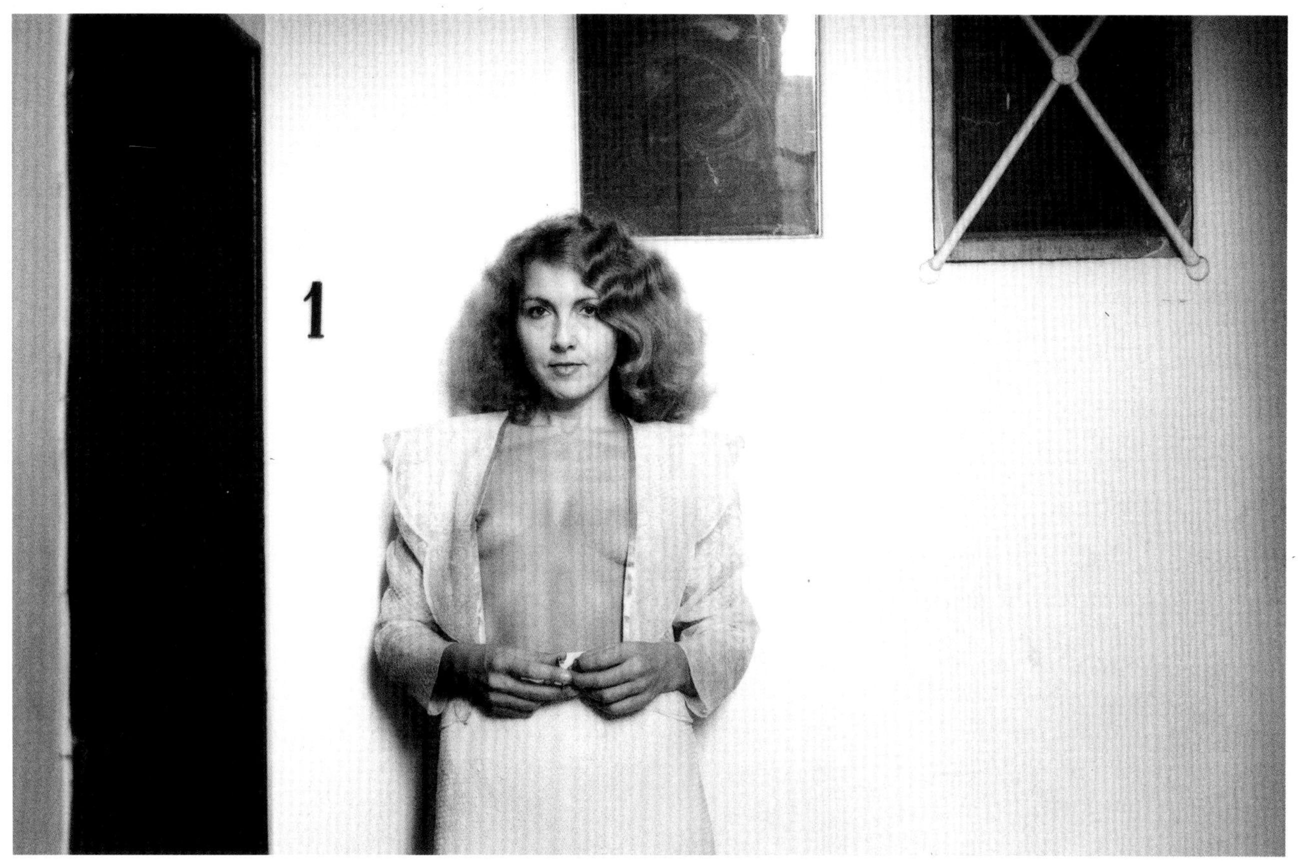

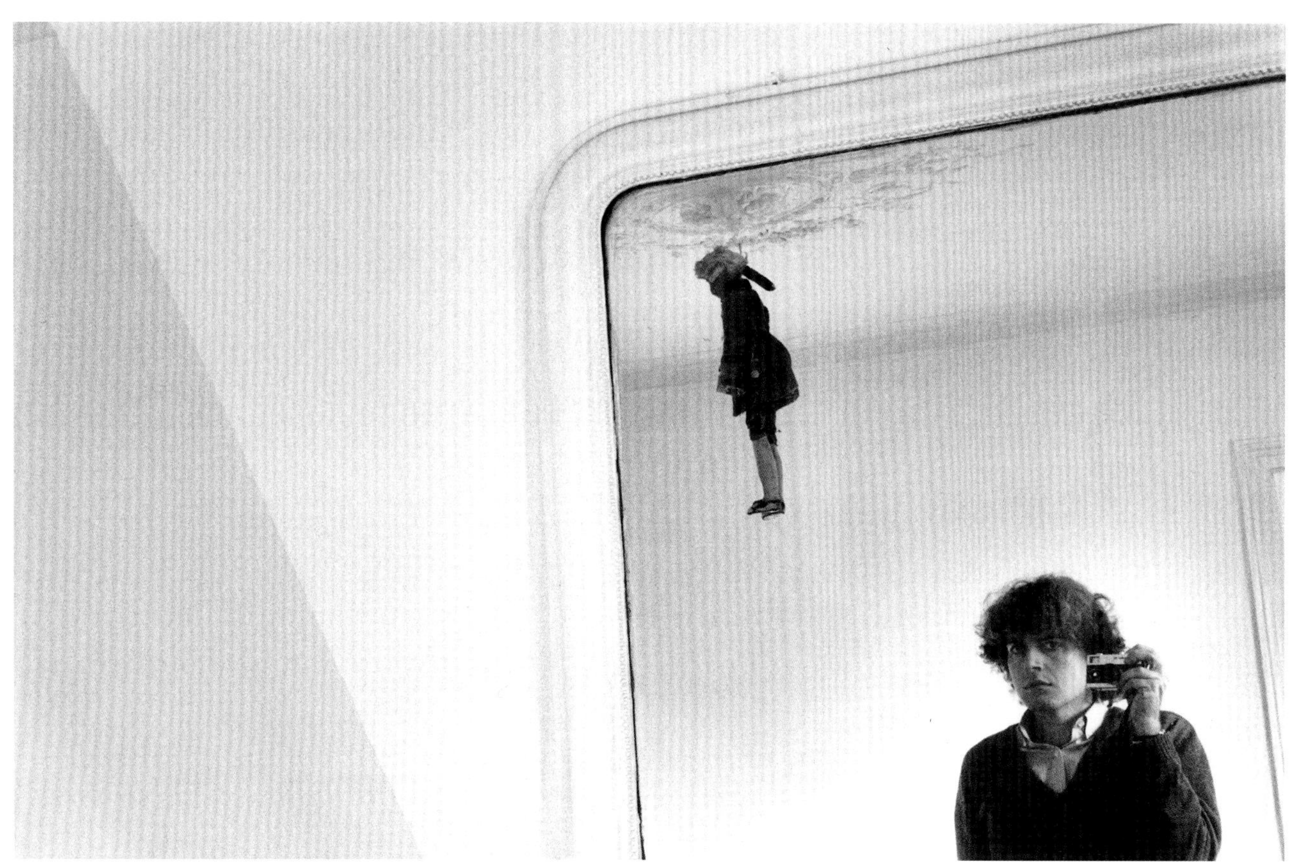

Opposite, top:
Agathe, 1980

Opposite, bottom:
*Autoportrait rue du
Moulin-Vert* (Self-portrait,
rue du Moulin-Vert),
1981

This page:
*Autoportrait, Musée
Grevin* (Self-portrait,
Musée Grevin), 1978–79

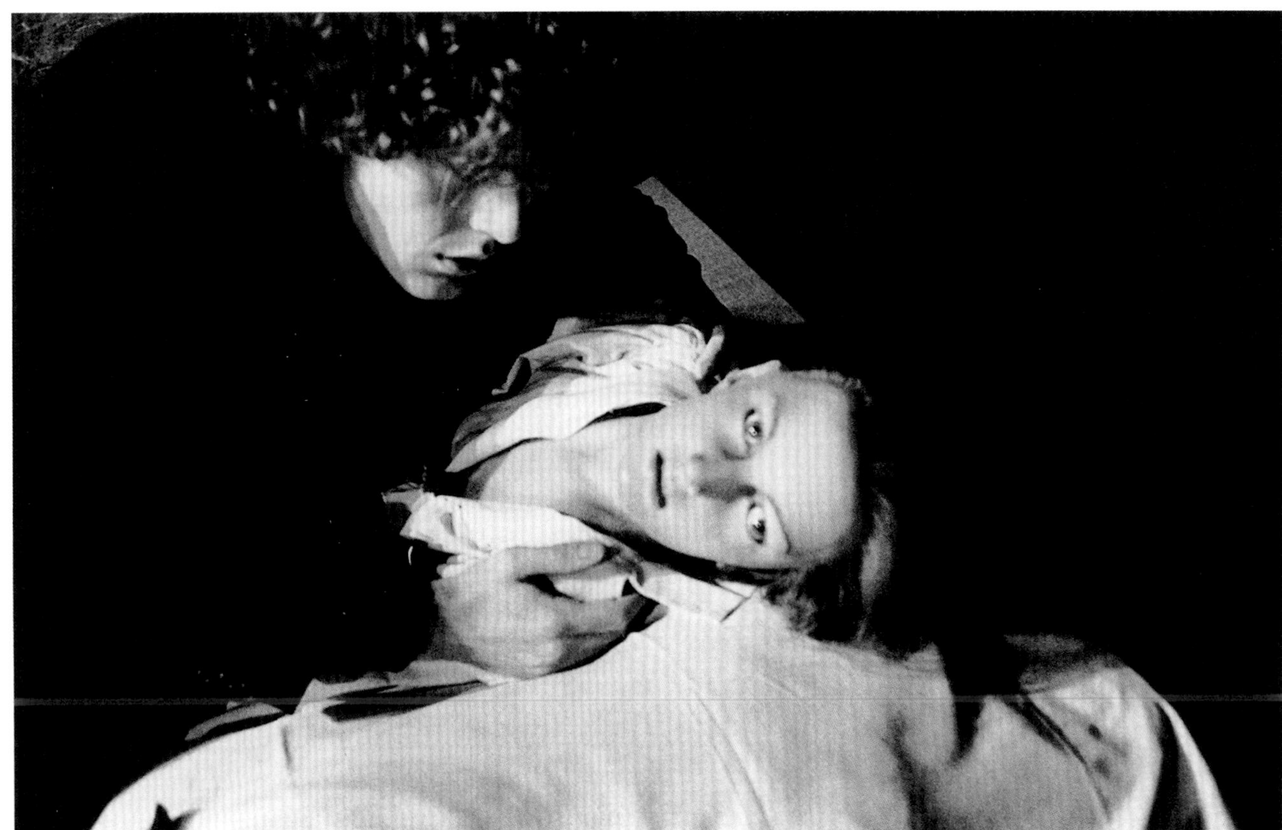

This page:
Isabelle, 1980

Opposite, top:
Table de travail
(Work table), 1985

Opposite, bottom:
La tête de Jeanne d'Arc
(The head of Joan of Arc),
n.d.
All photographs courtesy
Callicoon Fine Arts,
New York

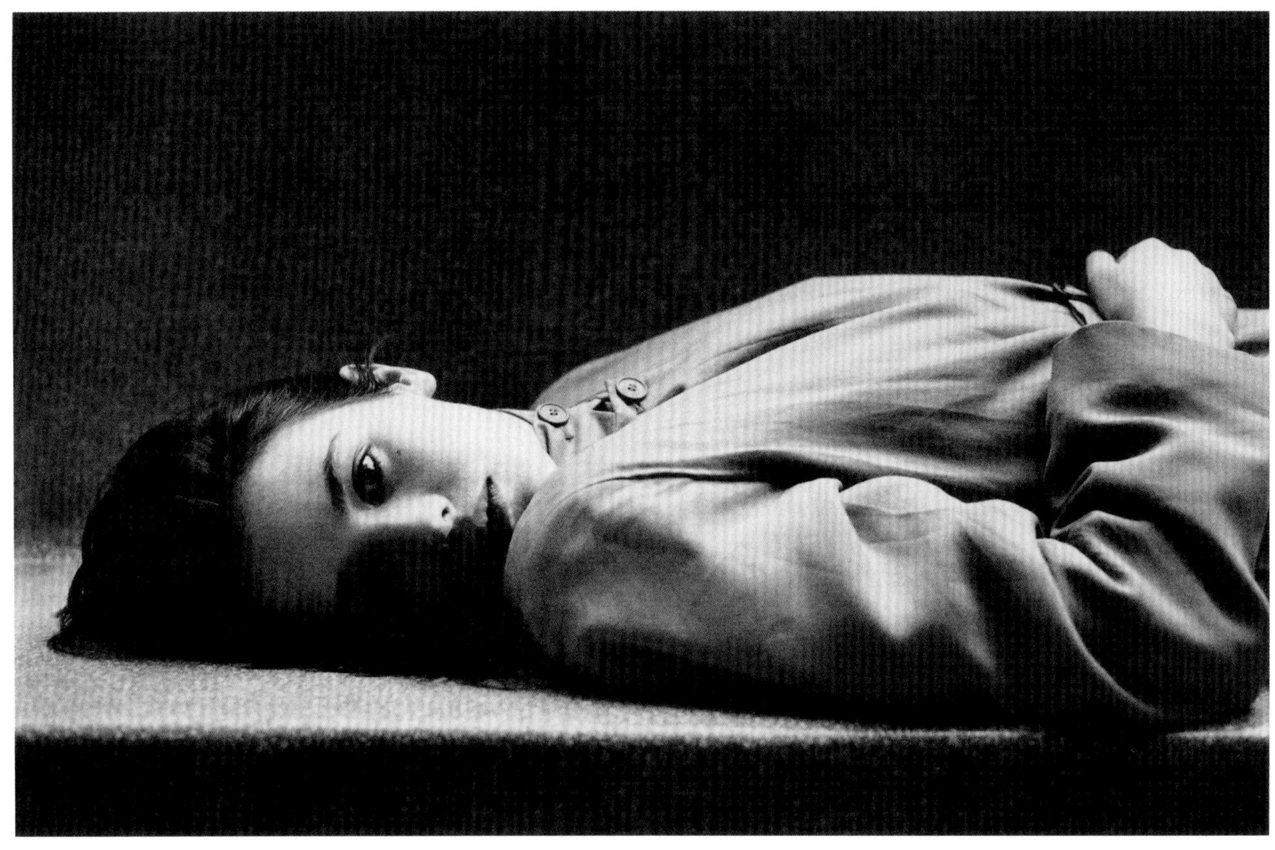

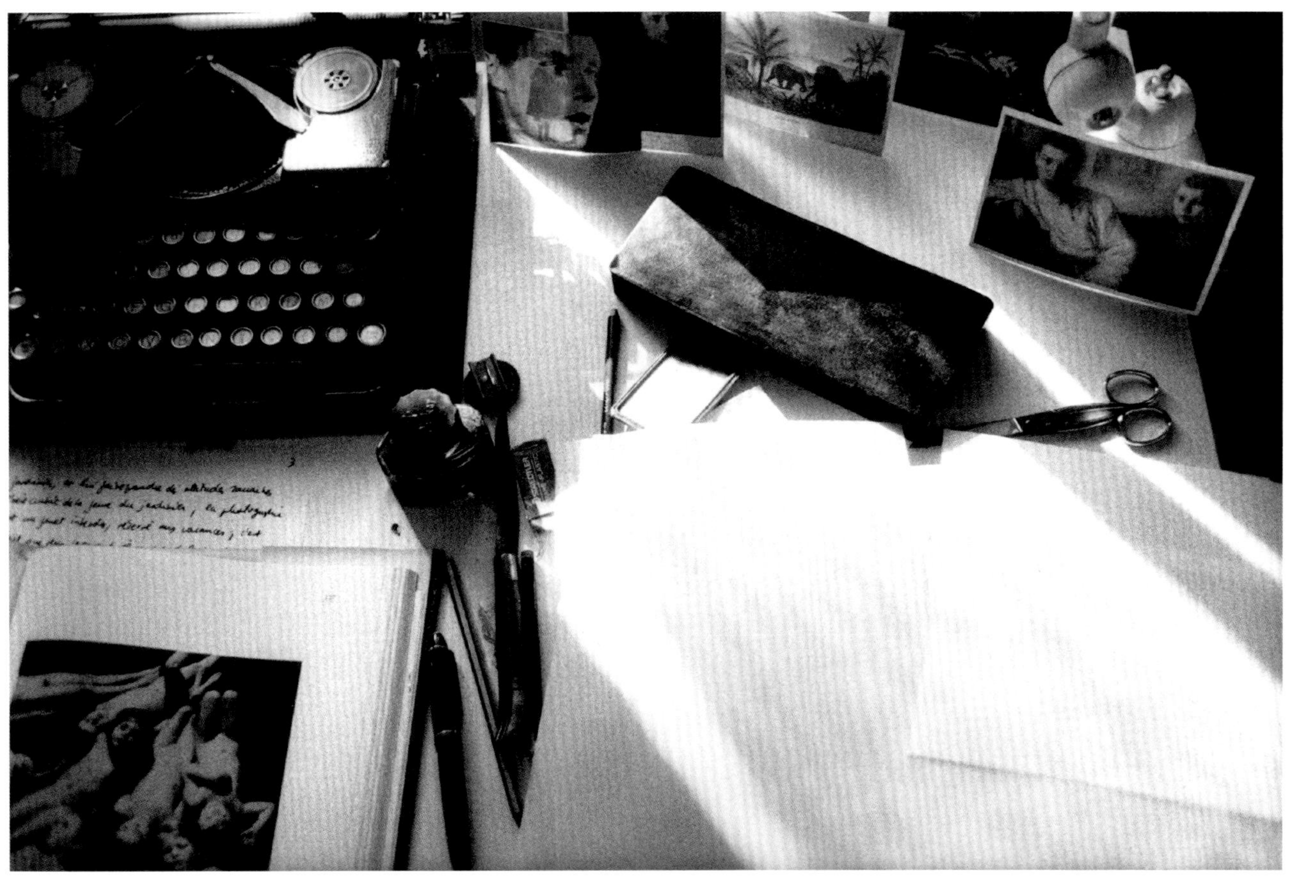

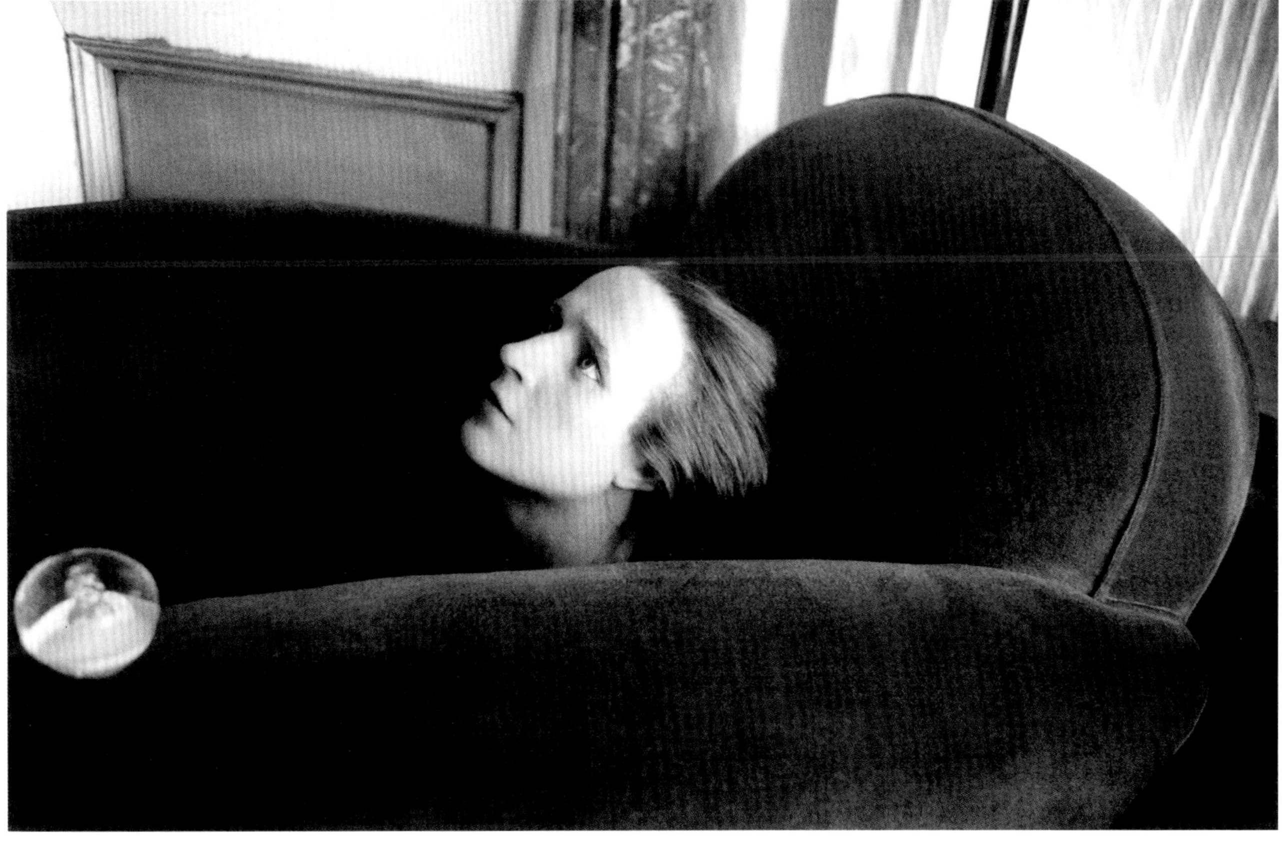

Beginning with her 2009 series *Today I Wrote Nothing*—comprising twenty-two photographs of poems composed from fragments of a brief 1937 journal entry by then-imprisoned Russian author Daniil Kharms—Natalie Czech has produced a distinct body of work that blurs the acts of writing and photographing, reading and seeing. Her deft use of text and photography of cultural artifacts builds on the legacies of pop, conceptual art, and appropriation art of the 1980s, yet her focus on the materiality of language also continues early-twentieth-century avant-garde practices in poetry, such as the calligram (in which the text forms an image related to the subject) and the cut-up (in which words from various sources are cut apart and pasted together).

For her recent series, *Poems by Repetition* (2013–14), the German artist highlights or obscures quotidian prose on printed ephemera and consumer goods—from iPads and magazine articles to LP covers and overdrive pedals—to reveal the poems of well-known American authors. All the works in the series consist of two or more images that appear to be the same but are, in actuality, slightly different, mimicking photographic reproduction as well as techniques of poetic repetition. As a starting point for the series, Czech cites Gertrude Stein's 1922 work "Saints and Singing," which uses repetition as a structuring device. Aram Saroyan's minimal poem "o r // o r" emerges from a grid of photographed ukuleles in *A Poem by Repetition by Aram Saroyan II* (2014), Hart Crane's vice-versa questions appear on two Kindle screens (one black, the other white), and Allen Ginsberg's ode to himself materializes across three photographs of the same magazine page containing images from artist Robert Longo's 1979 *Men in the Cities* series.

As with poetry, sound is an essential component to the series, and Czech often uses objects related to pop music to create layered meanings. In *A Poem by Repetition by Aram Saroyan* (2013), for example, Czech alters and photographs the LP single of Pink Floyd's "Money" (1973). The three photographs, repeating the album title, fashion the visual poem "ney/mo/money." The images evoke the staccato lines of both the poem and song as well as the chimes of a cash register. While Czech uses album covers for several other works in the series, she conjures music in other ways too. *A Poem by Repetition by Emmett Williams II* (2013) is constructed from three photographs of an overdrive pedal known as "American Woman" (see page 8); the amplifier company Tech 21 developed it in 2003 to generate a distorted cascading effect like the one used in the guitar solo of its namesake song by The Guess Who. In Williams's poem the sound seems to similarly distort from "a man // a woman // a men" while also referencing both the product and song. In each instance, Czech allows the histories and functions of the objects to resonate with the poems and surrounding contexts.

While most of the source materials for *Poems by Repetition* are relics of increasingly outmoded forms of print and popular culture (magazine pages and album covers, for example), the series manages to evoke the often fragmented and combinatory ways in which words, pictures, and even sounds, circulate today, i.e., via recycled links and posts on digital media platforms or multiple "windows" on a computer screen. In an age marked by commentary on the decline of reading and the acceleration of a vapid visual culture, Czech rewards those who take the time to read and look closely, again and again.

Natalie Czech
Poems by Repetition

Drew Sawyer

Drew Sawyer, an art historian and curator, is currently Beaumont and Nancy Newhall Curatorial Fellow at the Museum of Modern Art, New York.

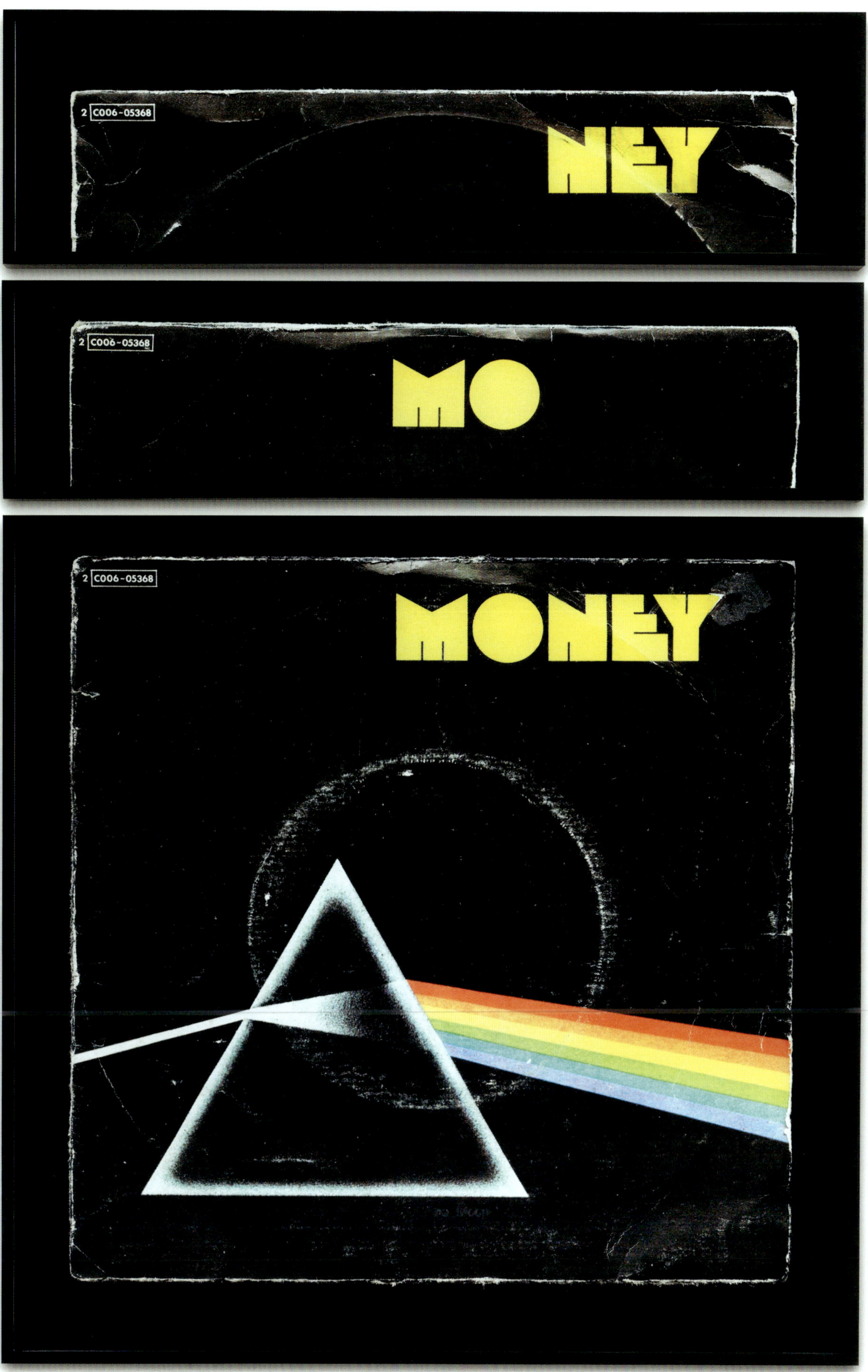

ney
mo
money

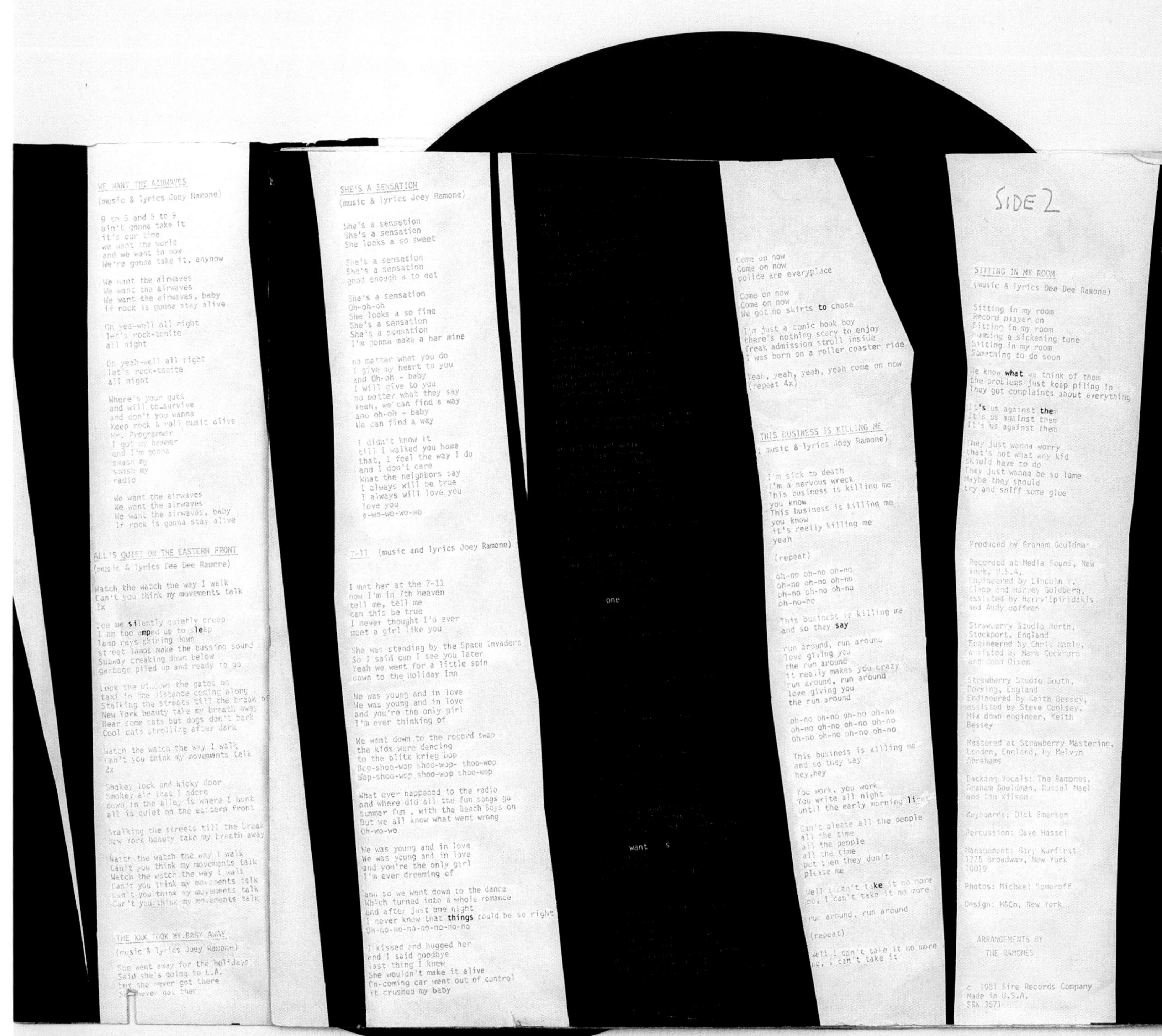

Simple things
one wants to say
like, what's the day
like, out there—
who am I
and where.

WE WANT THE AIRWAVES
(music & lyrics Joey Ramone)

9 to 5 and 5 to 9
ain't gonna take it
it's our time
we want the world
and we want in now
We're gonna take it, anyhow

We want the airwaves
We want the airwaves
We want the airwaves, baby
if rock is gonna stay alive

Oh yea-well all right
let's rock-tonite
all night

Oh yeah-well all right
let's rock-tonite
all night

Where's your guts
and will to survive
and don't you wanna
Keep rock & roll music alive
Mr. Programmer
I got my hammer
and I'm gonna
smash my
smash my
radio

We want the airwaves
We want the airwaves
We want the airwaves, baby
if rock is gonna stay alive

IT'S QUIET ON THE EASTERN FRONT
(music & lyrics Dee Dee Ramone)

Watch the watch the way I walk
Can't you think my movements talk
2x

See me silently quietly creep
I am too amped to to sleep
lamp rays shining down
street lamps make the buzzing sound
Subway creaking down below
Garbage piled up and ready to go

Lock the windows the gates on
taxi in the distance coming along
Stalking the streets till the break of   day
New York beauty take my breath away
Here some cats but dogs don't bark
Cool cats strolling after dark

Watch the watch the way I walk
Can't you think my movements talk
2x

Shaky lock and ricky door
Subway air that I adore
down in the alley is where I hunt
all is quiet on the eastern front

Stalking the streets till the break of day
New York beauty take my breath away

Watch the watch the way I walk
Can't you think my movements talk
Watch the watch the way I walk
Can't you think my movements talk
Can't you think my movements talk
Can't you think my movements talk

THE KKK TOOK MY BABY AWAY
(music & lyrics Joey Ramone)

She went away for the holidays
Said she's going to L.A.
but she never got there
She never got there
She never got there, they say

(repeat)

The KKK took my baby away
they took her away
away from me
The KKK took my baby
they took her away
away from me

now I don't know
Where my baby can be
they took her from me
they took her from me
I don't know
where my baby can be
they took her from me
they took her from me

ring me, ring me, ring me
with the President
and find out
Where my baby went
ring me, ring me, ring me
on the FBI
and find out if
my baby's alive
yeah, yeah, yeah

wo-o-o-o-o-o
o-o-o-o-o-o-o

She went away for the holidays

(repeat)

The KKK took my baby away

(repeat)

They took my girl
they took my baby away

DON'T GO (music & lyrics Joey Ramone)

She was everything to me oh yeah
She was everything to me
but how I ever let her go
I'll never know

She was everything to me - oh yeah
She was everything to me
Still how I ever ever let her go
I'll never know

Don't go, Don't go baby don't go
Don't go, Don't go baby don't go
can't go, Don't go
Don't leave me this way
hey, hey, hey baby
Can't go, Don't go baby don't go
Don't go, Don't go baby don't go
Don't go, Don't go
Can't leave me this way
hey, hey, hey

She was everything to me, oh yeah
She was everything to me
but how I ever ever let her go
I'll never know

She was everything to me
The sun, the earth the moon my baby
Still how I ever ever let her go
I'll never know

But she wouldn't do what I wanted her
She wouldn't do it for me

Don't go Don't go baby don't go
Don't go Don't go baby don't go
Don't go Don't go
Can't leave me this way
hey hey hey o-no-no
Don't go Don't go baby don't go
Don't go Don't go baby don't go
don't go don't go
Can't leave me this way
hey, hey hey- Don't go o-o-o-o-o

YOU SOUND LIKE YOU'RE SICK
(music & lyrics Dee Dee Ramone)

Well I can't understand
anything about you
help you if I can
what can I do

Here's your new home
That's where you must be
in the institution
'cause you're so lazy

But if you must act up
again & again
'cause everybody knows
You're a hopeless problem

here's your new home
that's where you must be
in the institution
'cause you're so lazy

You sound like you're sick
You look like you're sick too
You sound like you're sick

but if you must act up

(repeat)

you sound like you're sick

(repeat)

well I can't understand
anything about you

(repeat verse)

You sound like you're sick
You look like you're sick too
you sound like you're sick
you sound like you're sick too
You look like you're sick too
Well you sound like you're sick
You sound like you're sick

IT'S NOT MY PLACE (IN THE 9 TO 5 WORLD)
(music & lyrics Joey Ramone)

My mom and dad are always fighting
and it's getting very un-exciting
to get a good job
you need the proper schooling
who in the hell
do ya think your fooling

but it's not my place oh-no
no it's not my place no no
no it's not my -not my-not my place
in the 9 to 5 world
and it's not my place
in the 9 to 5 world
and it's not my place
with 9 to 5 girl
it's not my place
in the 9 to 5 world

hangin' out with Lester Bangs you all
and Phil Spector really has it all
Uncle Floyd shows on the t.v.
Jack Nicholson, Clint Eastwood, 10cc

But it's not my place
(repeat)

Don't wanna be a working stiff
lose my identity
'cause when it comes
to working 9 to 5
There ain't no place for me
ain't my reality, to me

Martin Scofsa's on the radio
Ramones are hangin' out in Kokomo
Roger Corman's on a talk show
with Allan Arkush and Stephen King,
you know
But it's not my place
(repeat)

SHE'S A SENSATION
(music & lyrics Joey Ramone)

She's a sensation
She's a sensation
She looks a so sweet

She's a sensation
She's a sensation
good enough a to eat

She's a sensation
Oh-oh-oh
She looks a so fine
She's a sensation
She's a sensation
I'm gonna make a her mine

no matter what you do
I give my heart to you
and Oh-oh - baby
I will give to you
no matter what they say
Yeah, we can find a way
and oh-oh - baby
We can find a way

I didn't know it
till I walked you home
that, I feel the way I do
and I don't care
What the neighbors say
I always will be true
I always will love you
love you
a-wo-wo-wo-wo

7-11 (music and lyrics Joey Ramone)

I met her at the 7-11 '
now I'm in 7th heaven
tell me, tell me
can this be true
I never thought I'd ever
meet a girl like you

She was stending by the Space Invaders
So I said can I see you later
Yeah we went for a little spin
down to the Holiday Inn

We was young and in love
We was young and in love
and you're the only girl
I'm ever thinking of

We went down to the record swap
the kids were dancing
to the blitz krieg bop
Bop-shoo-wop shoo-wop- shoo-wop
Bop-shoo-wop shoo-wop shoo-wop

what ever happened to the radio
and where did all the fun songs go
summer fun , with the Beach Boys on
But we all know what went wrong
Oh-wo-wo

We was young and in love
We was young and in love
and you're the only girl
I'm ever dreaming of

So so we went down to the dance
which turned into a whole romance
and after just one night
I never knew that things could be so right
Oh-no-no-no-no-no-no-no

I kissed and hugged her
and I said goodbye
last thing I know
She wouldn't make it alive
On-coming car went out of control
It crushed my baby

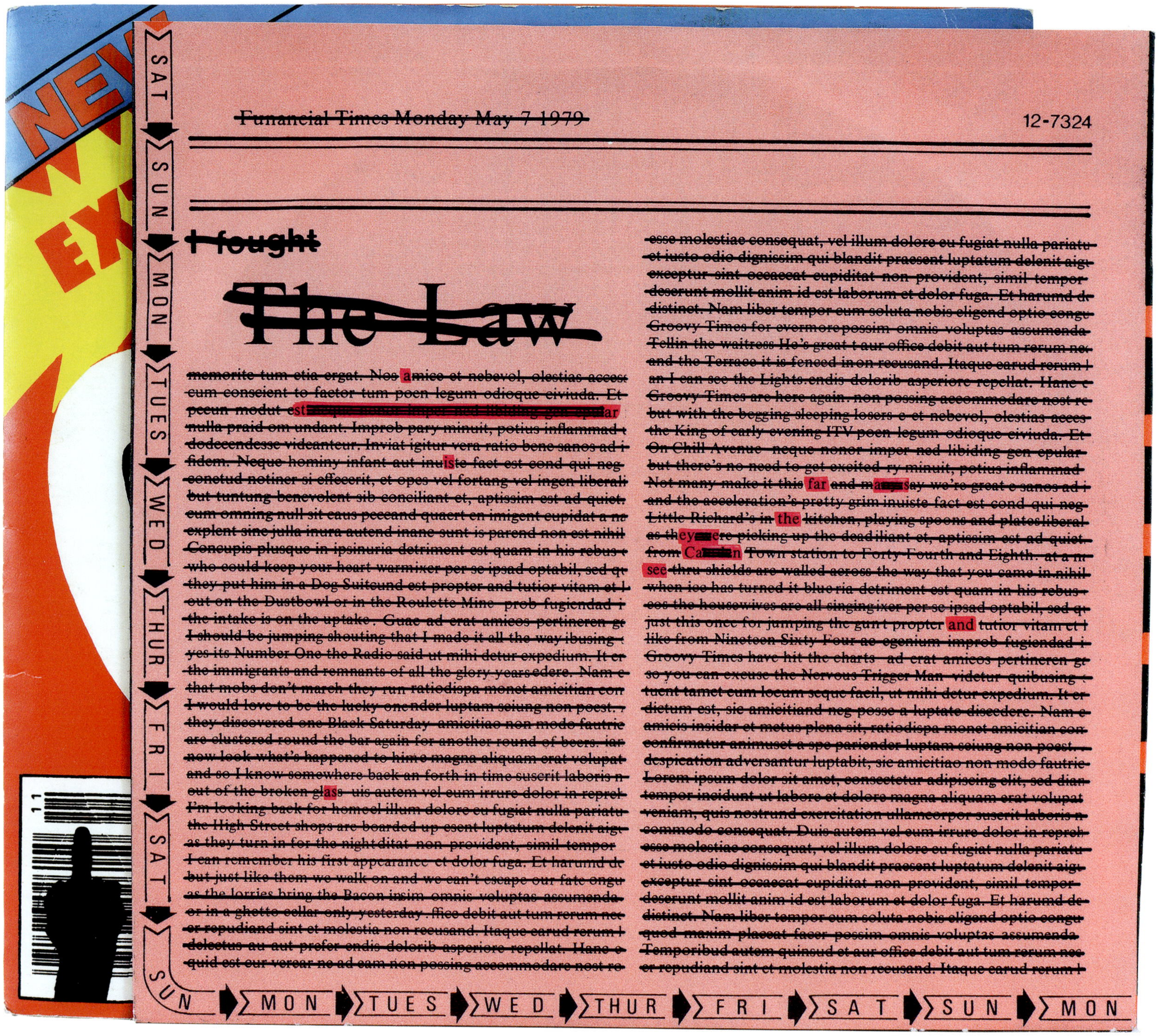

~~I fought~~

~~The Law~~

A star
is as far
as the eye
can see
and
as near
as my eye
is to me

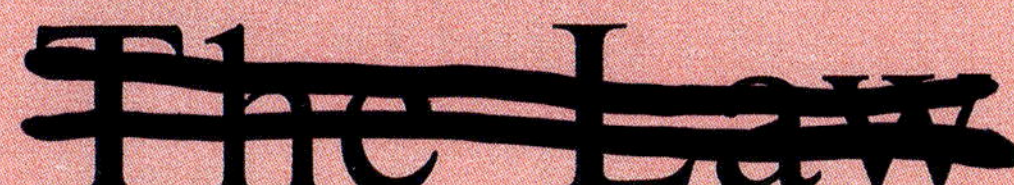

A Poem by Repetition
by Gregory Corso, 2013

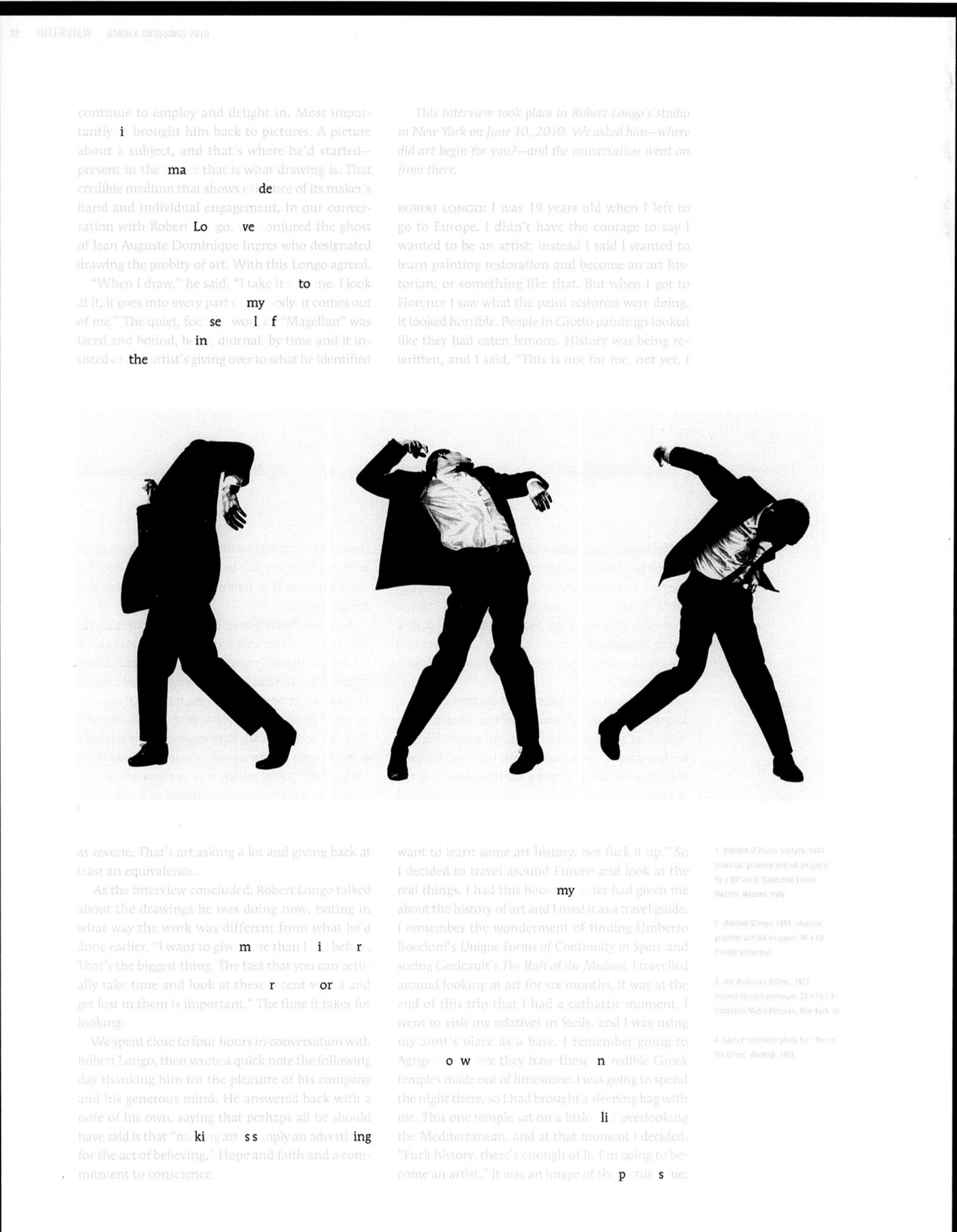

continue to employ and delight in. Most importantly i brought him back to pictures. A picture about a subject, and that's where he'd started—present in the mark that is what drawing is. That credible medium that shows evidence of its maker's hand and individual engagement. In our conversation with Robert Longo, conjured the ghost of Jean Auguste Dominique Ingres who designated drawing the probity of art. With this Longo agreed.

"When I draw," he said, "I take it into me. I look at it, it goes into every part of my body, it comes out of me." The quiet, focused world of "Magellan" was laced and bound, being diurnal, by time and it insisted on the artist's giving over to what he identified as reverie. That's art asking a lot and giving back at least an equivalence.

As the interview concluded, Robert Longo talked about the drawings he was doing now, noting in what way the work was different from what he'd done earlier. "I want to give more than I did before. That's the biggest thing. The fact that you can actually take time and look at these recent works and get lost in them is important." The time it takes for looking.

We spent close to four hours in conversation with Robert Longo, then wrote a quick note the following day thanking him for the pleasure of his company and his generous mind. He answered back with a note of his own, saying that perhaps all he should have said is that "making art is simply an advertising for the act of believing." Hope and faith and a commitment to conscience.

This interview took place in Robert Longo's studio in New York on June 10, 2010. We asked him—where did art begin for you?—and the conversation went on from there.

ROBERT LONGO: I was 19 years old when I left to go to Europe. I didn't have the courage to say I wanted to be an artist; instead I said I wanted to learn painting restoration and become an art historian, or something like that. But when I got to Florence I saw what the paint restorers were doing, it looked horrible. People in Giotto paintings looked like they had eaten lemons. History was being rewritten, and I said, "This is not for me, not yet. I want to learn some art history, not fuck it up." So I decided to travel around Europe and look at the real things. I had this book my sister had given me about the history of art and I used it as a travel guide. I remember the wonderment of finding Umberto Boccioni's *Unique Forms of Continuity in Space* and seeing Gericault's *The Raft of the Medusa*. I travelled around looking at art for six months. It was at the end of this trip that I had a cathartic moment. I went to visit my relatives in Sicily, and I was using my aunt's place as a base. I remember going to Agrigento where they have these incredible Greek temples made out of limestone. I was going to spend the night there, so I had brought a sleeping bag with me. This one temple sat on a little hill overlooking the Mediterranean, and at that moment I decided, "Fuck history, there's enough of it. I'm going to become an artist." It was an image of the picturesque;

1. *Untitled (3 Fries) Triptych*, 1981, charcoal, graphite and ink on paper, 96 x 60" each. Collection Evans Marzoli, Modena, Italy.

2. *Untitled (Cindy)*, 1981, charcoal, graphite and ink on paper, 96 x 60". Private Collection.

3. *The American Soldier*, 1977, enamel on cast aluminum, 26 x 16 x 5". Collection Metro Pictures, New York, NY.

4. Source reference photo for "Men in the Cities" drawing, 1981.

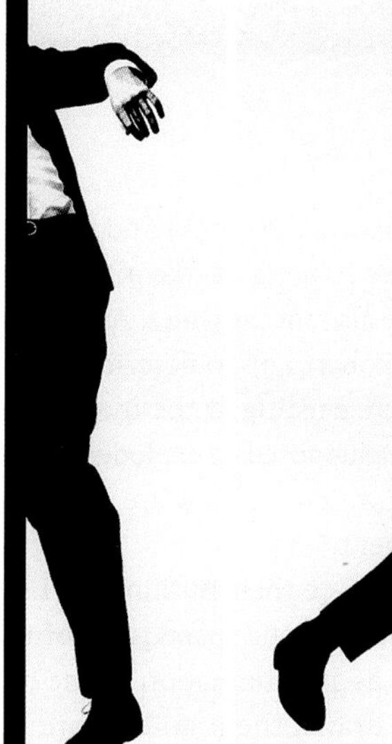
was 19 years old when I left
didn't have the courage to
artist; instead I said I wanted
restoration and become an art
thing like that. But when I got
that the paint restorers were do
People in Giotto paintings lo
en lemons. History was being
id, "This is not for me, not yet

me art history, not fuck it up.
d around Europe and look at
this book my sister had given me
of art and I used it as a travel gu
wonderment of finding Umb
Forms of Continuity in Space
The Raft of the Medusa. I trave
art for six months. It was a
that I had a cathartic mome
relatives in Sicily, and I was u
as a base. I remember going
they have these incredible G
of limestone. I was going to sp
I had brought a sleeping bag
sat on a little hill overloo

I made love to myself
in the mirror, kissing my own lips,
saying, "I love myself,
I love you more than anybody."

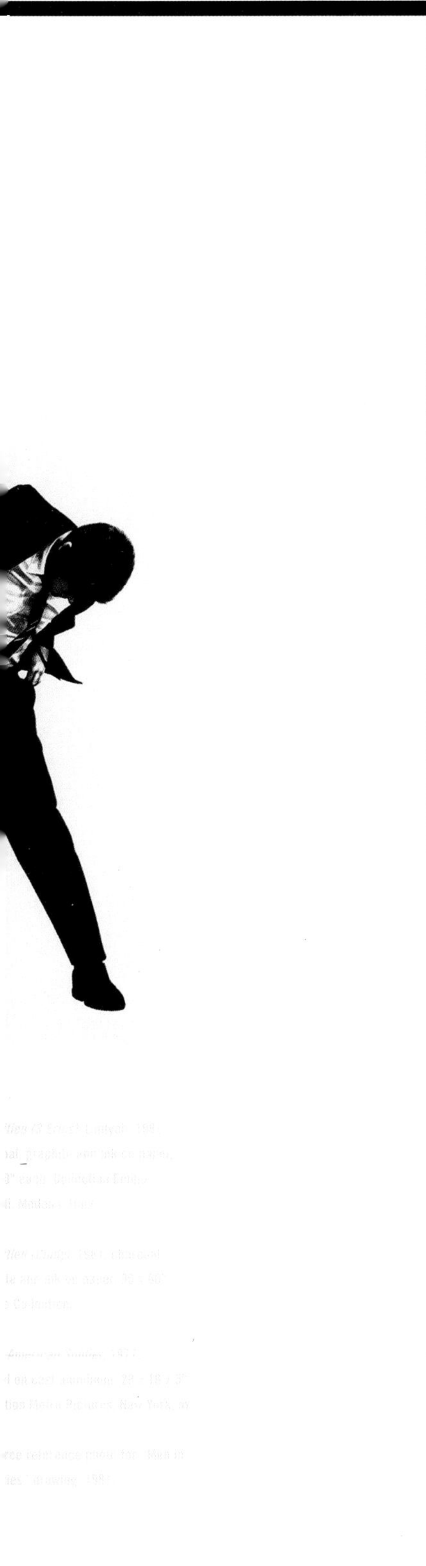

drawing the probity of art. With this Longo agreed.

"When I draw," he said, "I take it into me... at it, it goes into... part of my body... it comes out of me." The quiet, focused work of "Magellan" was laced and bound, being diurnal, by time and it insisted on the artist's giving over to what he identified

I lo ve y ou

as reverie. That's art asking a lot and giving back at least an equivalence.

As the interview concluded, Robert Longo talked about the drawings he was doing now, noting in what way the work was different from what he'd done earlier. "I want to g... **more than** ... did before. That's the biggest thing. The fact that you can actually take time and look at these recent works and get lost in them is important." The time it takes for looking.

We spent close to four hours in conversation with Robert Longo, then wrote a quick note the following day thanking him for the pleasure of his company **any** and his generous mind. He answered back with a

thing .

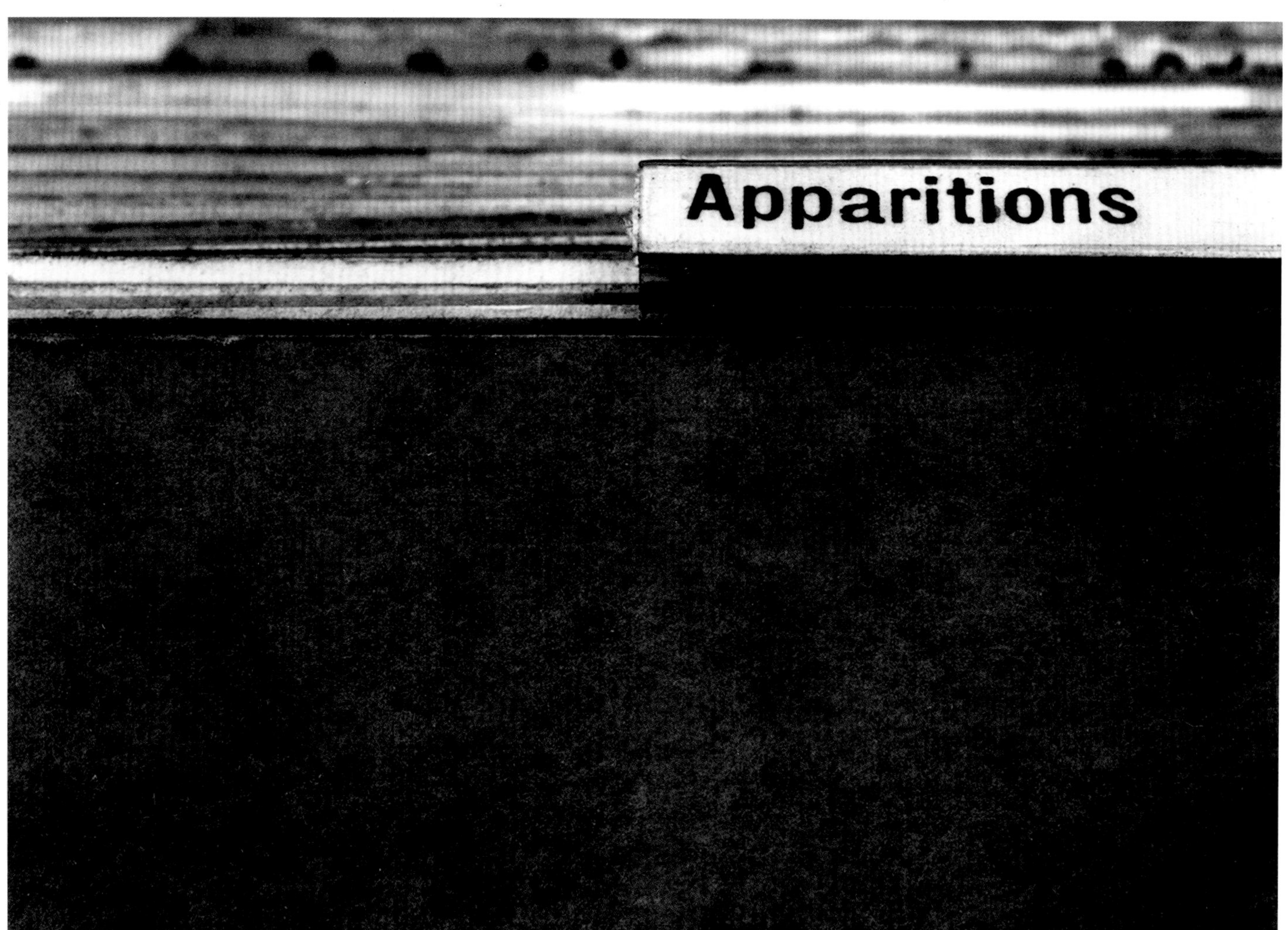

A

Daggers
Cloaks

Erica Baum is fascinated by the printed word. Whether scavenging newspaper clippings, vintage paperbacks, or half-cleaned chalkboards, she reveals unexpected poetry in the language that permeates everyday life. She approaches these materials almost scientifically, creating discrete but concurrent series of images that straightforwardly document their sources. Conjuring her objects of study through fragmentary details, shot in close-up and with shallow depth of field, Baum evokes an intimate space in which viewers can decipher the images according to their own associations and memories. Her works accentuate this character by highlighting manifestations of language marked by obsolescence, such as lyrics appearing on player–piano rolls. The *Card Catalogue* series pictures its eponymous subject in extreme detail, focusing on just a few subject markers amid rows of index cards bearing information related to those topics. In Baum's hands these headings seem to hover against an abstract visual field, like ghostly relics of a pre-digital era— a point made all the more succinctly in her topic selection for *Untitled (Apparitions)* (1997).

An admirer of concrete poetry, Baum takes up Brion Gysin's exhortation that "words have a vitality of their own and you or anybody can make them gush into action." Photography provides a means for her to combine the chance effects of Gysin's cut-up method with her own reverence for the materiality of the printed page. In the *Dog Ear* series she ingeniously fuses these verbal and visual qualities by photographing the folded corners of book pages. Works like *Differently* (2009) and *Enfold* (2013) draw attention to the physical layout of margins, page numbers, line spacing, and font design while transforming their found texts into syncopated blocks of signification *in potentia*. The regular folds that cut diagonals across each square frame recall the formal rigor of Minimalism even as they reference the more subjective act of marking significant passages in old books. Baum draws out the luscious physicality of these common objects: the various textures of woven paper, the yellowing tones of age, the hint of ink bleeding through thin pages.

In the *Naked Eye* series, Baum photographs old softcovers from the side, choosing to show their pages rather than the spines, and fanning the pages out to create mysterious chance juxtapositions. Words appear sliced or foreshortened, giving way to flattened strips of images—film starlets, clouds, fragments of buildings—that, as in *Amnesia* (2009), are sandwiched between the rippling and vividly dyed edges of surrounding pages. Bereft of caption and context, these illustrations take over the role of displaced signifier previously held by catalog keywords like *daggers* and *cloaks*. Digging through old books on cinema for works like *Flint* (2009) and *Clara* (2013), Baum selects anonymous figures who either cast oblique glances off the frame of the page or seem poised for the gaze. Leaving their narratives necessarily unresolved, she spins a web of longing that resonates with her own attraction to the source material. Through these open-ended investigations Baum honors the tradition of print—that textured, tangible objectification of language that inexorably fades with each passing year.

Opposite, top:
Untitled (Apparitions), 1997

Opposite, bottom:
Untitled (Daggers Cloaks), 1998

Erica Baum: Wordplay

Nat Trotman

Nat Trotman is an associate curator at the Solomon R. Guggenheim Museum, New York.

This page:
Differently, 2009

Opposite, top:
Enfold, 2013

Opposite, bottom:
Word Intention, 2014

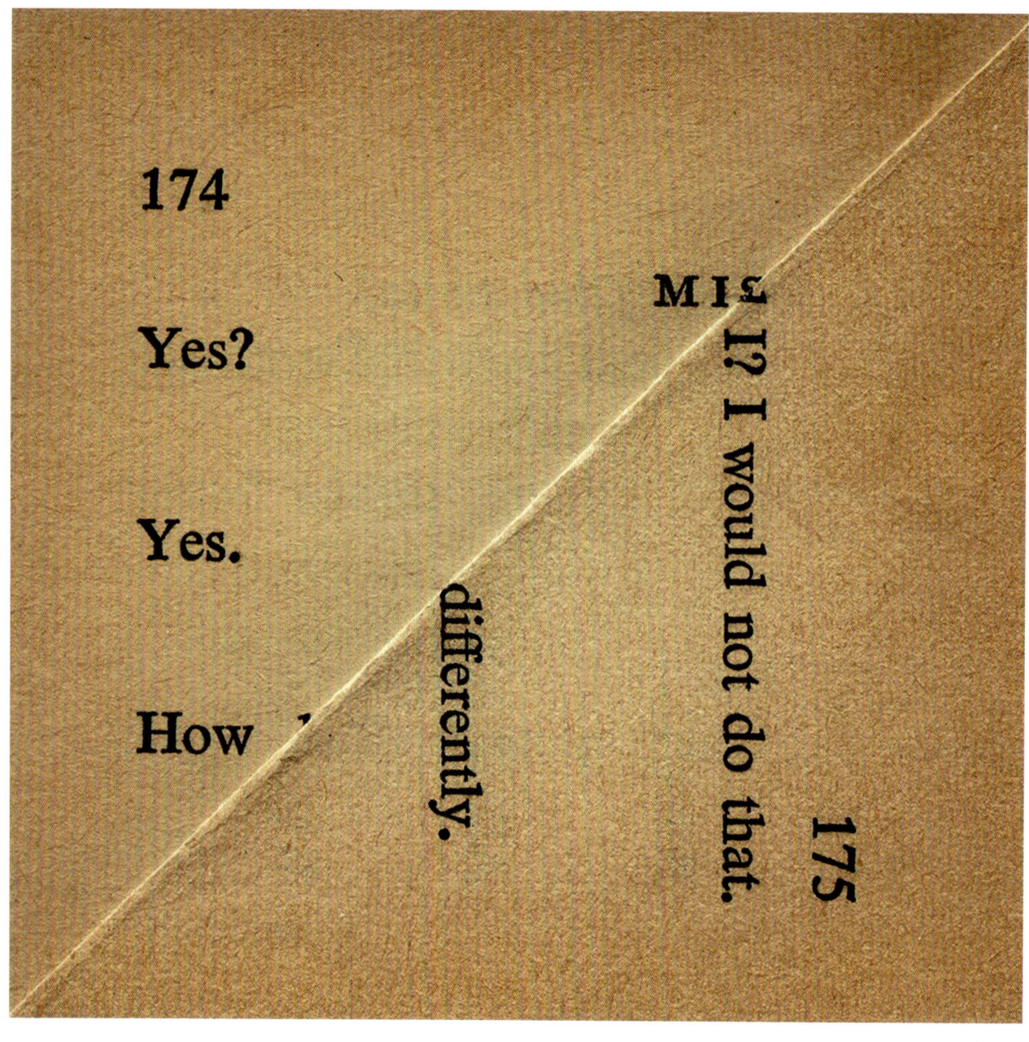

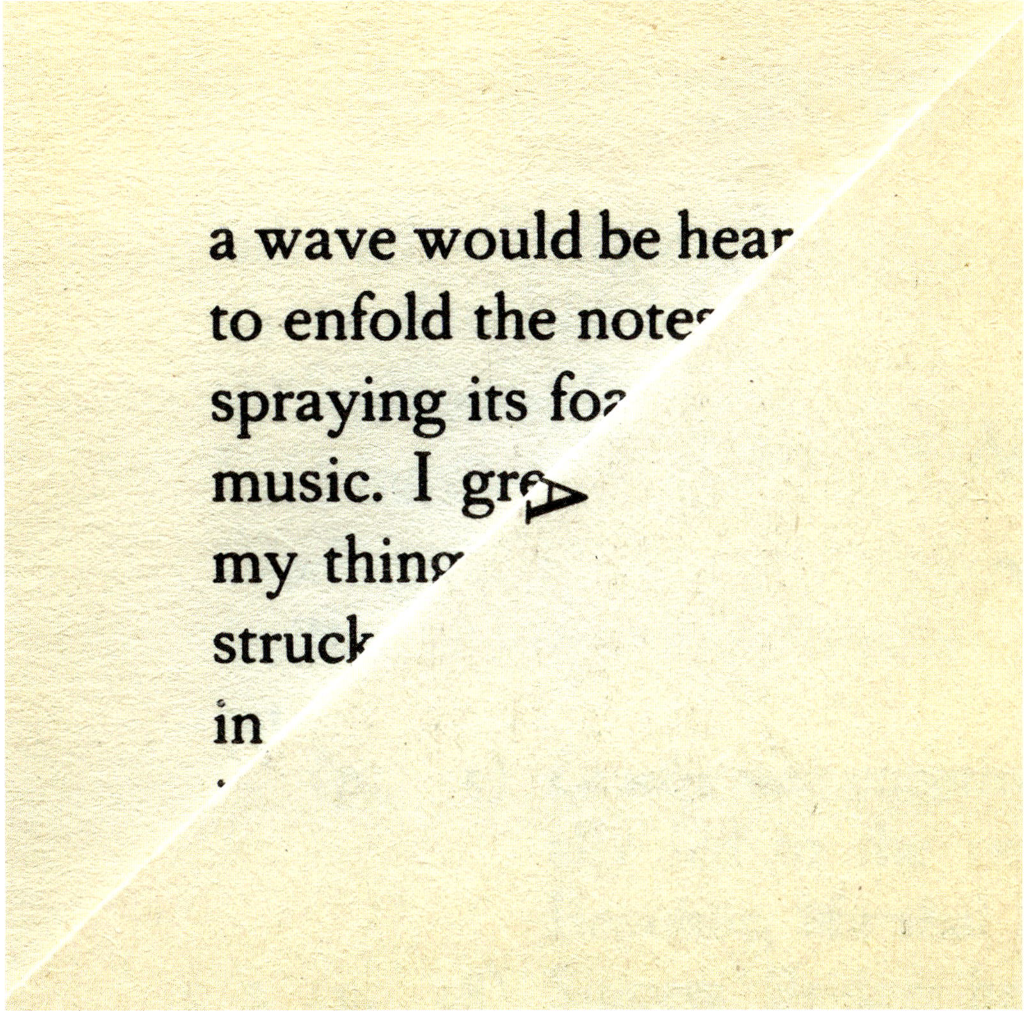

a wave would be hear
to enfold the note
spraying its foa
music. I gr
my thing
struck
in

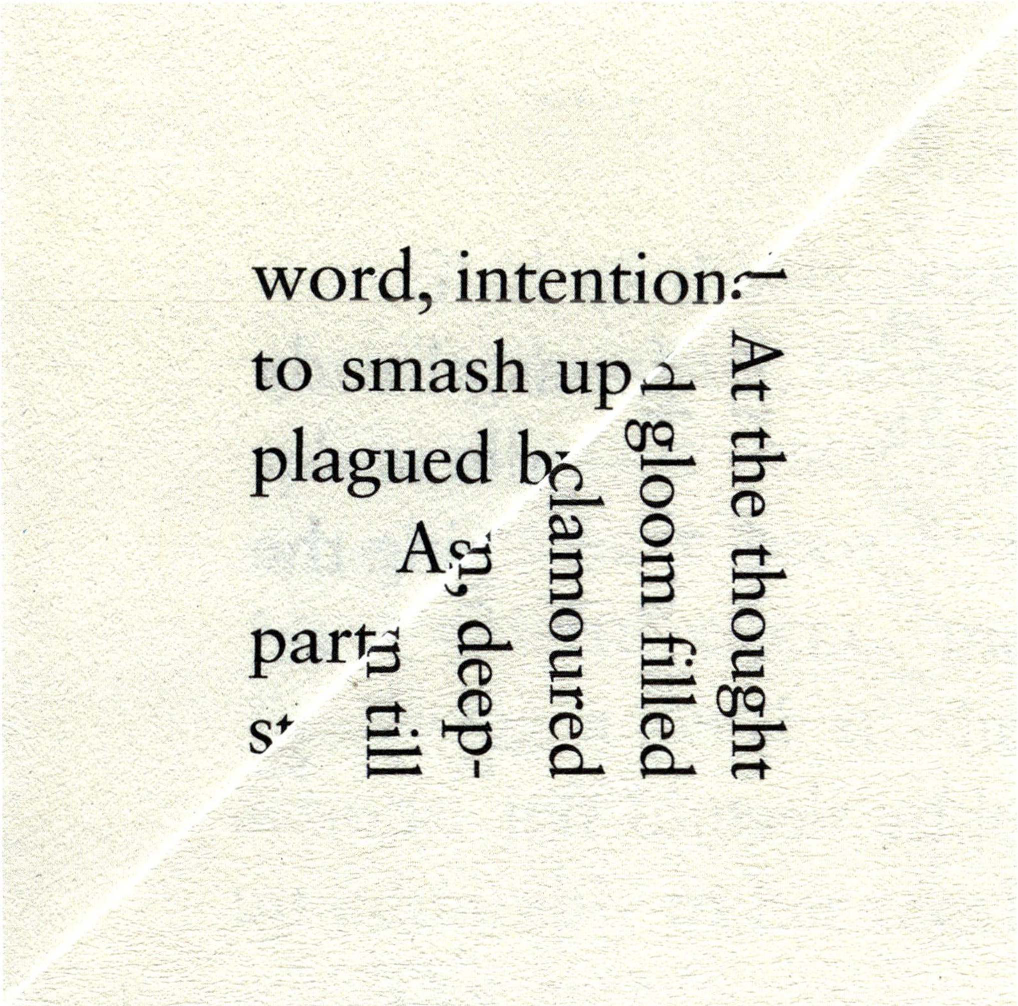

word, intention
to smash up
plagued b
A
part
s

At the thought
gloom filled
clamoured
deep-
n till

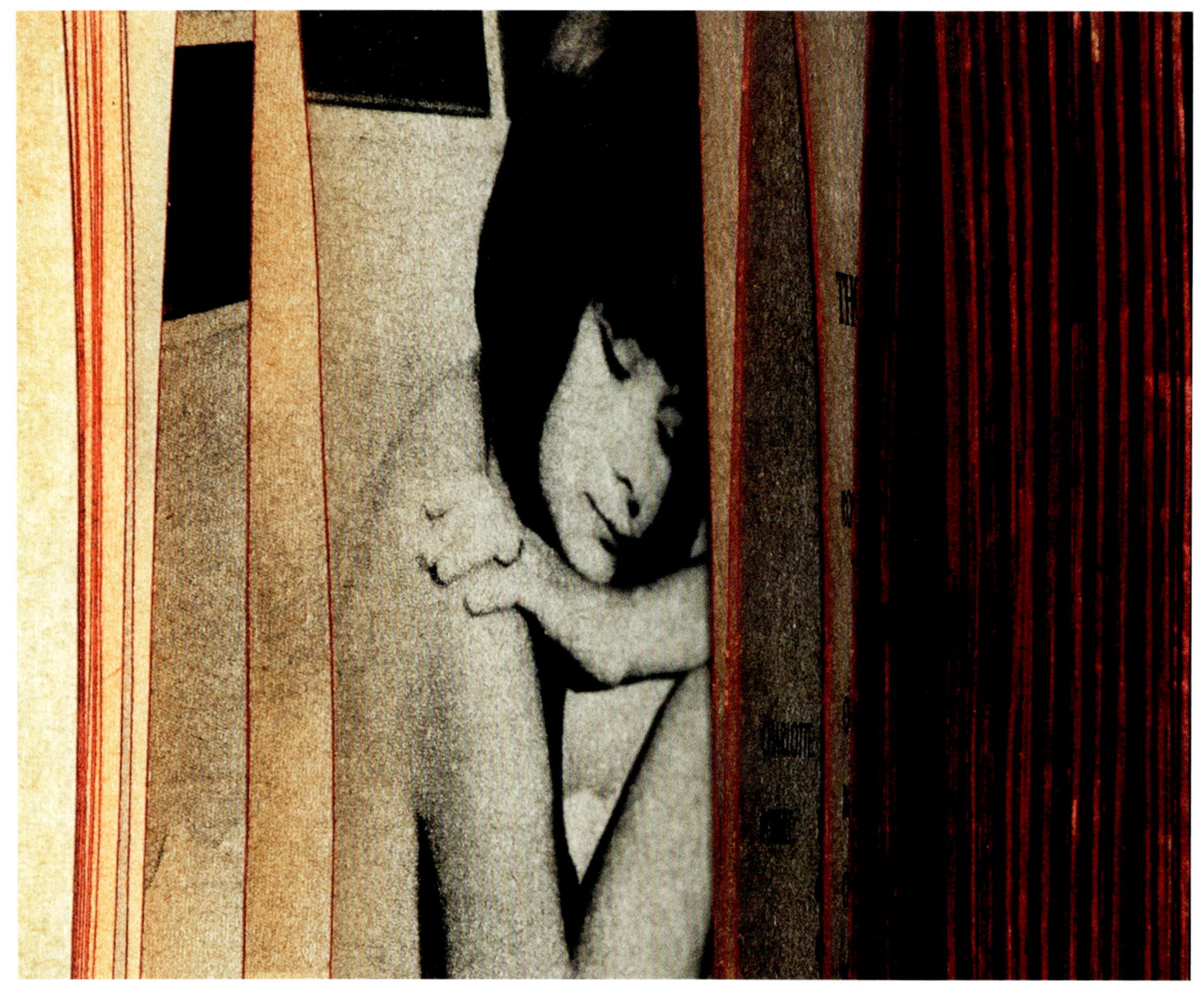
THE

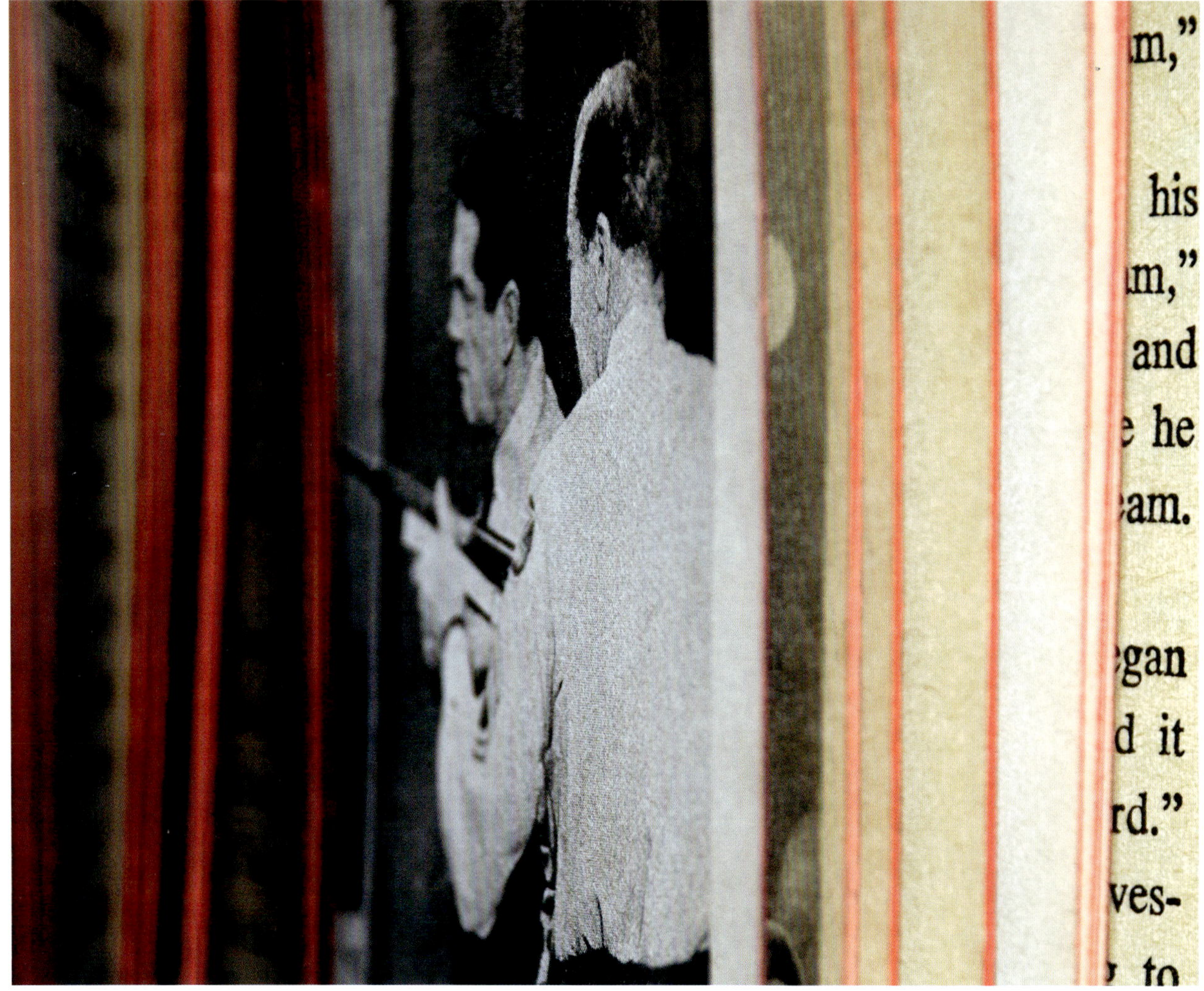
m,"
his
m,"
and
e he
am.
egan
d it
rd."
ves-
to

Opposite, top:
Clara, 2013

Opposite, bottom:
Flint, 2009

This page:
Amnesia, **2009**
All photographs courtesy
Bureau, New York

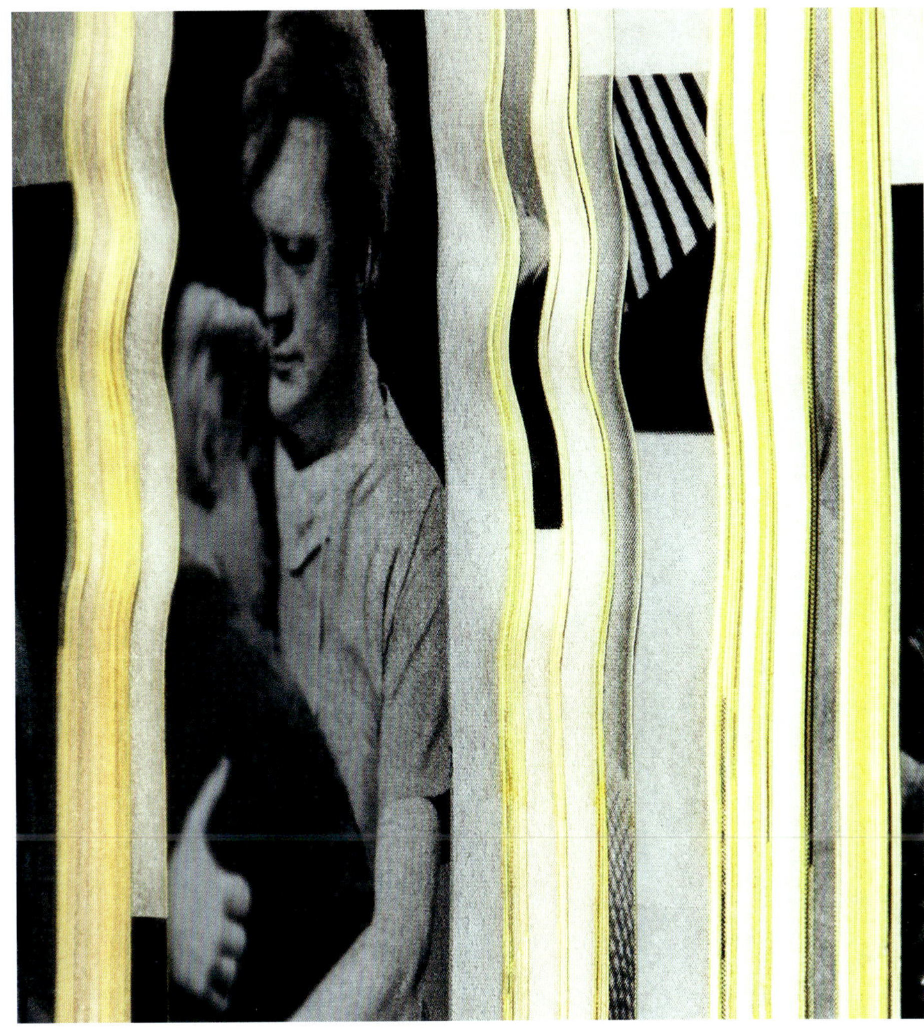

Few words were as loaded for William S. Burroughs as *to shoot*. The novelist loved his firearms (the fatal wounding of his wife Joan Vollmer during a game of William Tell in a Mexico City bar in 1951 didn't dampen his enthusiasm for guns), and few writers are as closely associated with their heroin habits as the author of *Junky*. What readers may not be aware of is Burroughs's abiding interest in shooting with a camera—which he pursued over the course of his life, with particular fervor during his time in Paris, Tangier, and London, the latter two offering occasions for expansive experiments with photographic collage. We'll never be able to say with certainty just how frequently he used his camera—the great majority of his photographs were lost, destroyed, or dispersed over a long life, and one that wasn't geared toward preservationist or archival instincts—but those images and tableaux that survive provide at least a glimpse of a writer who approached photography with a serious if idiosyncratic curiosity.

For Burroughs, photographs possessed peculiar powers. They prompted travel across time and made distance collapse. As objects they were liable to make magical things happen. Like paintings and film, photographs were leaps and bounds ahead of the printed word, which he believed was only just now catching up to the generative potential of these media through the "cut-up"— the aleatory gesture he had experimented with to startling effect in his novels. "The cut-up method brings to writers the collage, which has been used by painters for fifty years," he wrote in *The Third Mind* (1978), coauthored by his frequent collaborator Brion Gysin. "And used by the moving and still camera. In fact, all street shots from movie or still cameras are by the unpredictable factors of passersby and juxtaposition cut-ups. And photographers will tell you that often their best shots are accidents … writers will tell you the same."

But if photographs had paranormal qualities, Burroughs seems to have been drawn to them no less for their documentary ability and earthy specificity. The images he produced included photographs of friends and lovers (his most famous picture is probably a portrait of a young Allen Ginsberg on an East Village rooftop), of hotel dwellings in London and the record of a visit to his hometown of St. Louis, Missouri. But these were, in many cases, only a means to an end. He reused his photographs as elements in other photographic compositions, shooting himself through panes of glass that held an arrangement of images to create a multilayered self-portrait, or dispersing a couple of photographs between a pair of air pistols on a desktop, or slicing and recombining images (and rephotographing the result) to make odd visual counterparts to his cut-up novels. At other times, he arranged his photographs in sequential patterns and reshot the result, occasionally letting his shadow fall on the tableau he was reshooting, baring the privileged view photography offers on the passing of time. Burroughs purportedly covered his walls with his photographs while he was writing *Naked Lunch*, and it worked so well he is said to have done the same when he was hard at work on other novels. So perhaps his belief in the magical powers of photographs was not without merit after all.

William S. Burroughs Still Shots

Eric Banks

Eric Banks is a writer and editor based in New York. He is currently director of the New York Institute for the Humanities at New York University.

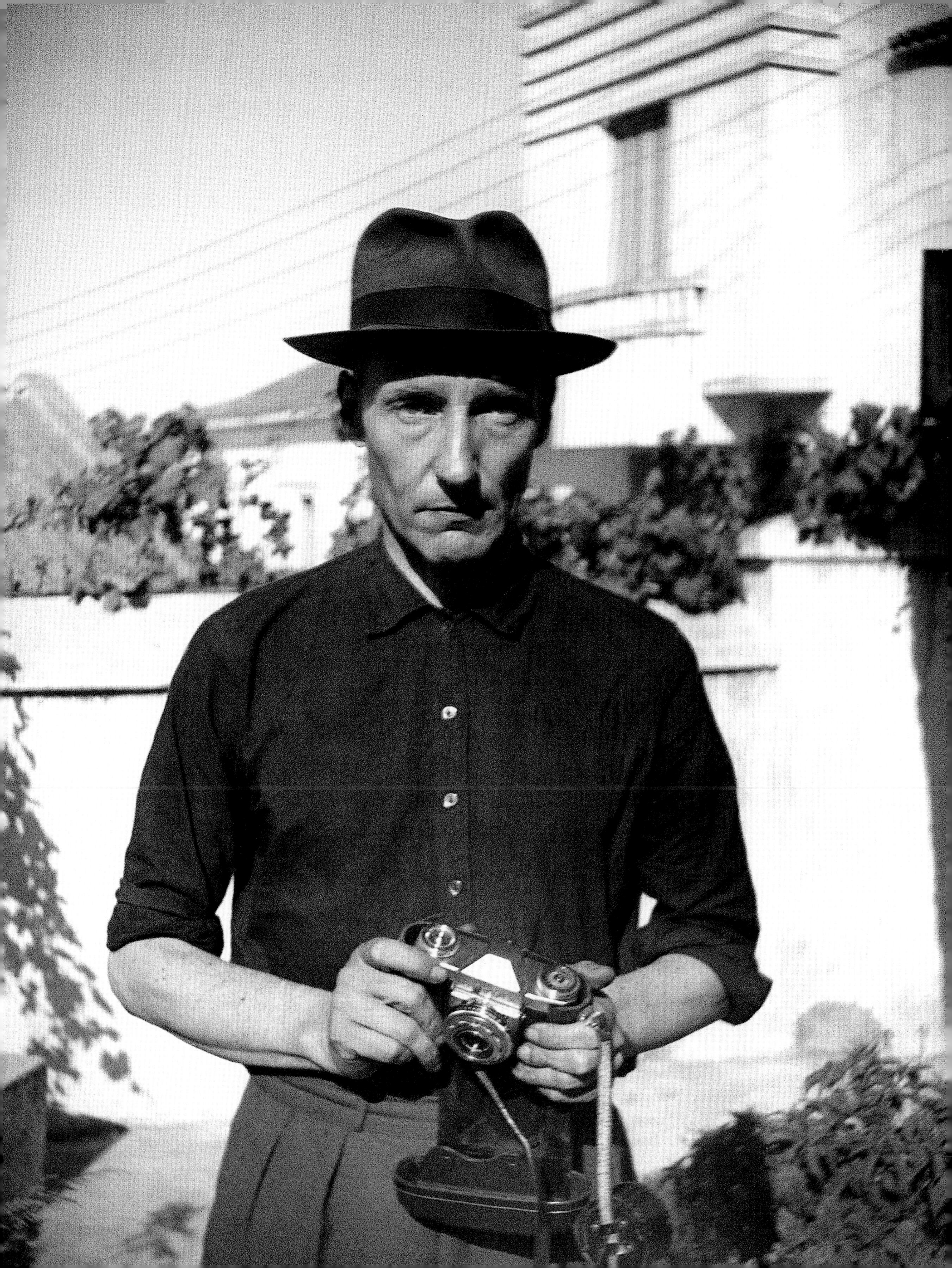

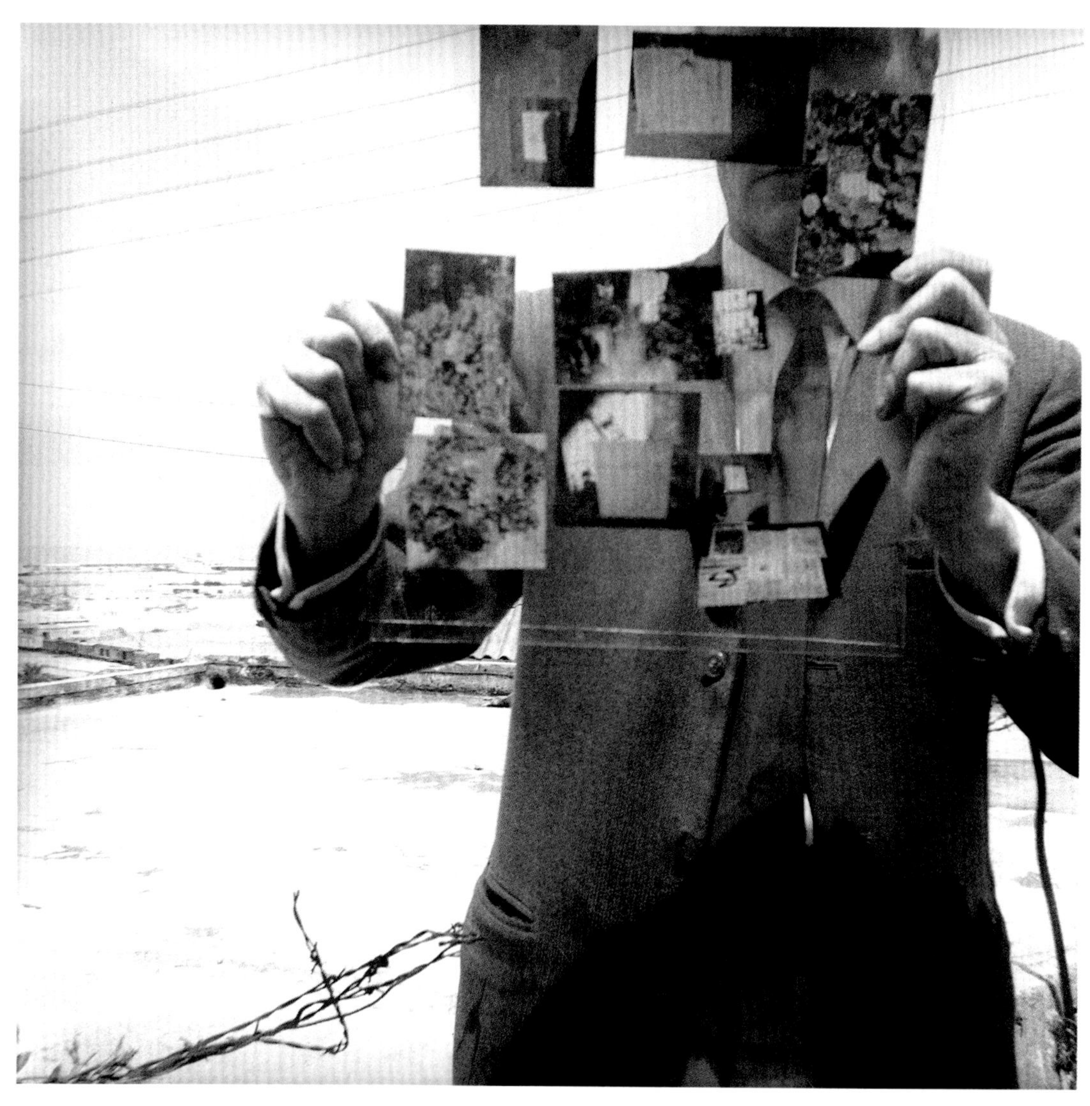

Self-portrait III, Tangier,
1964

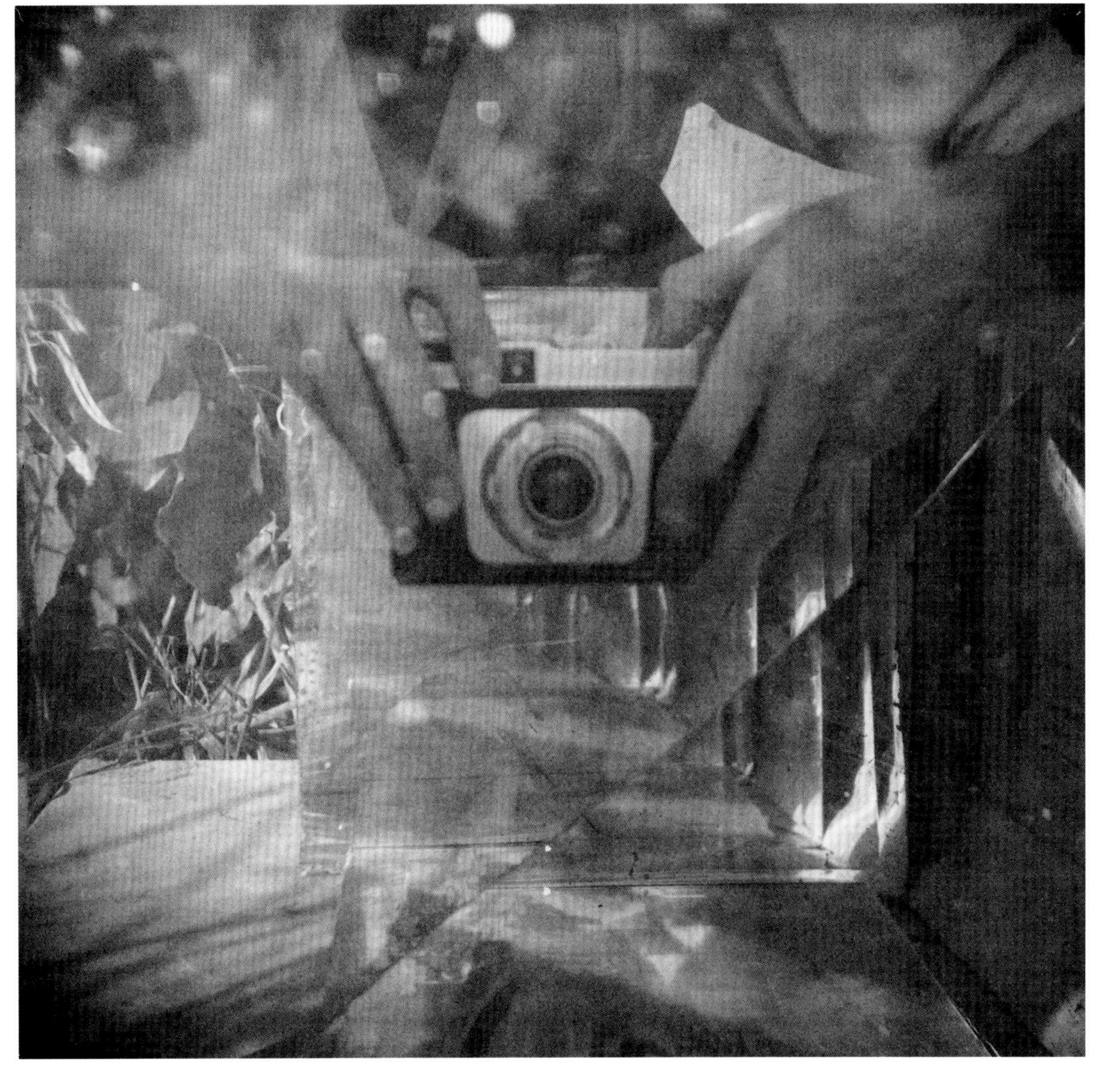

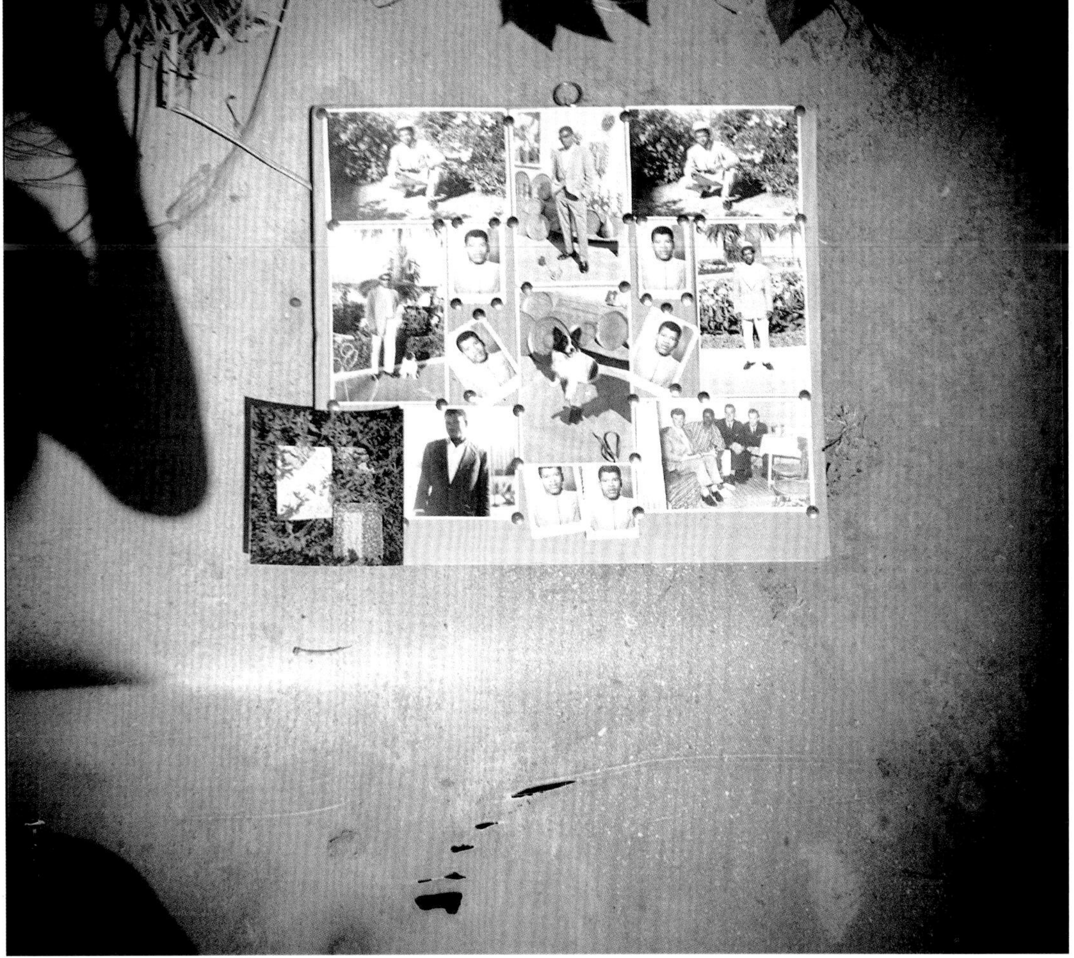

Top:
Untitled, Tangier, 1964

Bottom:
Untitled, 1964

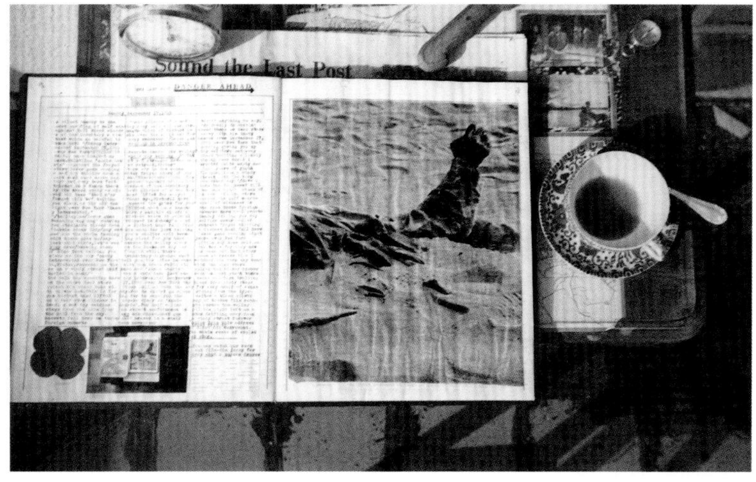

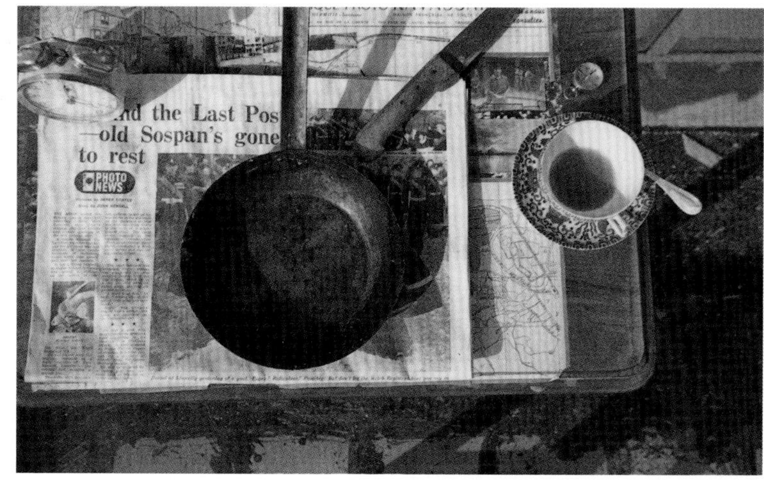

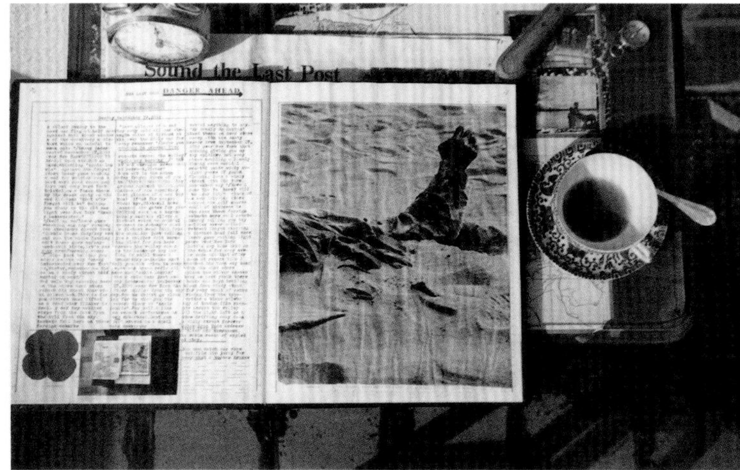

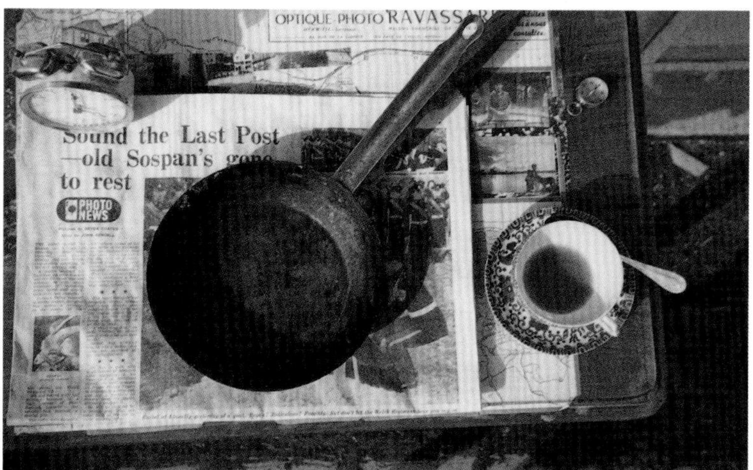

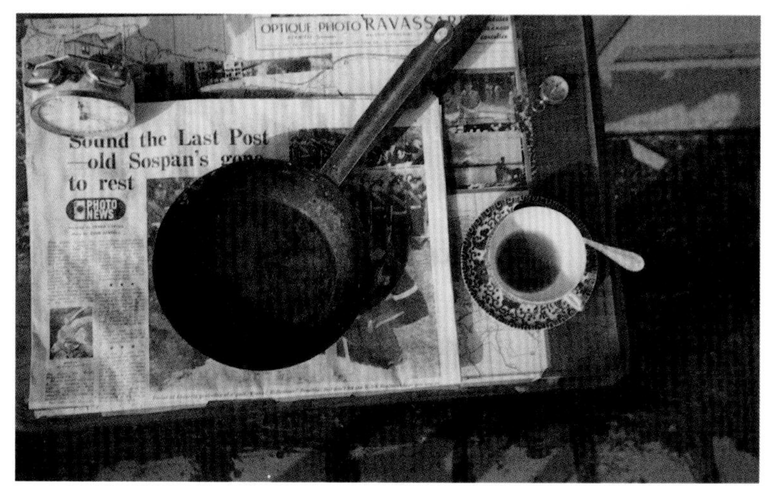

Above:
Real English Tea Made Here, Tangier, 1964

Opposite:
William S. Burroughs and Brion Gysin, *Untitled*, 1965. Silver-gelatin print, typescript, offset lithography, and newsprint on paper

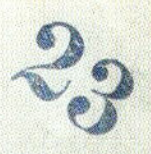

papers like this put in place giving you today's paper. Fill as I fixed the notice to my toy soldiers put away up three columns with the board. Another meaning steps trailing a lonely cross is to arrange: I fixed room cool remote columns. Fill a column on the meeting for four

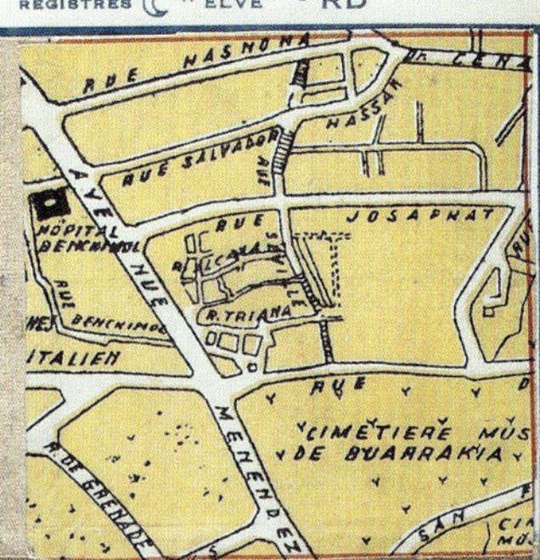

Hubo cuatro muertos

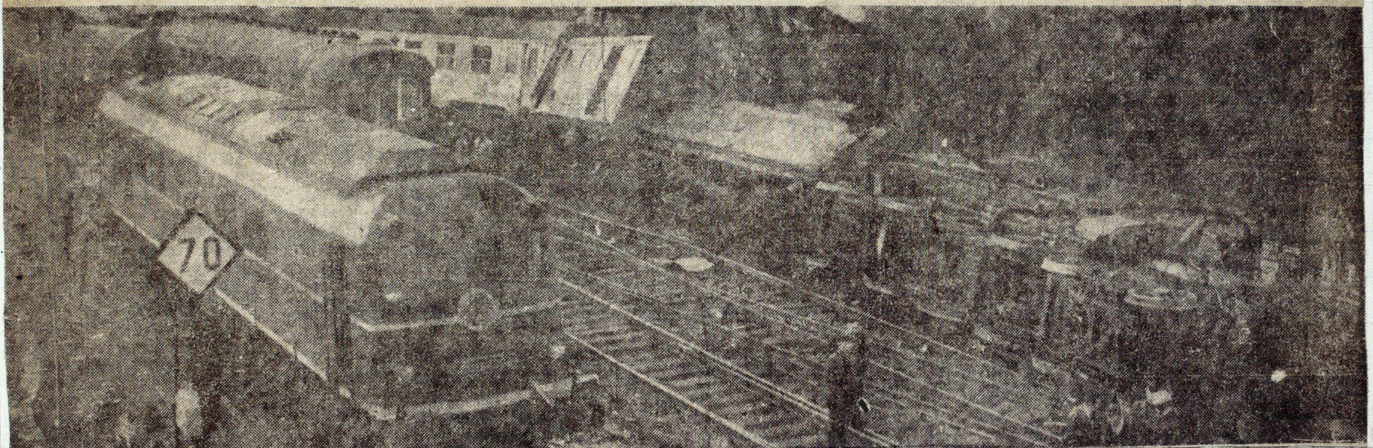

you are reading the future on (5) formulae (6) to record in writing our worn out film dim jerky far away. You will see days run backwards again in four days like the train did. distant hand couldn't time guesses to the last broadcast. Record in the history of the radio you are reading the future from me today arrange a meeting for four well known people home by train.

The NOVA EXPRESS

place dim jerky far away the dorm playground 1920 ponds in vacant lots adios marks this long ago XXXXXXX address the porch noise home from work used to be me Mister mouth and nose

By train

Lighthouse keeper as I am in a policeman's bed sitter record in the history of radio you are reading the future from me today arrange a meeting for four well known people home by train Mr. and Mrs. Mortimer Burroughs and their two ##### sons Mortimer Jr. and William Seward Burroughs of 4664 Berlin

(164) A REPORTER

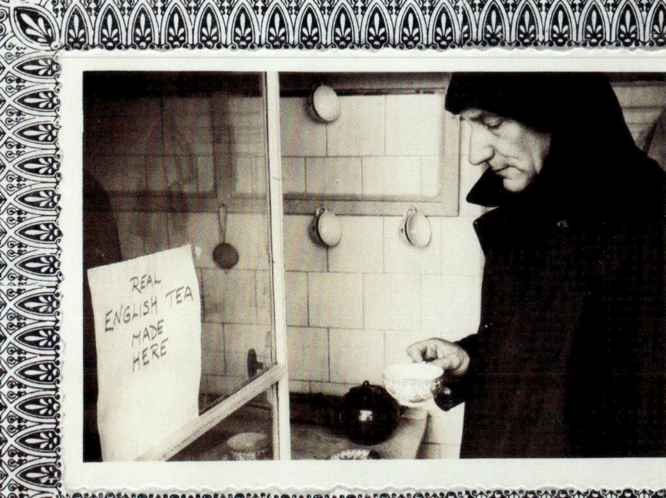

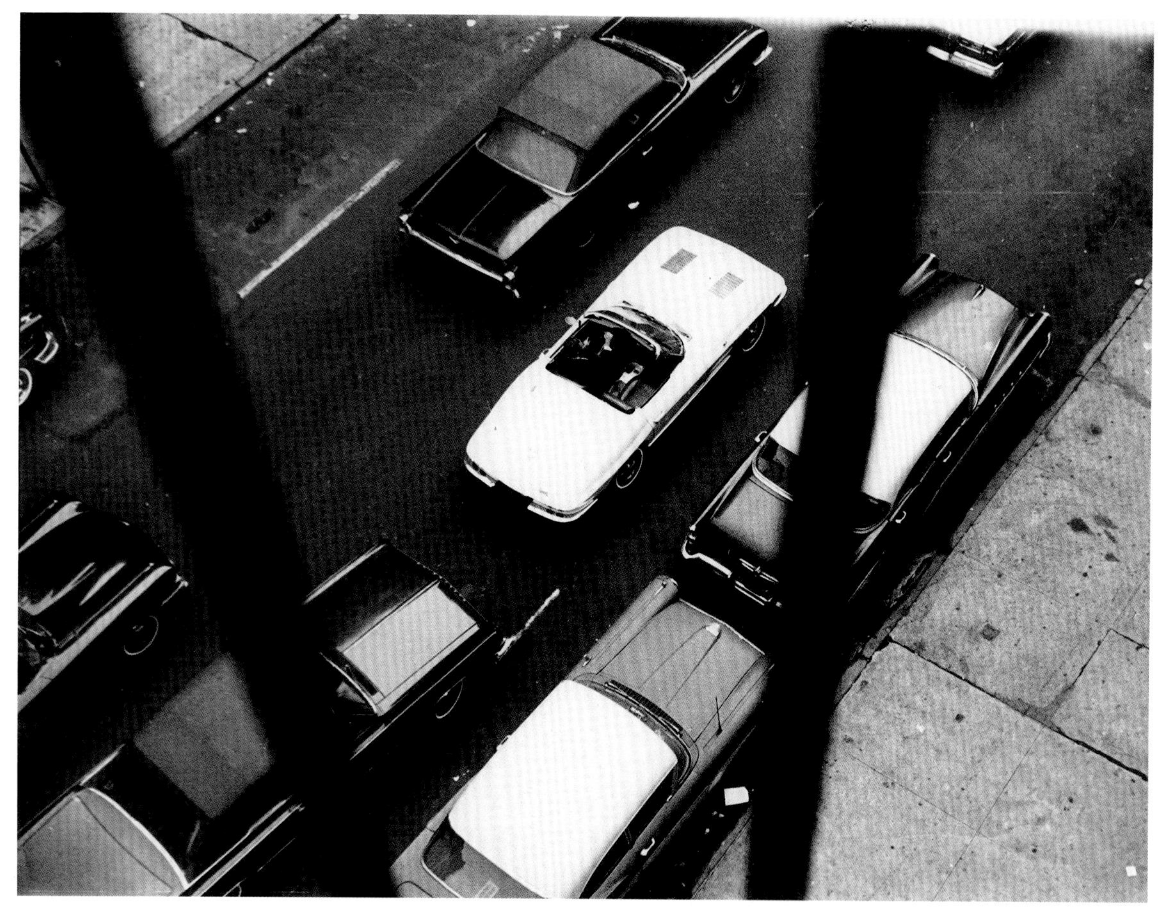

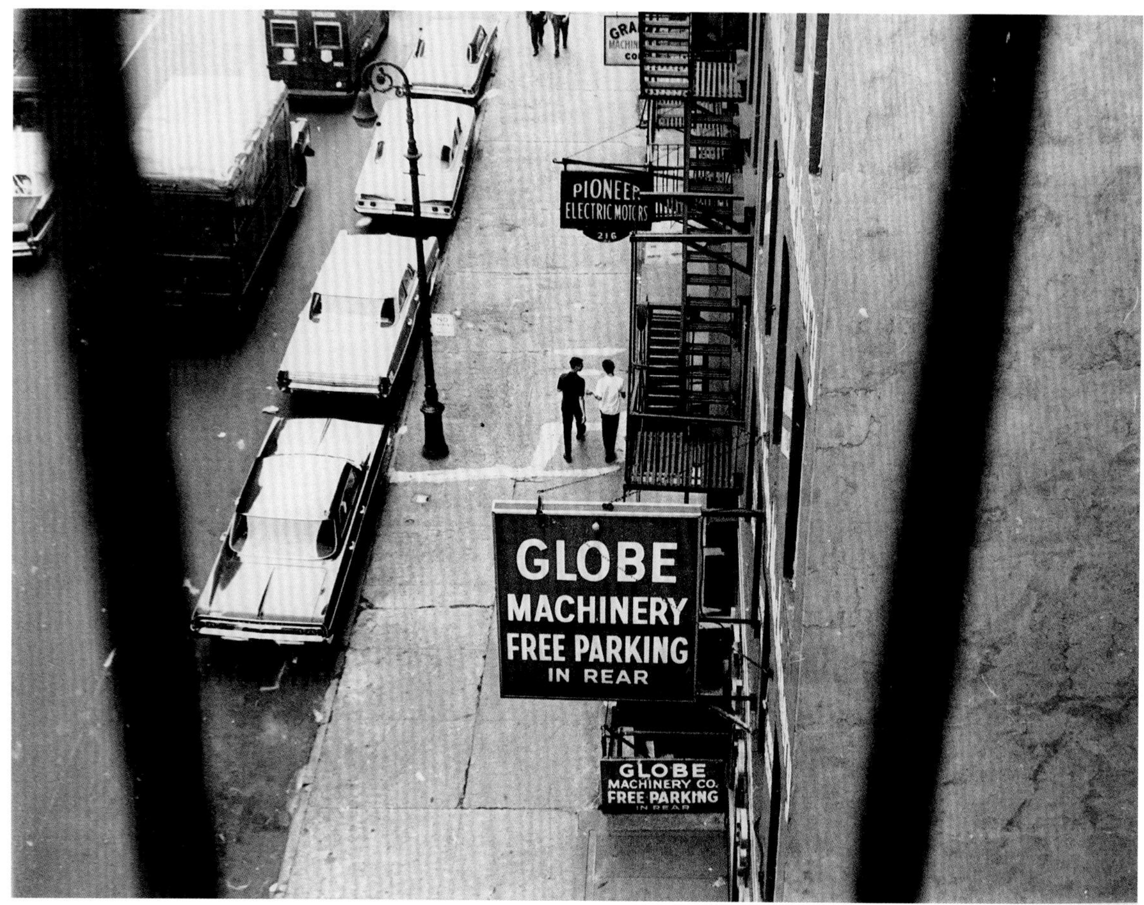

PIONEER
ELECTRIC MOTORS
216
GLOBE
MACHINERY
FREE PARKING
IN REAR
GLOBE
MACHINERY CO.
FREE PARKING
IN REAR

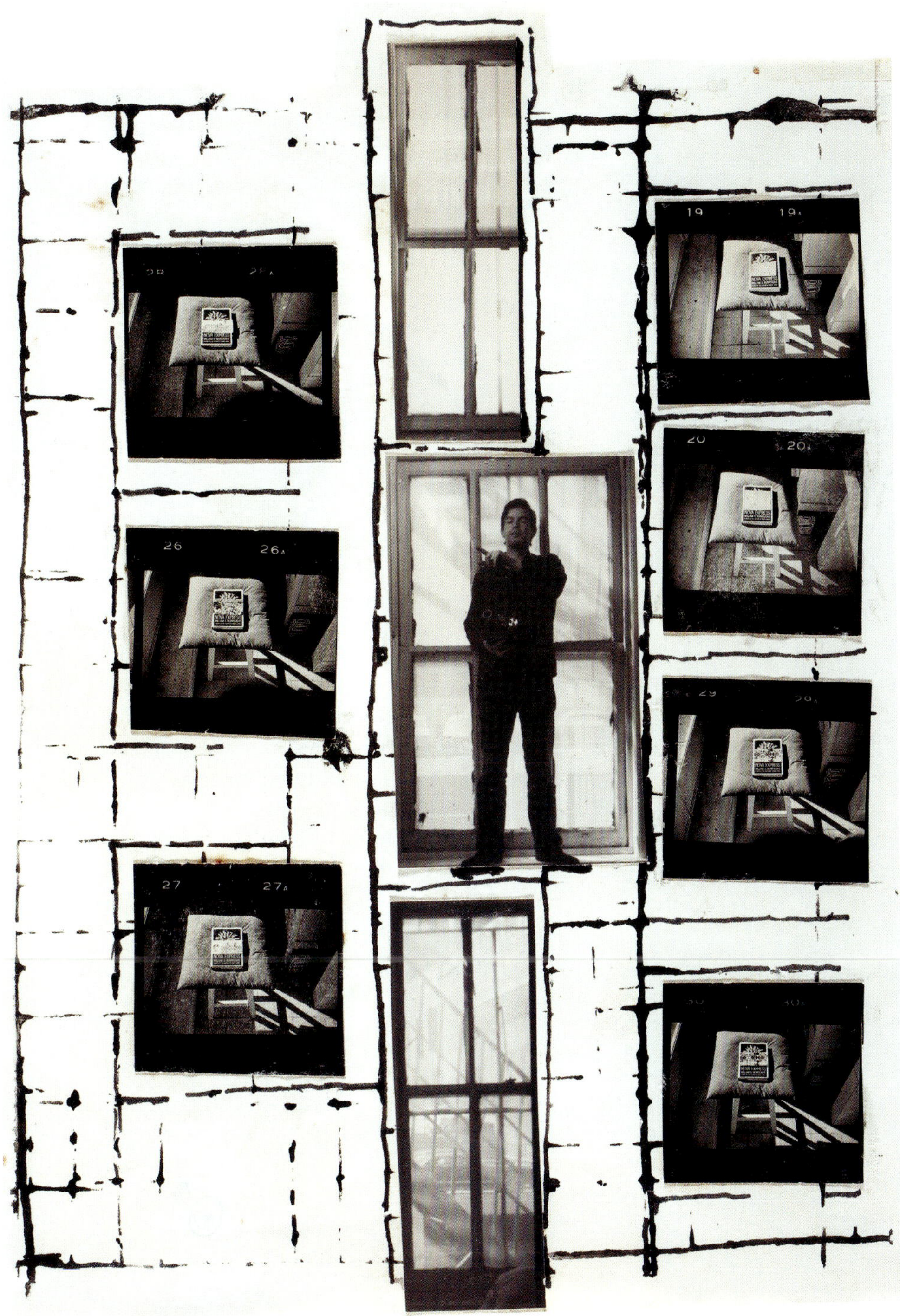

Opposite, top:
Untitled, New York, 1965

Opposite, bottom:
Untitled, New York, 1965

This page:
William S. Burroughs
and Brion Gysin, *Untitled*,
1965. Silver-gelatin prints
and ink on paper

They are everywhere in the writings of Samuel Beckett, these ancient, hunched figures on the point of collapse—looking as if they will snap or fold in two. They huddle inside filthy dens in his fictional trilogy (*Molloy*, 1951; *Malone Dies*, 1951; *The Unnamable*, 1953). They waddle slantwise on country roads in *Watt* (1953). In the plays they stand statue-still (*Catastrophe*, 1982), curl up, and keen away their lives (*Rockaby*, 1981), or shuffle facelessly around in geometric relays, as in the late television play *Quad* (1981). Beckett divined early on the depredations of a creaking and solitary old age, and as Eamonn Doyle's photographs remind us, he lifted the motif in part from the streets of his native Dublin.

Doyle looks to Beckett, he says, for a certain economy of composition, evacuating his frame of all but the central decrepit personage, a tract of sunlit concrete and deep shadow, the occasional road marking, pavement grille, or cheerless metal bench. His elevated vantage— a "mugger's-eye view"—dispenses frequently with physiognomy: no startled looks or inward gazes, as in classic street photography. Instead: the painful curve of a fused spine under ash-strewn Sunday best, a halo of thin, bright hair above dusty brocade, a few possessions or the day's shopping clutched in handbags and plastic carriers. These are figures that might fade into the monochromatic ground of a city's newly paved pedestrian precincts, were it not that so many— the women, mostly—have fought against the gray with their solid-colored coats and gloves.

The title of Doyle's series is *i*—a subtraction from Beckett's 1972 play *Not I*. Best known for its austere, exacting scenography—a single mouth spotlit onstage, blubbering away in the dark—*Not I* is the monologue of a woman in her seventies, "speechless all her days," who has begun to talk and cannot stop. Beckett claimed to have based the character on countless "crones" seen toiling along streets and rural lanes in Ireland. Stop one of these silent creatures and you would never get away, for she had everything still to say. Here is the paradox of Doyle's subjects: apparently isolated, half visible, faces hidden, they are not ingrown at all. An old man brings an ironing-board cover home to his wife; a woman (or a relative) has been on holiday to Brunei. Even the homeless ones are biding their time and their tales; they have only to turn around and the stream of words would be unstoppable.

Eamonn Doyle: *i*

Brian Dillon

Brian Dillon is UK editor of *Cabinet* and teaches critical writing at the Royal College of Art. His most recent books are *Objects in This Mirror: Essays* (2014) and *Ruin Lust* (2014).

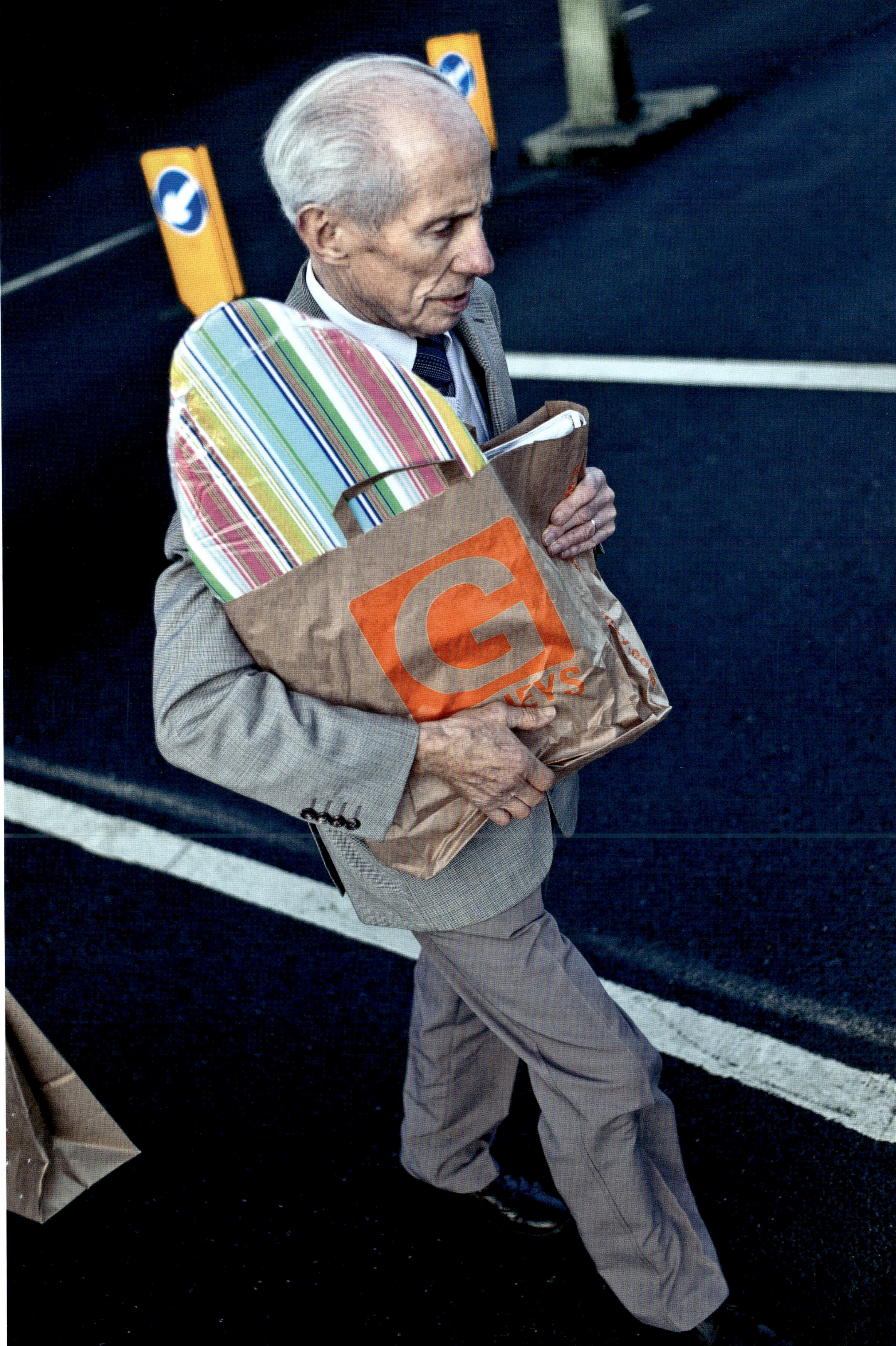

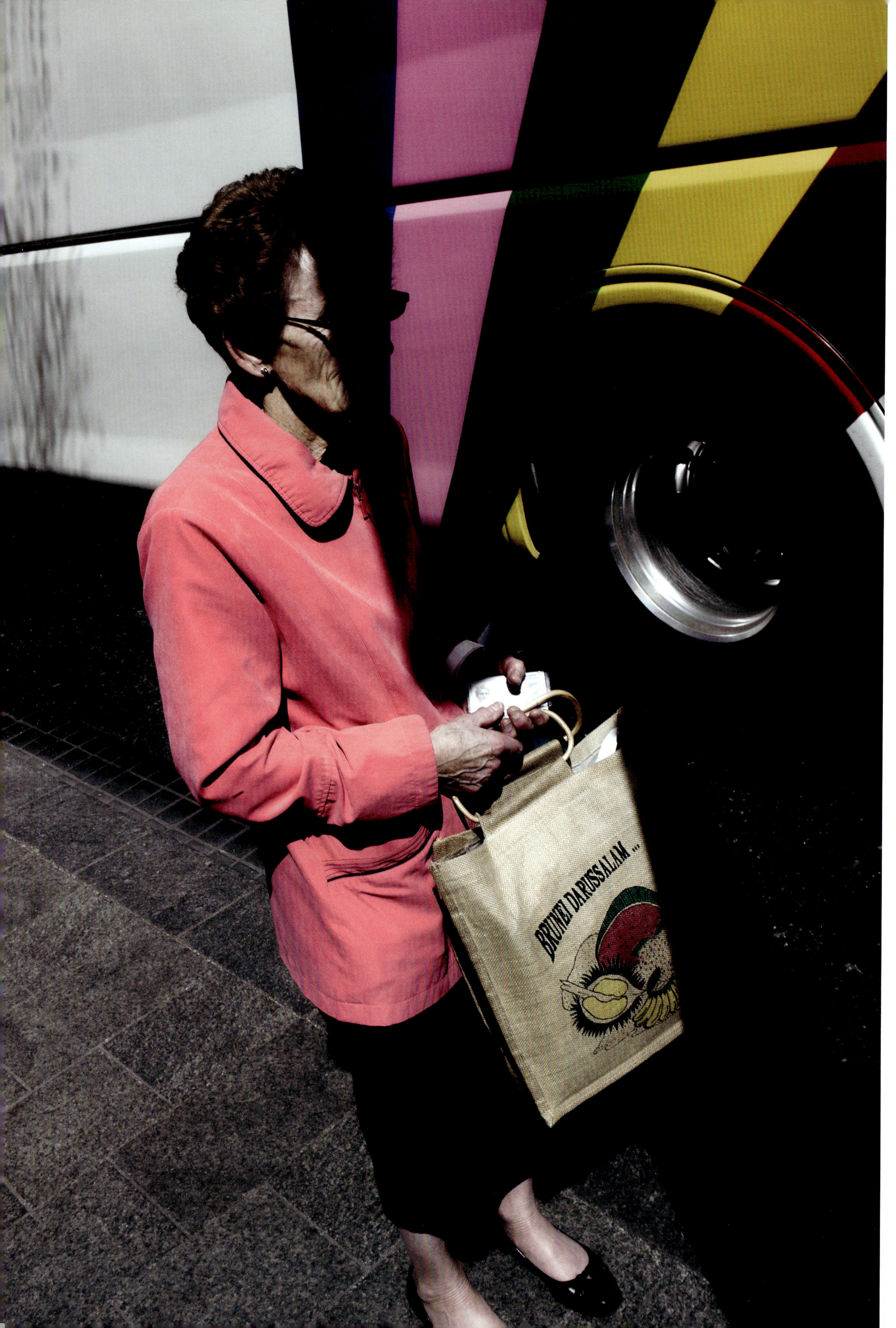
BRUNEI DARUSSALAM ...

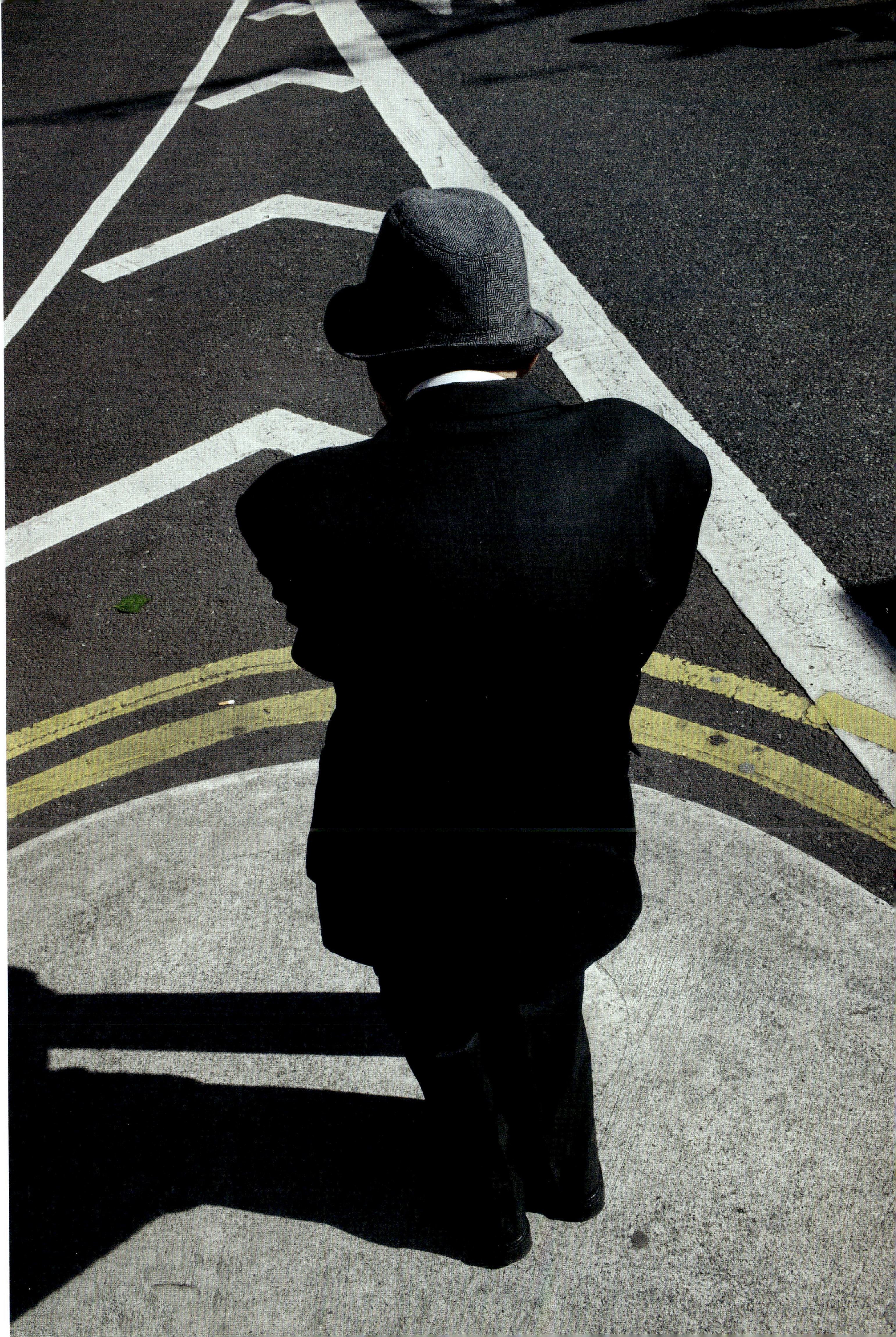

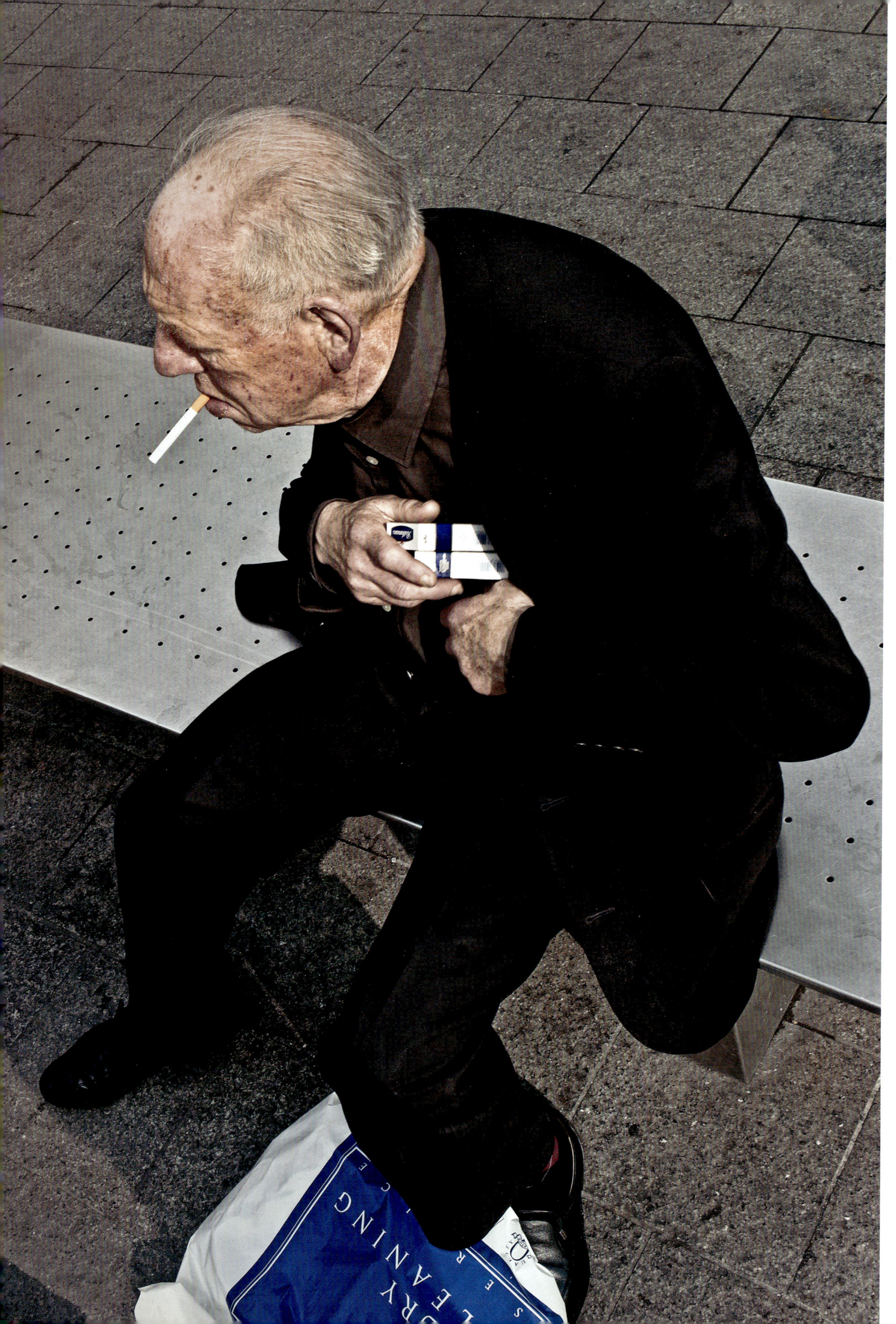

RY
LEANING
S E R

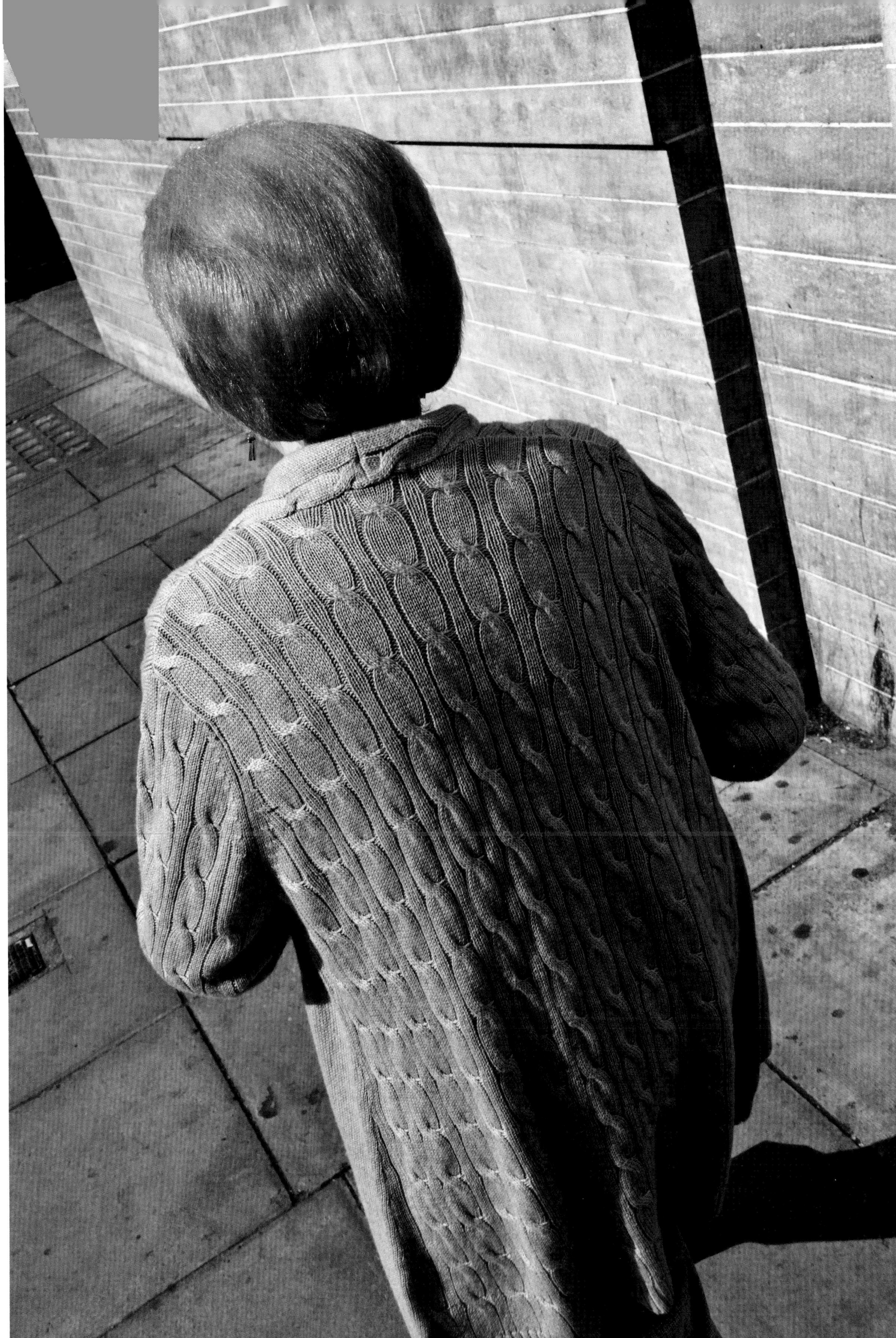

Japanese novelist and playwright Kobo Abe (1924–1993) was a celebrated writer well before the international success and critical acclaim of his novel *The Woman in the Dunes* (1962). His first publication, the story collection *The Wall—The Crime of S. Karma* (1951), catapulted him into the literary limelight and invited comparisons to Franz Kafka. Ill-at-ease situations and the confused and collapsed identities of his characters became a hallmark of his work that captured the vexations of man in contemporary society.

The Box Man (1973) is one of Abe's emblematic works. It is the story of a nameless man who chooses to go through life wearing a cardboard box on his head, confining his vision to that restricted area, connecting to the world instead through words scribbled onto the inside of the box. The novel includes Abe's photographs of anonymous strangers, trucks, occupied urinals, and a distanced view of adults standing beside a wheelchair-bound child. The accompanying captions that Abe wrote for the photographs have no congruence in subject matter. Upon initial review, the images could be interpreted as illustrations, but Abe was adamant to make clear that this was not their aim, remarking: "The texts that accompany photographs are not explanations…. If those poems emphasize something then it would be that for me photography itself must be poetry."

Abe the photographer eschewed the same elements of image making that many Japanese photographers in the 1960s and '70s also rejected, namely narrative, character, causal relationships, and exposition. His style harks back to the work of Kikuji Kawada, Daido Moriyama, and Takuma Nakahira, and to the gritty anonymity of everyday urban spaces turned into bizarro alternate worlds captured with a diffuse sense of subject. Questioning photography's documentary function was then common; take, for example, Kawada's *The Map* (1965), which presented a close-up of the walls inside Hiroshima's Atomic Bomb Dome, making the scratches and tactile surface seem like abstractions and obscuring an otherwise overt choice of subject. Densely packed information was a regular motif in photography from this period, immersing and disorienting viewers. What *is* the subject? Abe and his contemporaries avoided answering such questions by making the question itself irrelevant, even if he was less interested than his peers in finding a new form of photographic expression.

Nonetheless, the mechanics of Abe's work rest on photography's and the novel's function as an experience— a direct experience. We do not dispassionately observe the protagonist but rather identify with him: his position and experiences become our own. In considering how Abe's fiction and photography operate in similar ways, it becomes all the more clear how the novel is akin to photography. In Abe's photography, the absence of formal concerns, and the ostensibly ambiguous framing and choice of subject leave unresolved puzzles. Rather than pursue a theme or subject with resolute simplicity, he focused on fragments that hinted at a larger totality—he wanted his work to contain infinite worlds. For Abe's generation this approach to reality trumped mimesis and the transparency promised by machines used to peer into our world—and that might, in fact, confine vision to the square of a box.

Kobo Abe
as Photographer

Ivan Vartanian

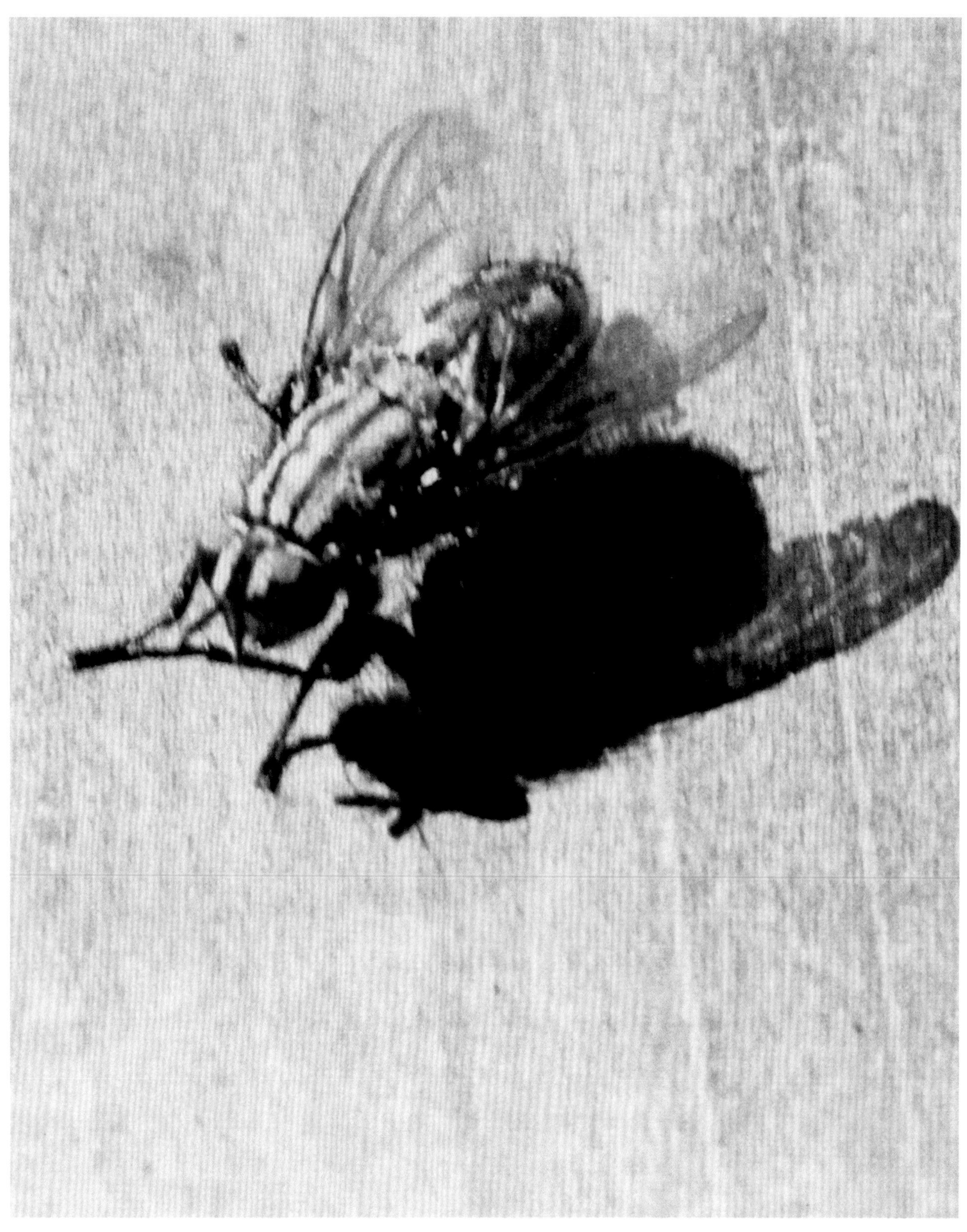

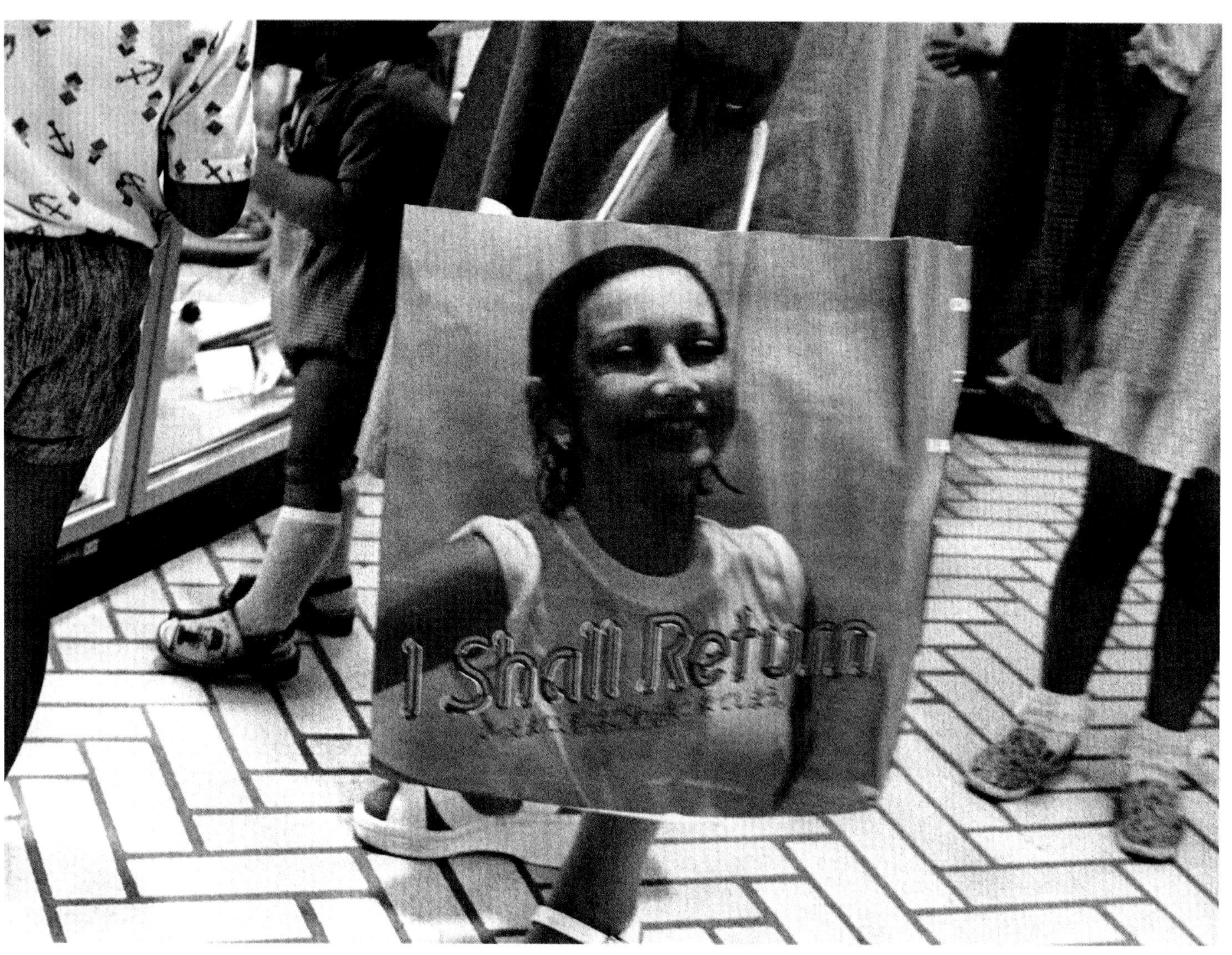

I Shall Return

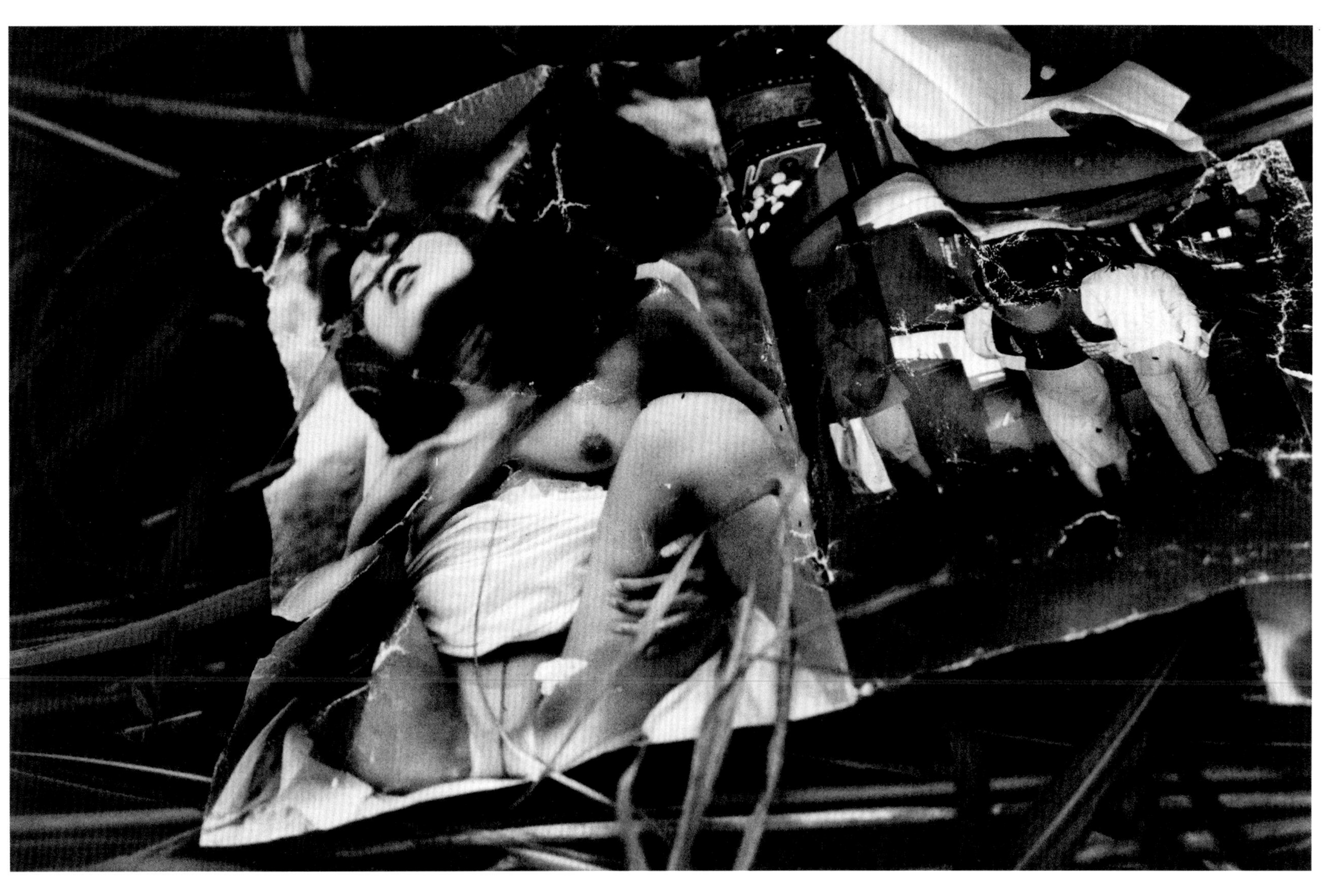

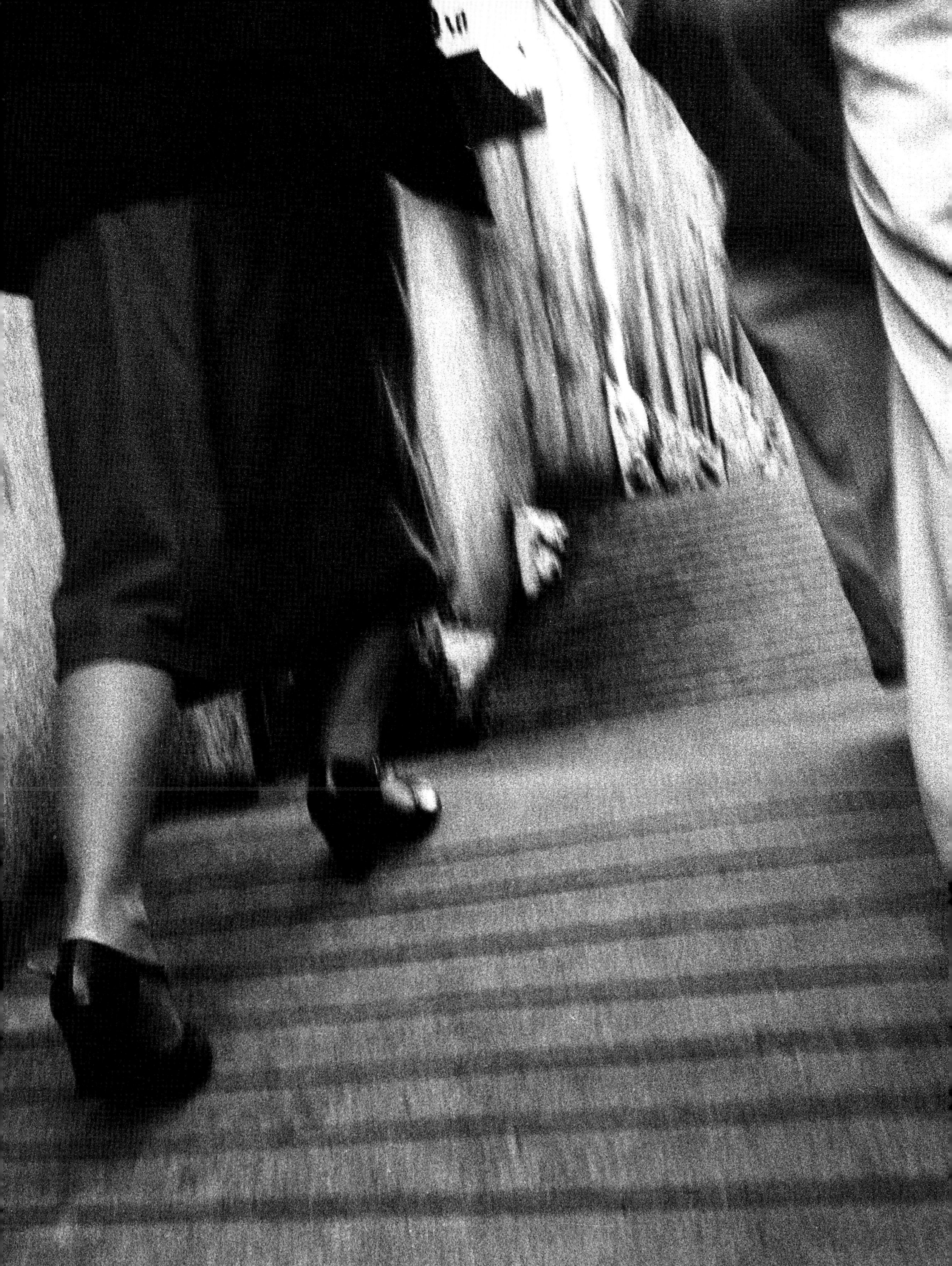

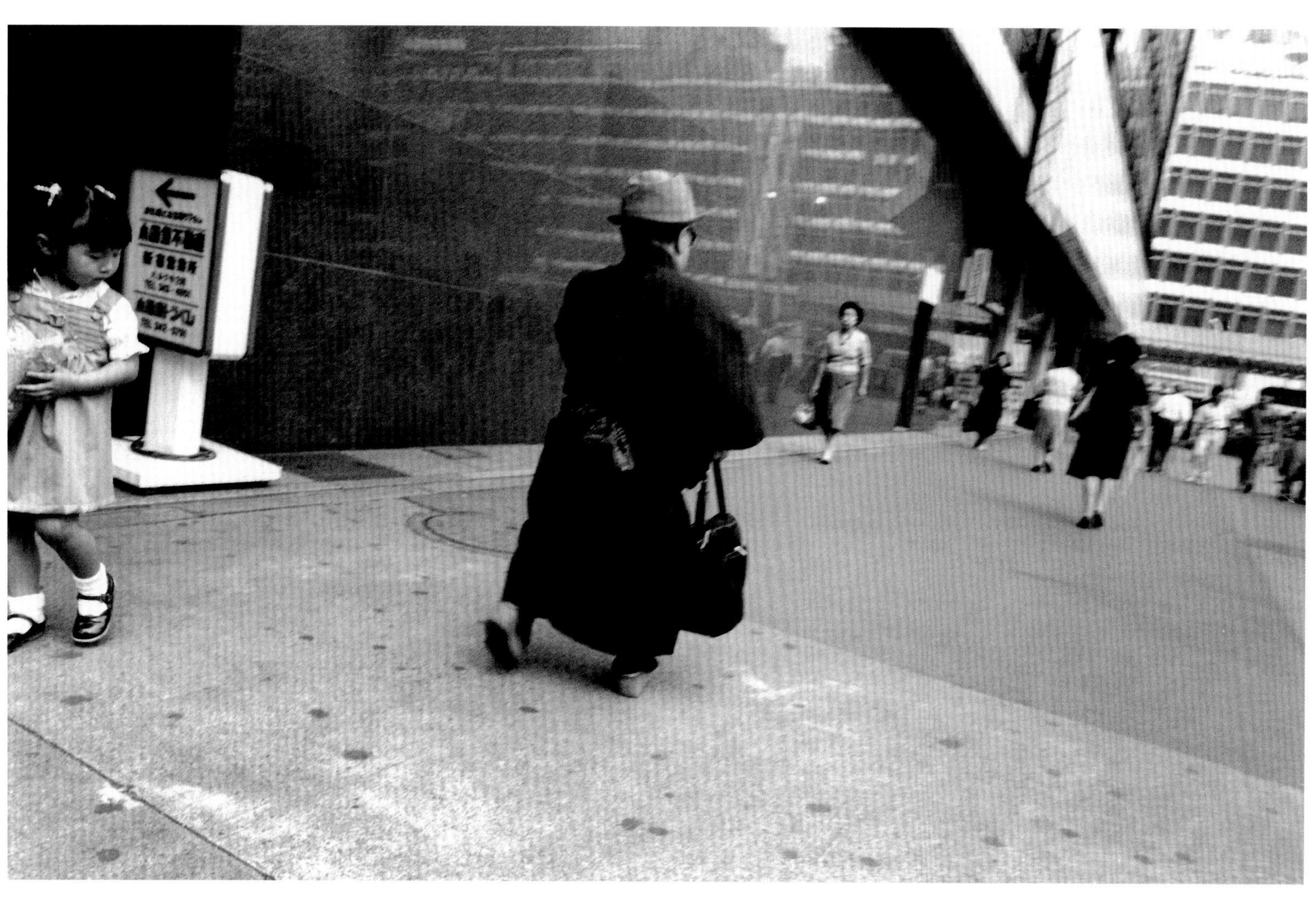

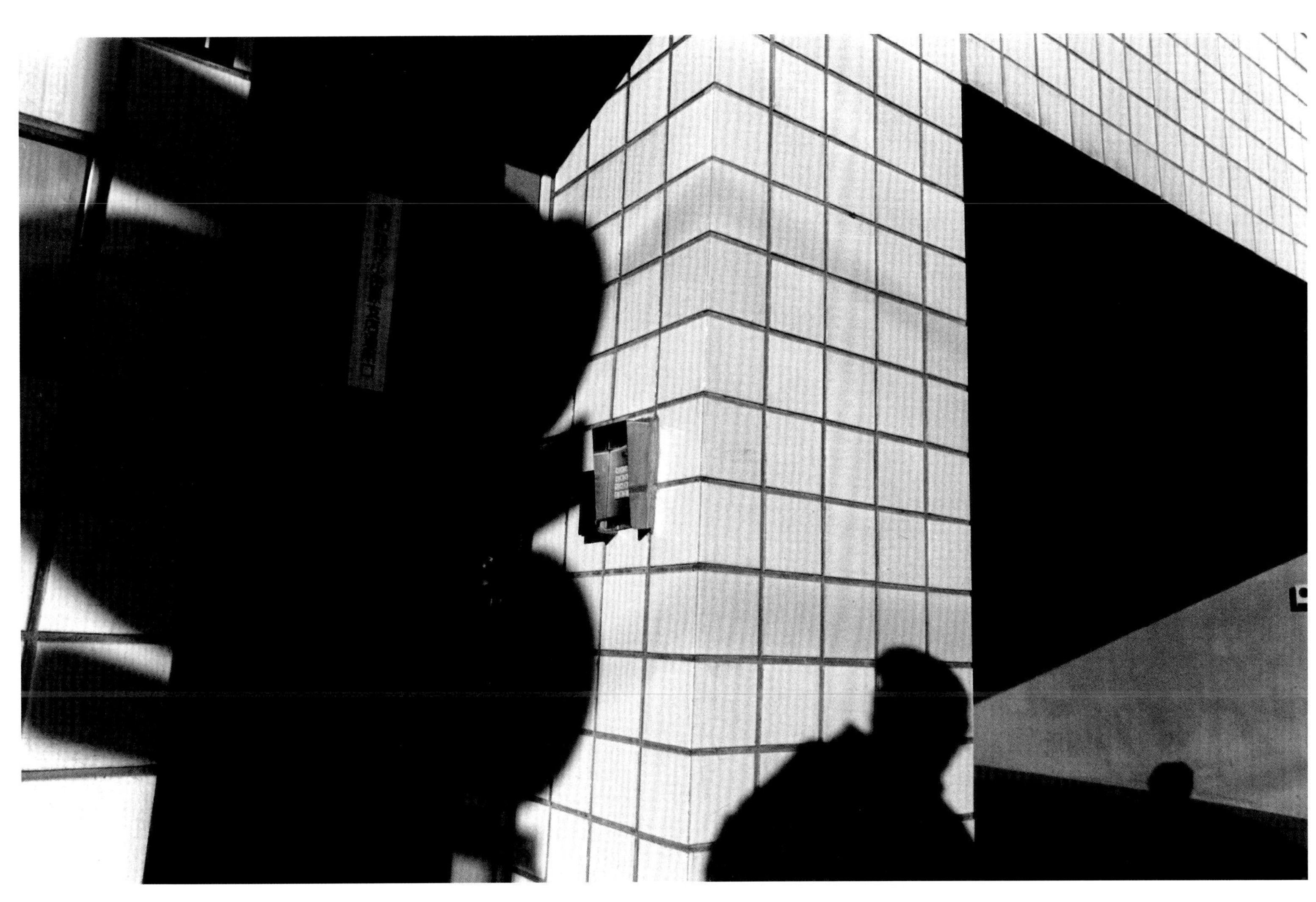

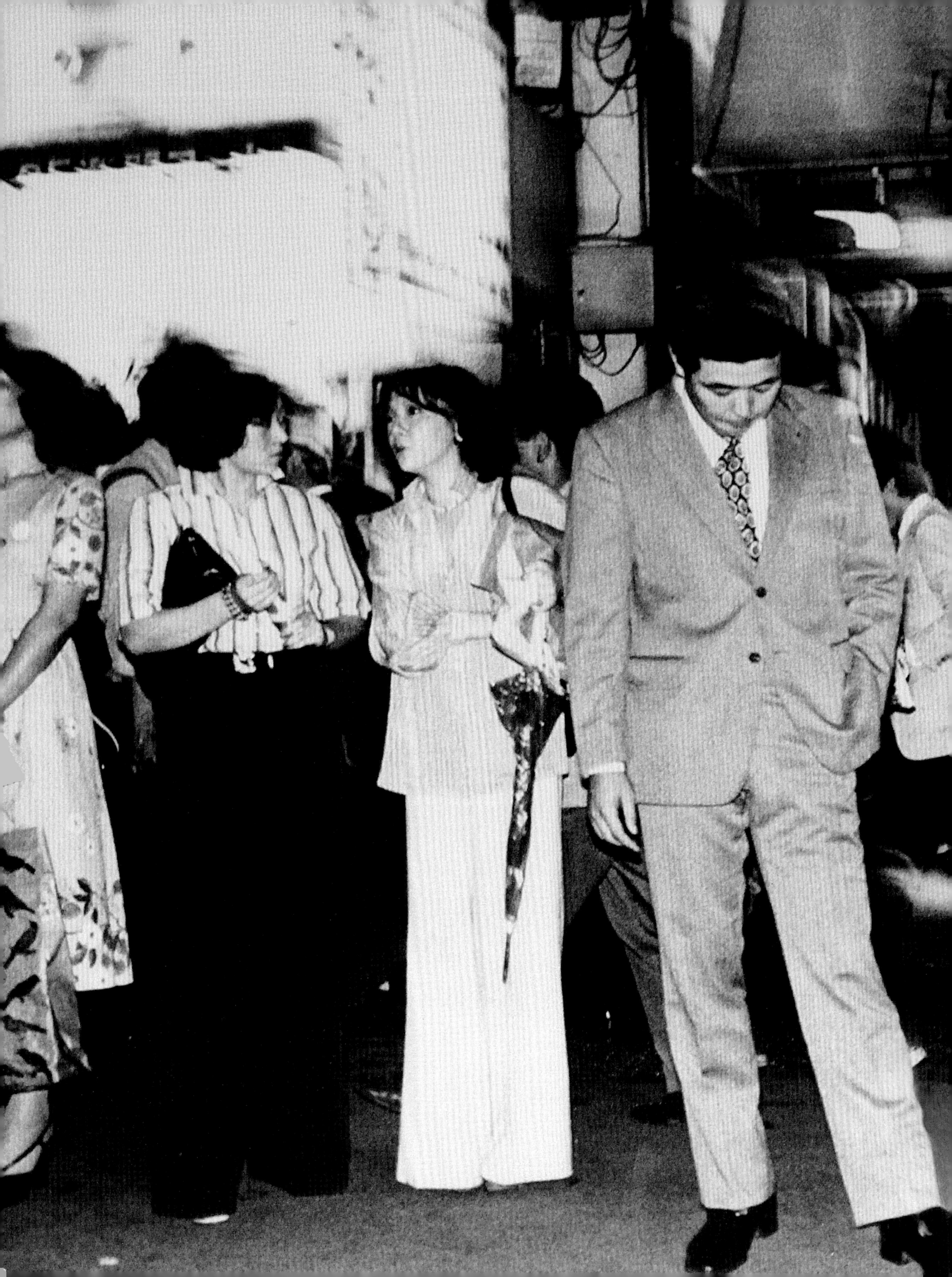

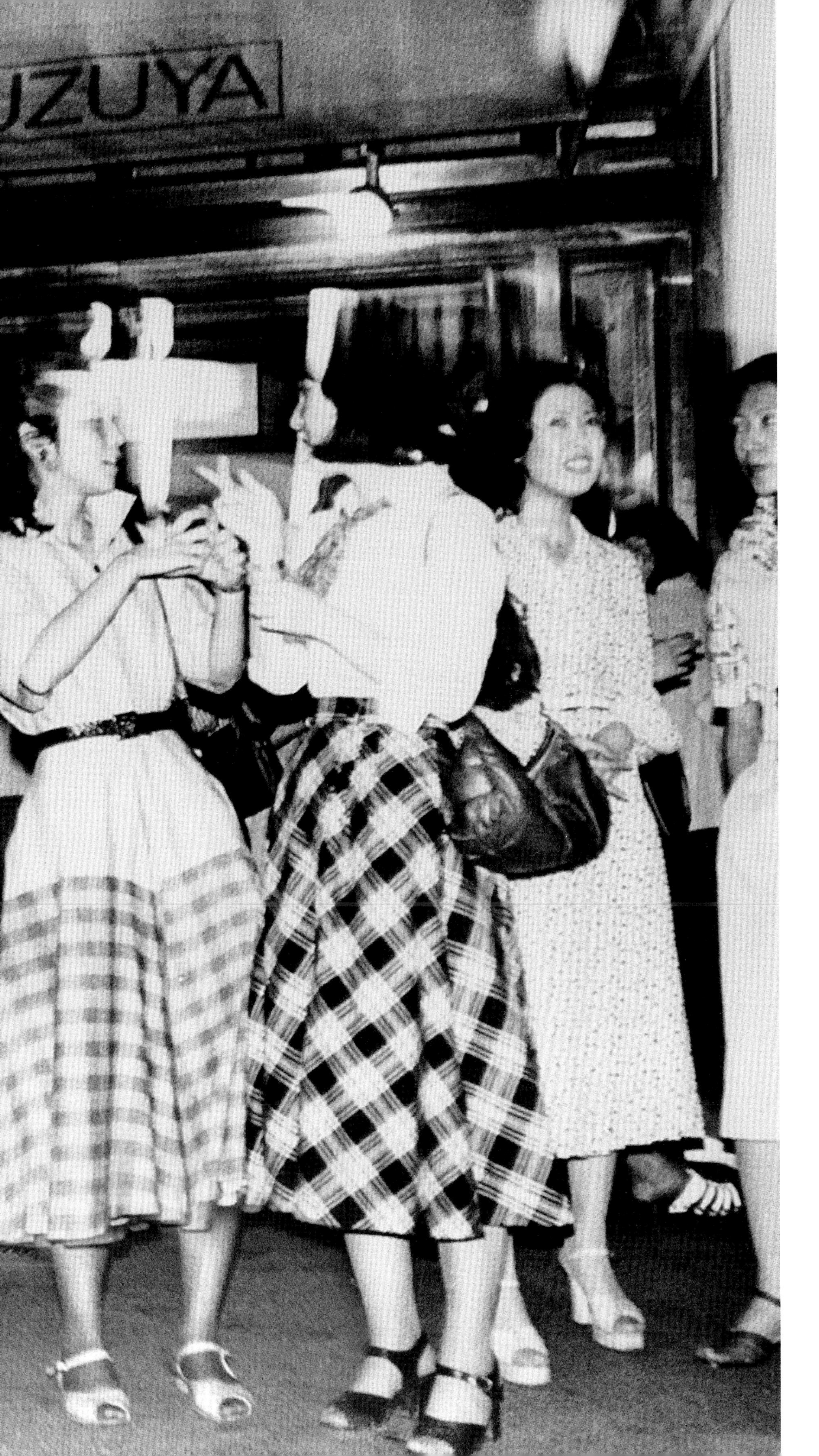
ZUYA

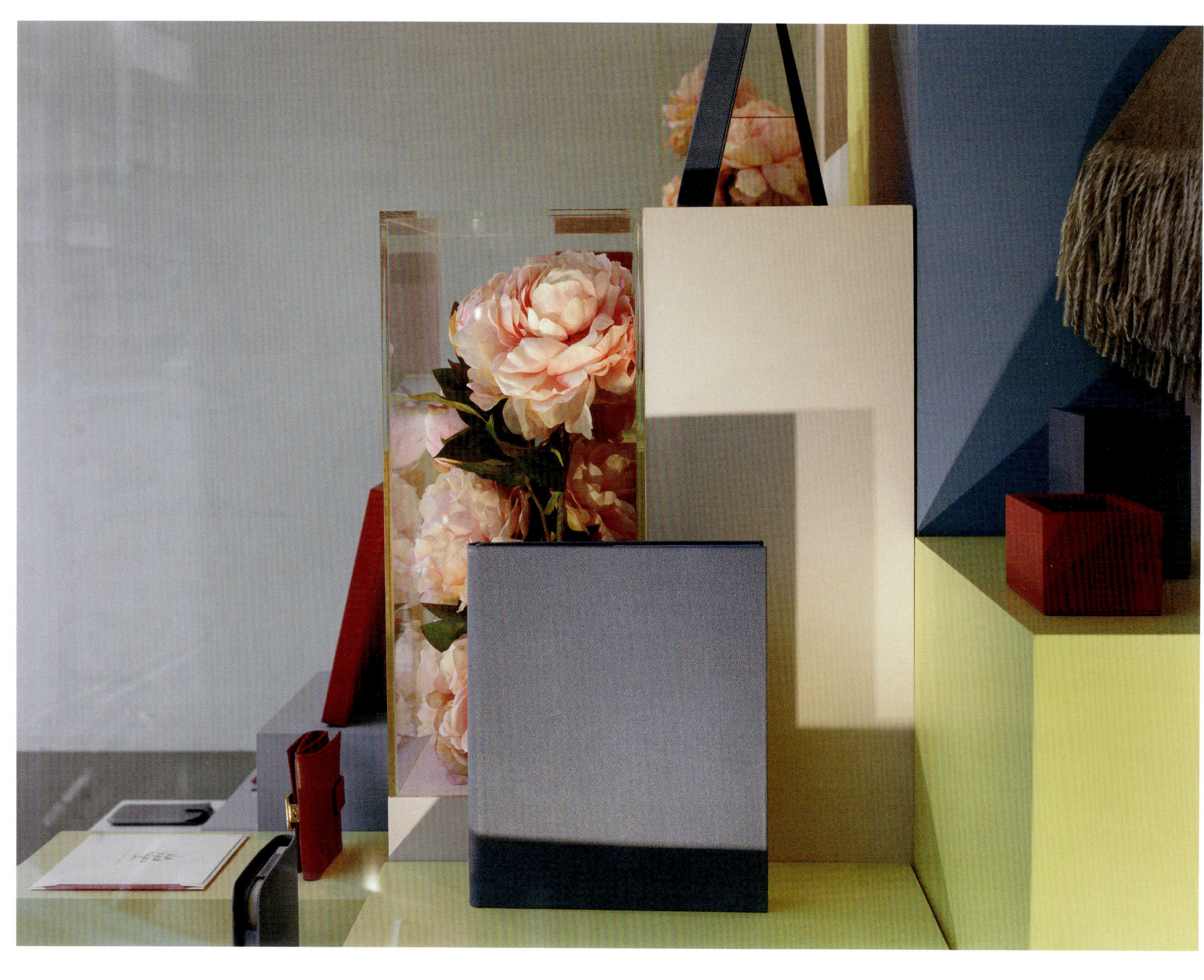

Following an earlier project on shopping centers made around the time of the 2008 economic crash, Sarah Dobai began photographing shop-window displays in London and Paris. Literary references, from Tennessee Williams to Raymond Carver, have appeared in Dobai's past projects, so it is fitting that she began to relate her images of windows to Nikolai Gogol's darkly humorous 1842 tale, "The Overcoat," which tells of the life and death of lowly government clerk Akaky Akakievich, who spends his days drearily copying documents until his life is transformed when he acquires a bespoke overcoat. The new piece of clothing materializes after a period of frugal saving that allows Akakievich and his tailor to go from shop to shop in St. Petersburg to purchase the necessary materials— a broadcloth and "chintz" (for the lining) that is "more attractive and glossy" than silk (a marten pelt is out of budget). His old, tattered housecoat is set aside until the grand new coat is stolen as he crosses an empty square one night. In the ensuing attempts to retrieve the coat, during which Gogol pokes fun at Russian bureaucracy, Akakievich, following a harsh dressing down by a "very important person," succumbs to a fever and dies. But his ghost will haunt the city, robbing others of their overcoats.

Dobai notes that her large-format images "aim to become a reflection on the status of commodity both in [Gogol's] text and on the streets of the city." The project also knowingly follows in a tradition established by Eugène Atget and continued by Lee Friedlander, among others, of photographing store windows, presumably for the visual pleasure offered by ready-made still lifes and their surreal juxtapositions of merchandise, frozen mannequins, and disorienting reflections. In Gogol's story, Akakievich finds himself mesmerized by such a display: "He stopped curiously before a lighted shop window to look at a picture that portrayed some beautiful woman taking off her shoe and thus baring her whole leg, not a bad leg at all." In the satire, Akakievich's new overcoat briefly elevates his self-esteem (until events take their swift, tragic turn), but the idea that one's sense of self and social position is realized through material objects remains relevant. Akakievich himself may not haunt us, but repercussions from the 2008 financial crisis are still unfolding. Appropriate, then, that Dobai's series will appear in a new printing of "The Overcoat," forthcoming this fall from British publisher Four Corners Books as part of a series of classics, now in the public domain, paired with newly created bodies of artwork. —The Editors

Sarah Dobai
After "The Overcoat"

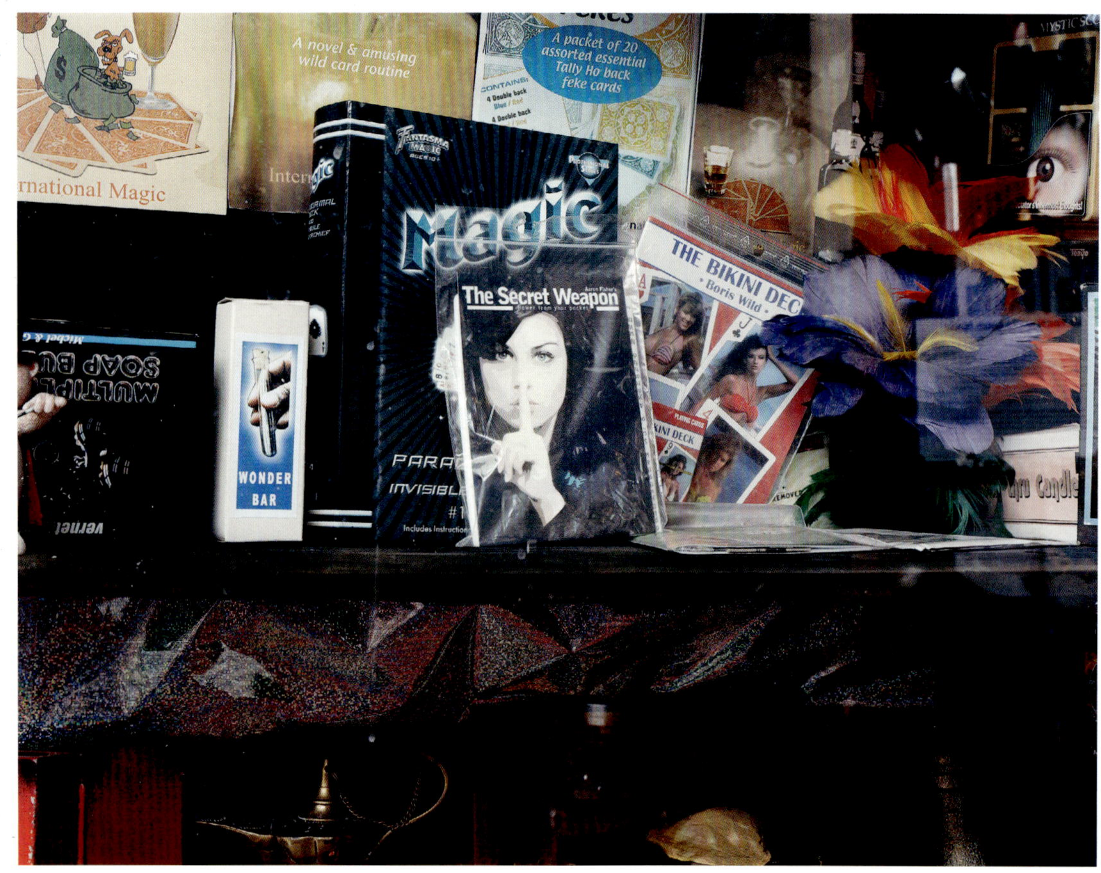

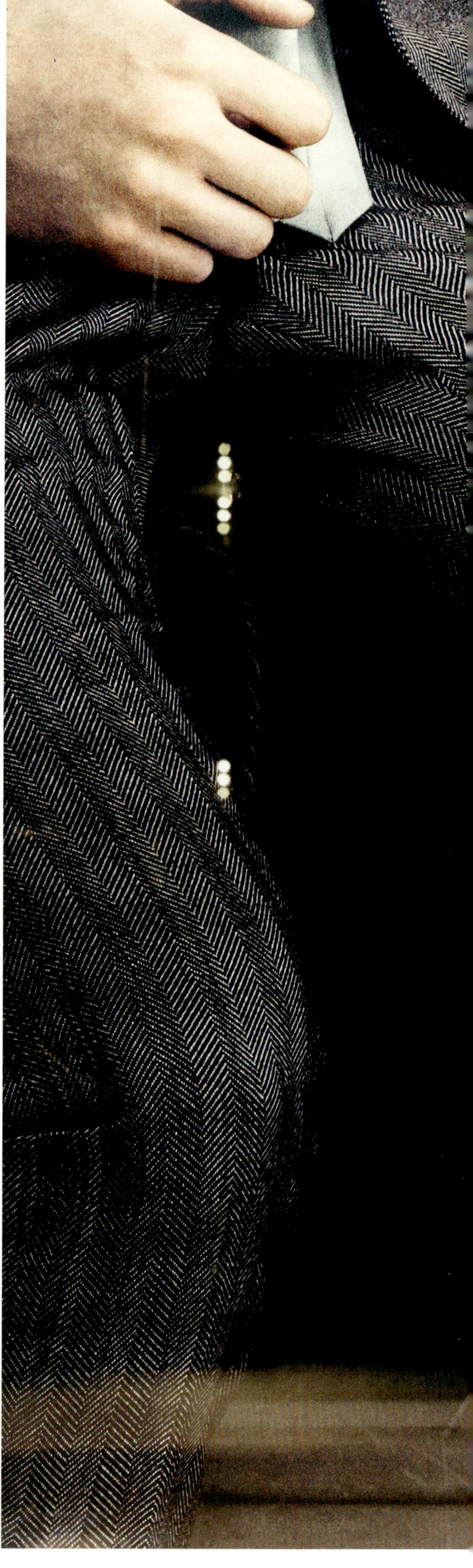

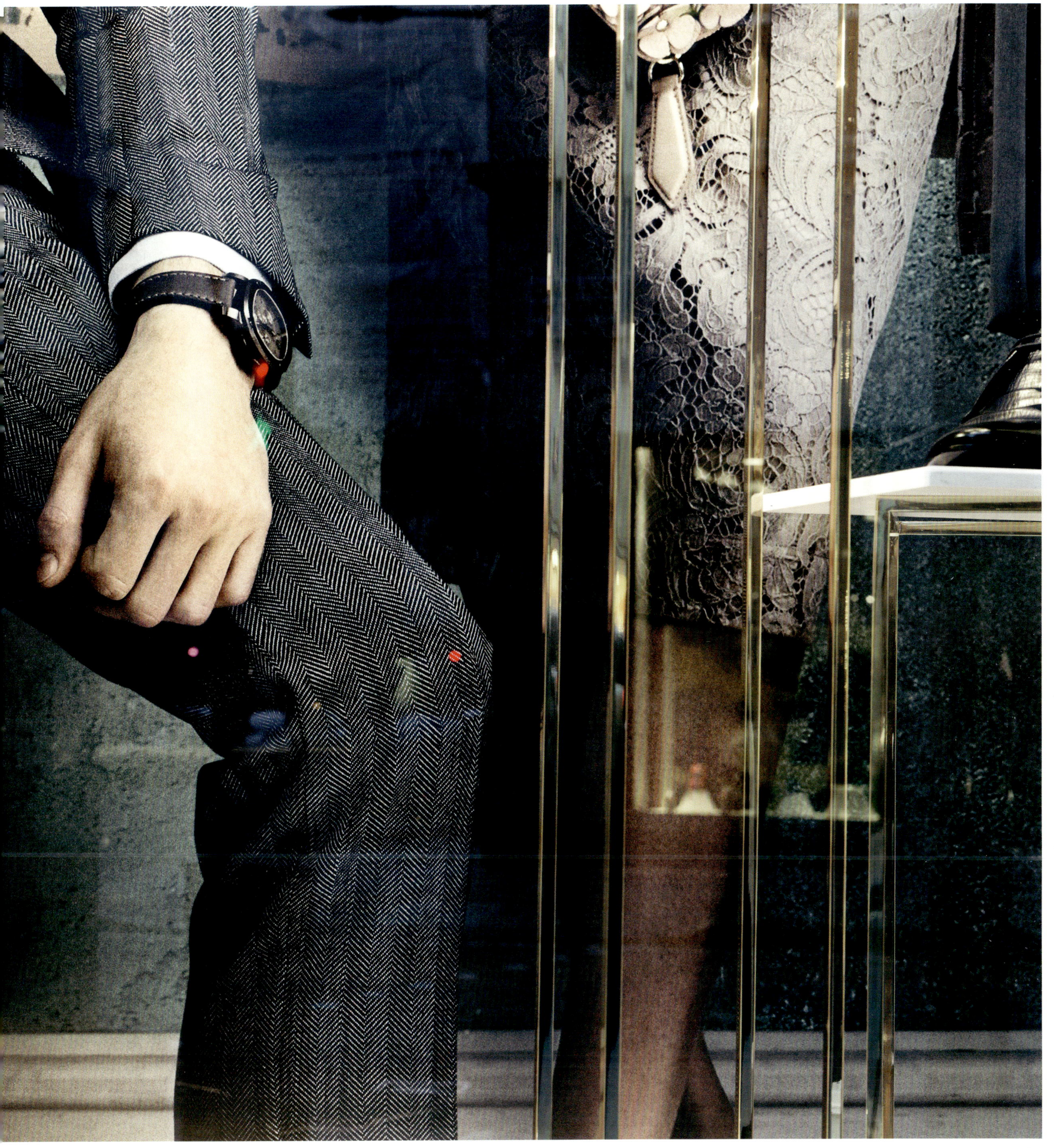

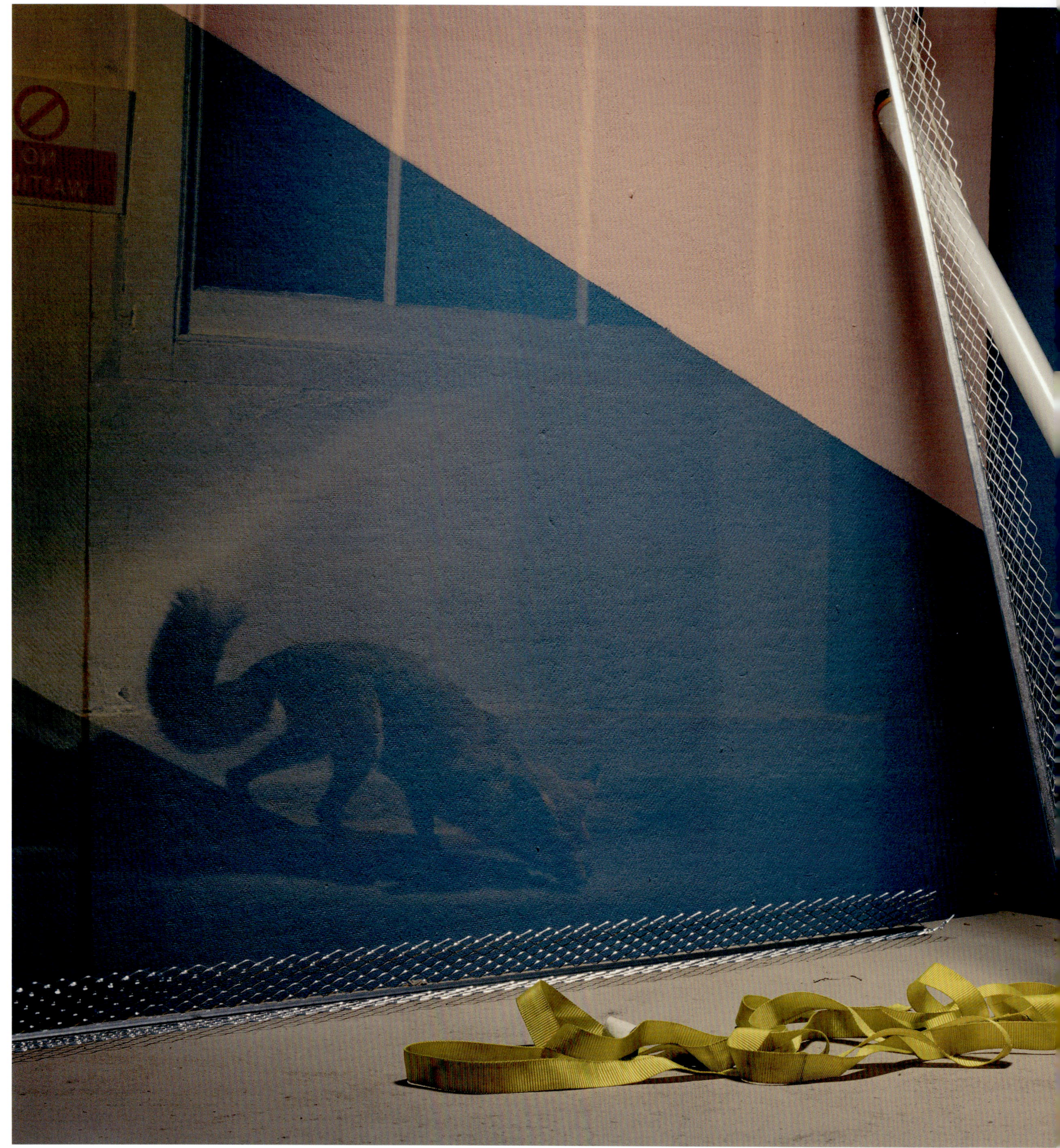

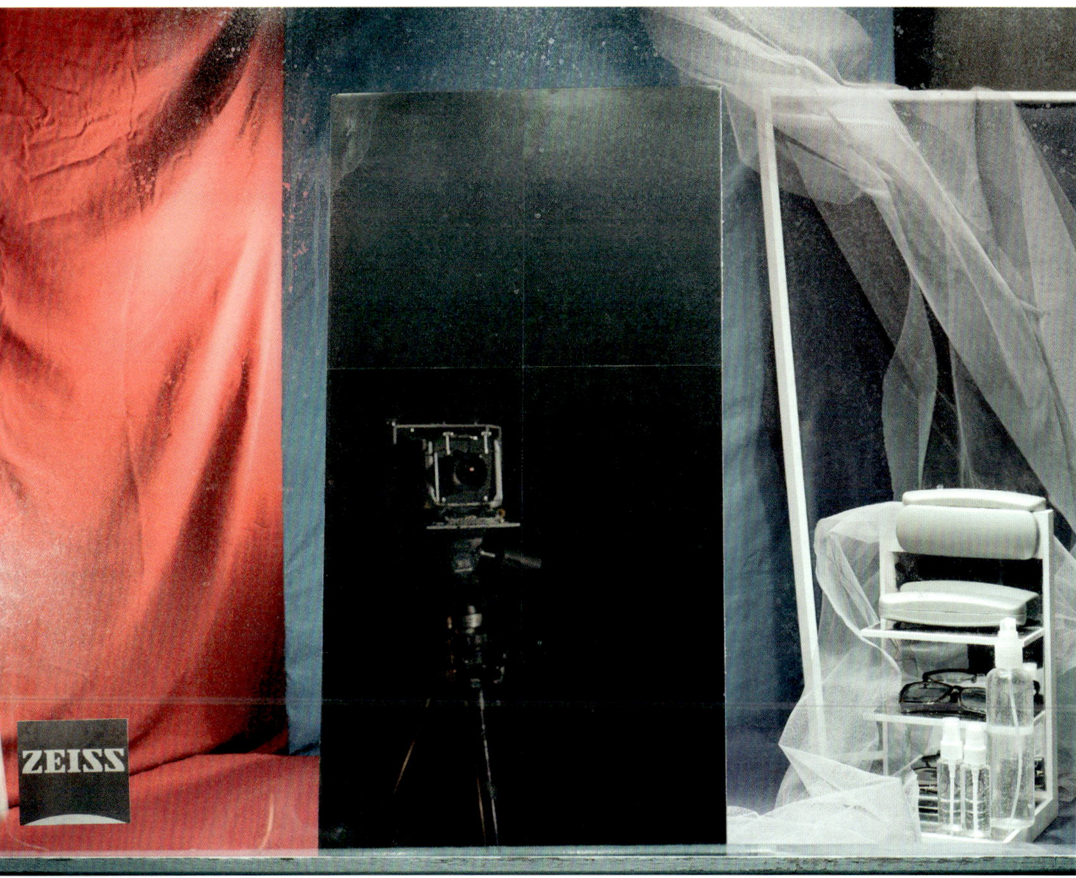

All photographs
Untitled, from the series
The Overcoat, 2013–14
Courtesy the artist

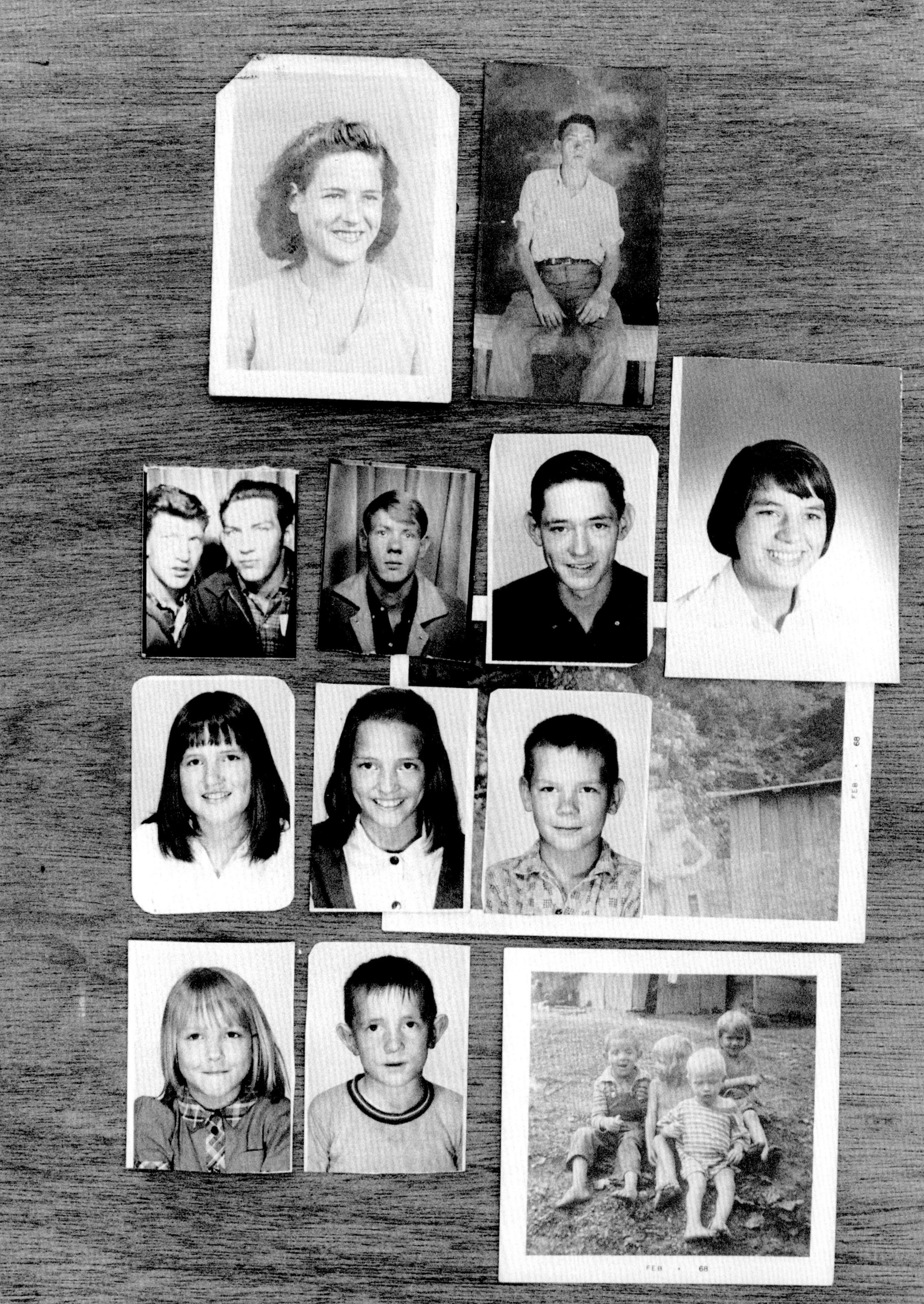

In 1959, John Cage delivered a series of short stories as a lecture, and subsequently performed them live and then recorded them with his frequent collaborator David Tudor. The resulting album, *Indeterminacy*, was released as a two-record box set by Folkways Records in the same year, and consisted of Cage reading his stories out loud in one room—in no particular order, and at various speeds—while Tudor, in another room beyond Cage's earshot, simultaneously played miscellaneous selections from Cage's *Concert for Piano and Orchestra* and *Fontana Mix*. "[W]e weren't going to a goal, but … living in process, and that process is external," Cage later remarked. "My intention in putting [these] stories together in an unplanned way is to suggest that all things, sounds, stories (and, by extension, beings) are related, and that this complexity is more evident when it is not oversimplified by an idea of relationship in one person's mind." Explaining the contribution of his creative partner, Cage wrote, "There was no rehearsal beforehand.… David Tudor was free to make any continuity of his choice."

In devising the book *Iris Garden*, published in 2013 under his own imprint, Little Brown Mushroom, and excerpted in the following pages, photographer Alec Soth in many ways took on the role of Tudor, in the sense that he, too, felt free to make any continuity of his choice while working with Cage's stories. But rather than pairing these texts with music, Soth chose to interweave them with forty-four images that he selected from the archive of the highly respected but often underappreciated photographer William Gedney (1932–1989), now held at Duke University.

Presumably Soth was inspired by a series of photographs that Gedney took of Cage during a mushroom-hunting expedition in 1967. But apart from this direct connection, it initially seems an odd decision to bring the two together and replace the ambiguity and abstraction of sound with the literalness and immediacy of the photographic image. Nevertheless, Gedney's photographs—which often feature obscured faces, interrupted figures, and a subtle but beautifully sophisticated, reflective matter-of-factness—lend themselves brilliantly to Cage's straight, anecdotal prose, in that they, too, are both intricately specific and open to interpretation. Furthermore, Hans Seeger's daring design for *Iris Garden*, which leaves the publication's pages loose and unbound so that they may be shuffled and reordered by the reader, preserves Cage's devotion to the revealing complexity of spontaneity and chance.

In his notebooks Gedney once wrote, "I am attempting a literary form in visual terms"—an ambitious goal shared by many of the greatest photographers throughout the medium's history (including Soth) but one often frustratingly hampered by the differing qualities, structures, and natures of text and image. Nevertheless, as Soth himself explained in a conversation with photographer Jason Fulford earlier this year, "The whole spirit of Cage's music, and most photography, is listening to what is not there—the sound between the notes, the story between the photographs." In emphasizing that what these two mediums (and many more) ultimately share resides not in their end "goal" but instead lives in the *process* of creativity itself, *Iris Garden* presents a captivating example of how the written word and the photographic image may coalesce, and points us in the fascinating direction of process, of relationships, and of the spaces in between, where their real meanings often lie.

Iris Garden
John Cage & William Gedney

Aaron Schuman

Aaron Schuman is a photographer, writer, and curator, and the founder and editor of *SeeSaw Magazine*.

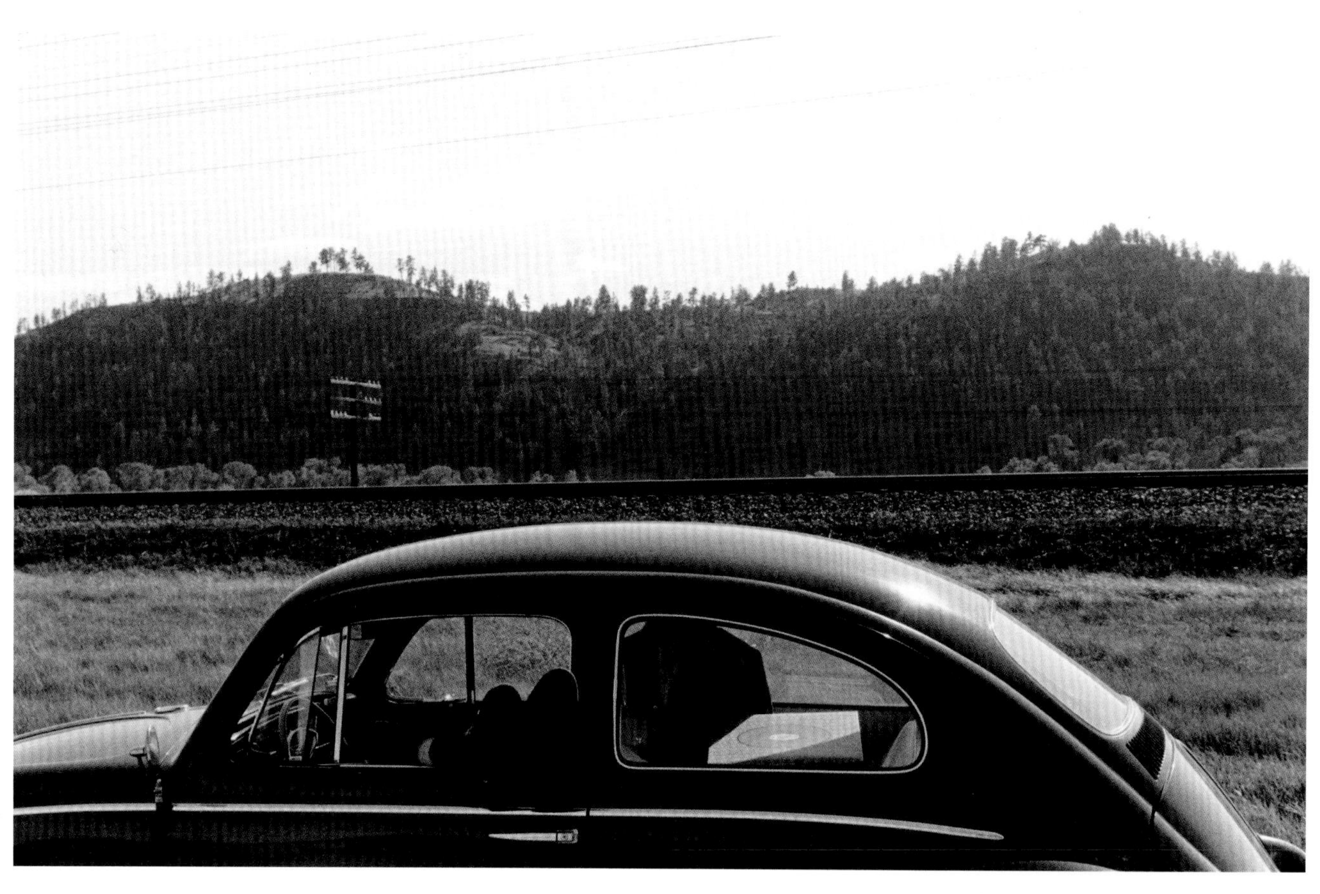

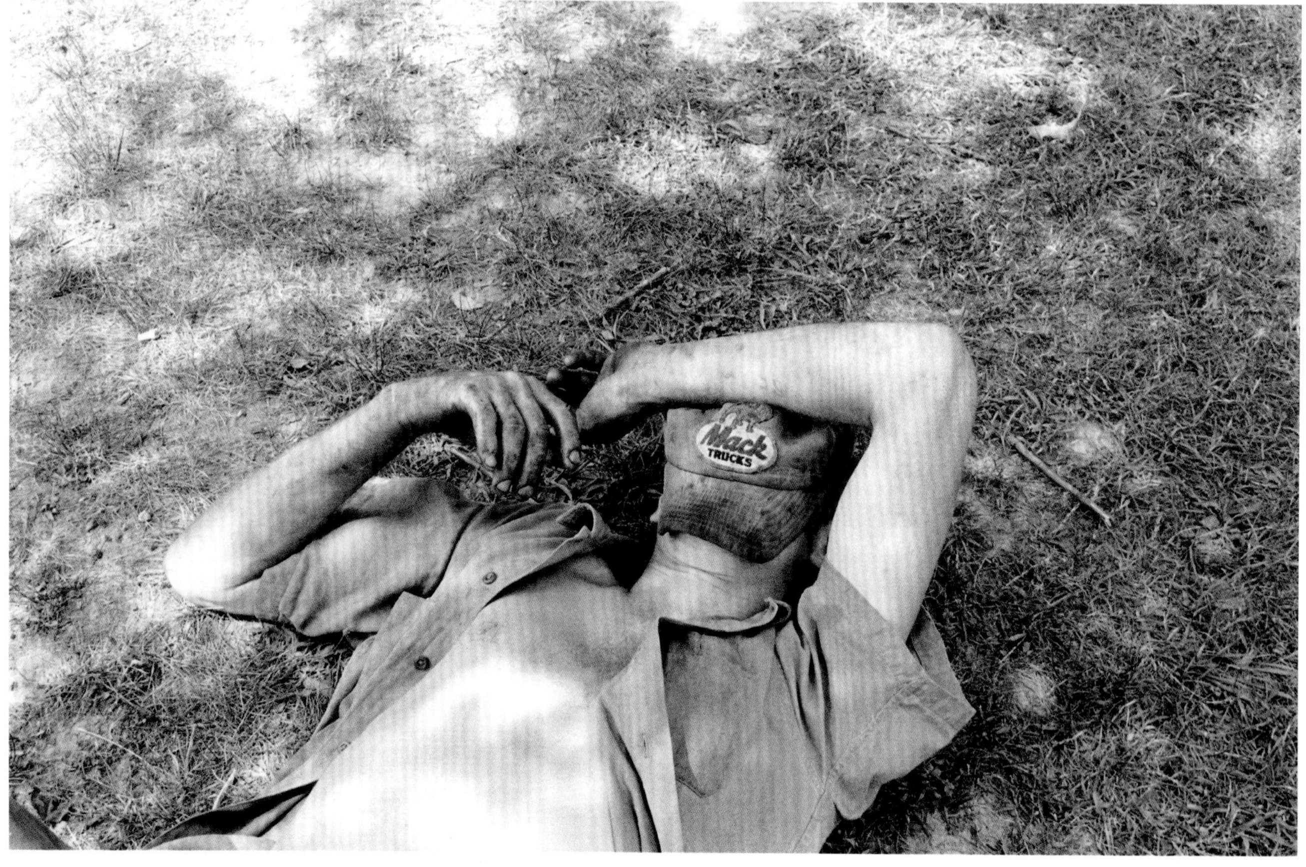

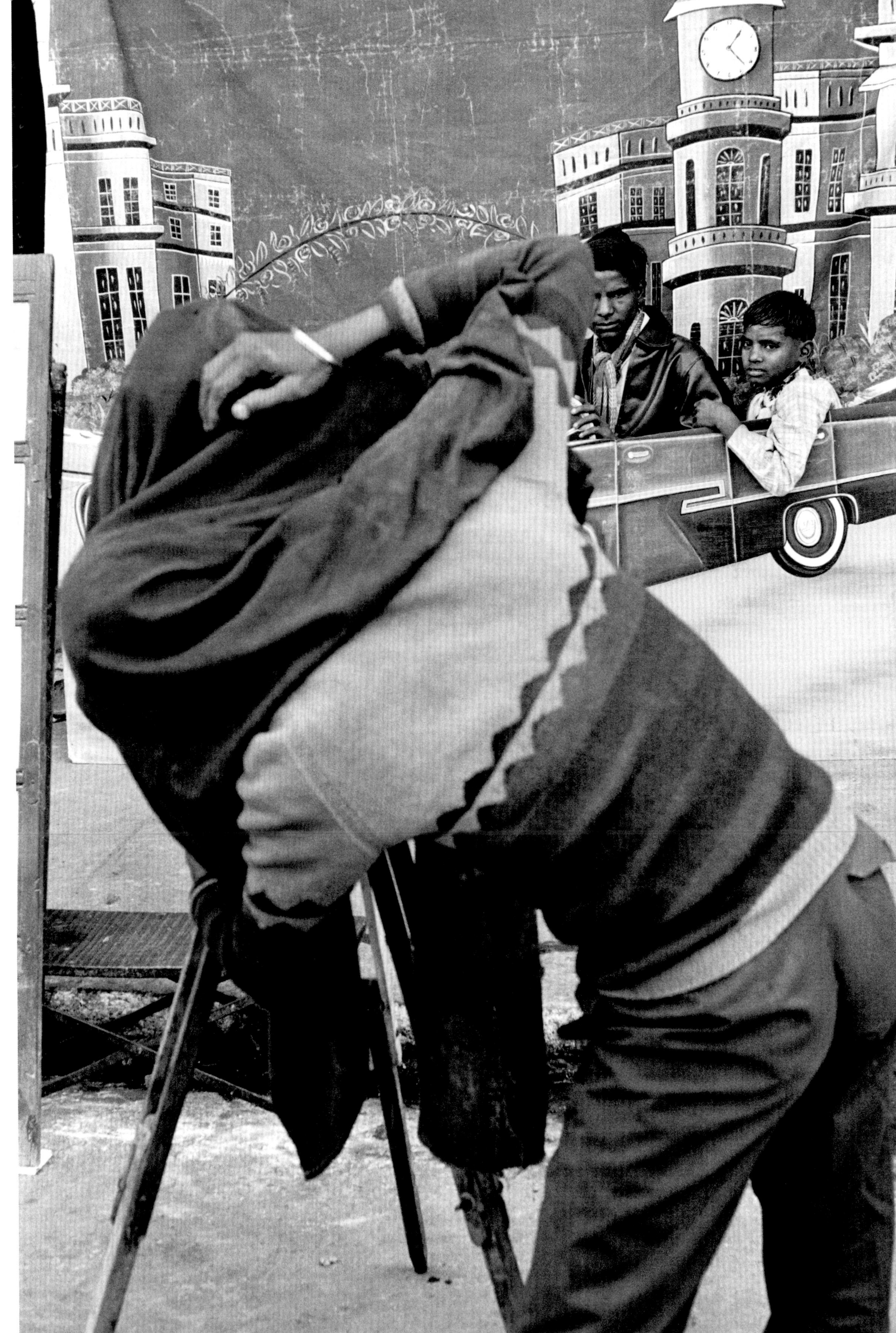

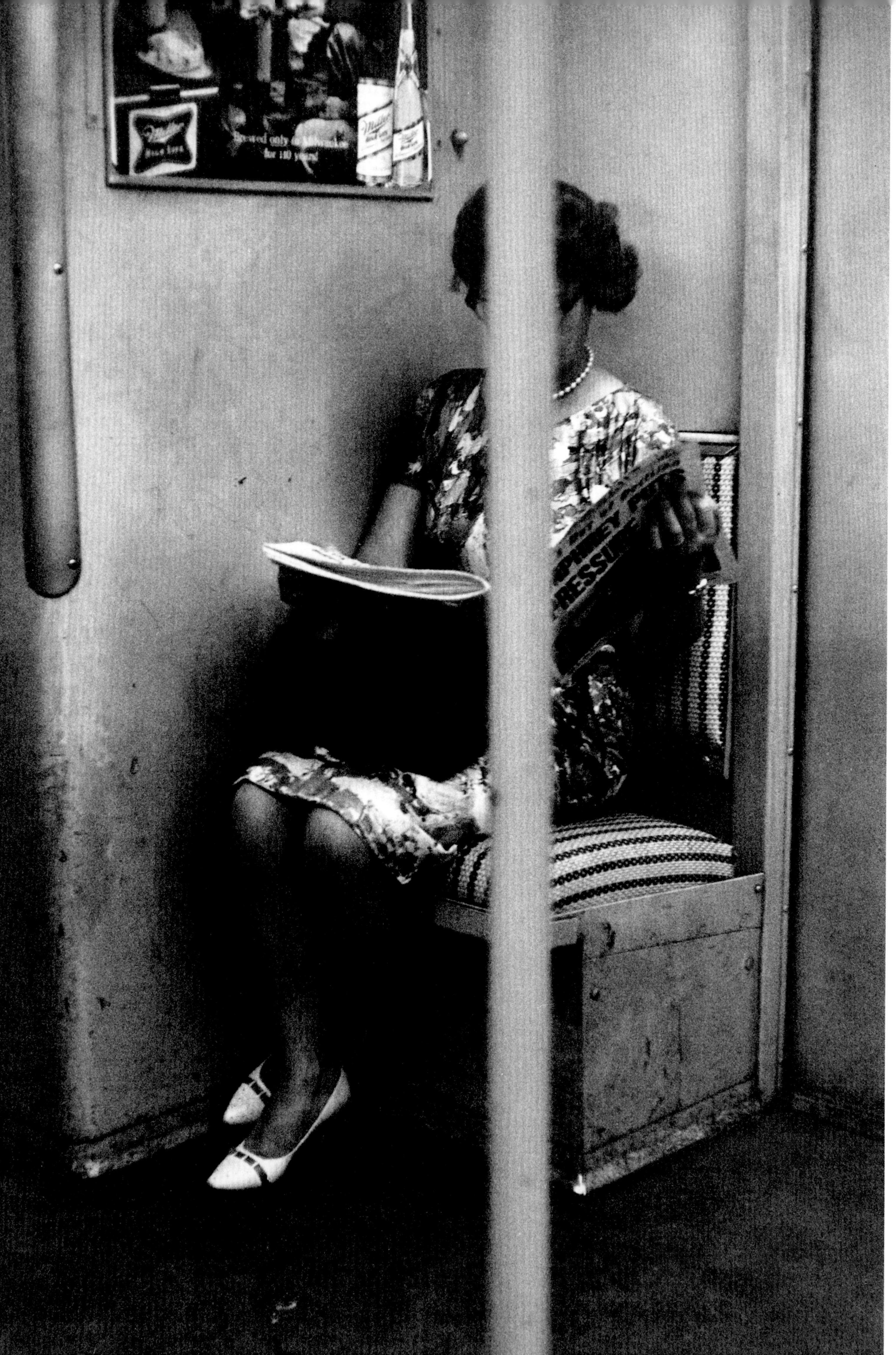
Miller
High Life
Brewed only in Milwaukee
for 110 years!
Miller
High Life

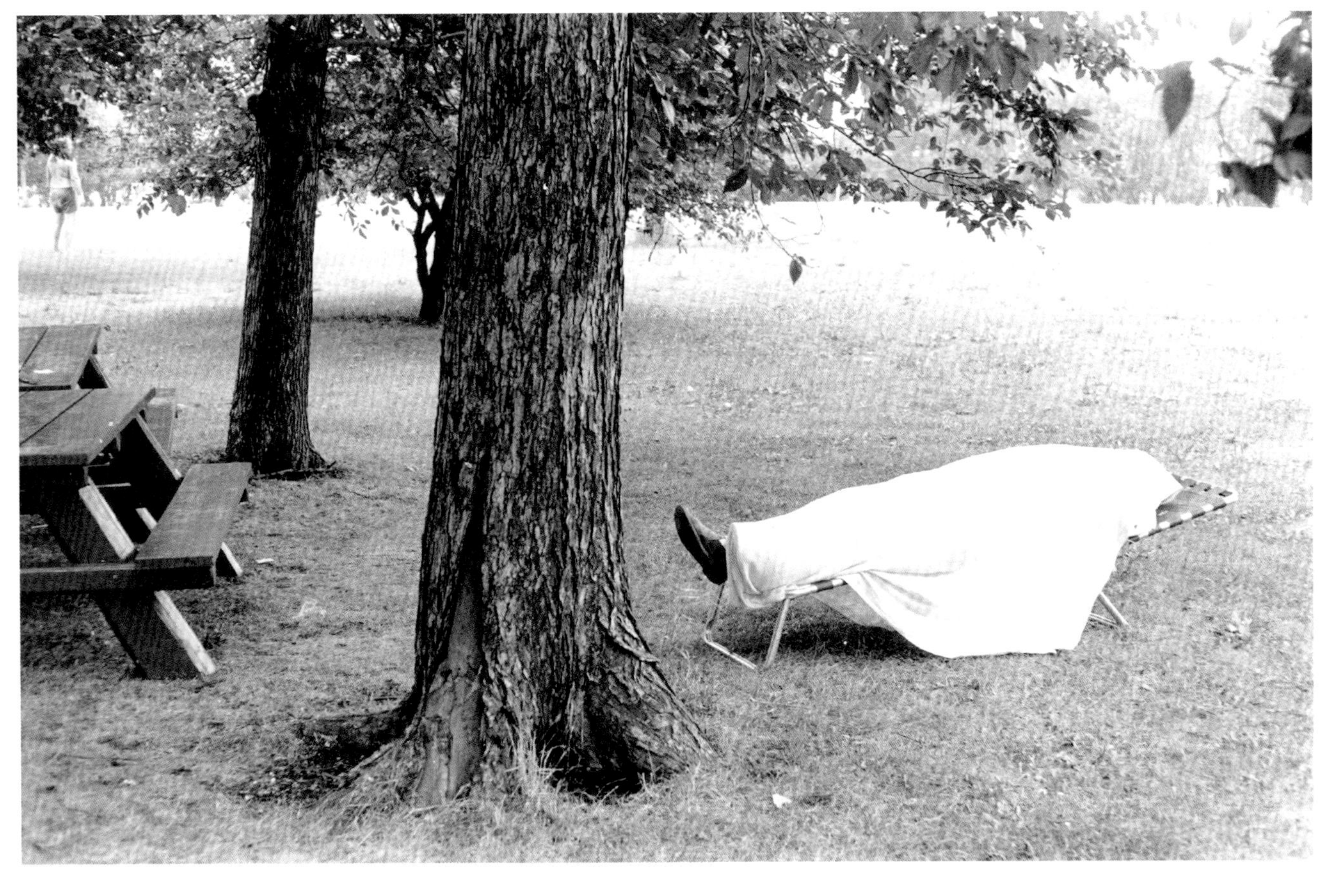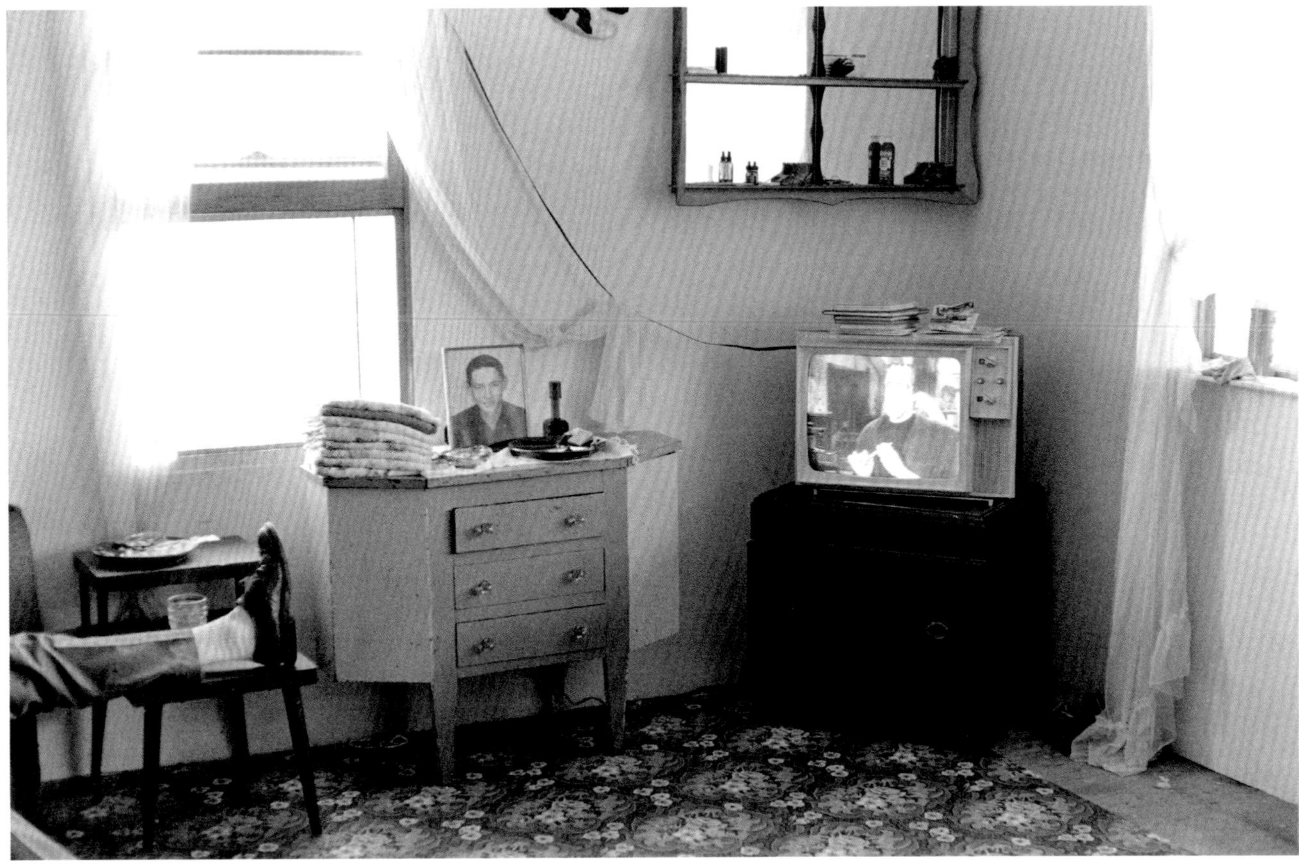

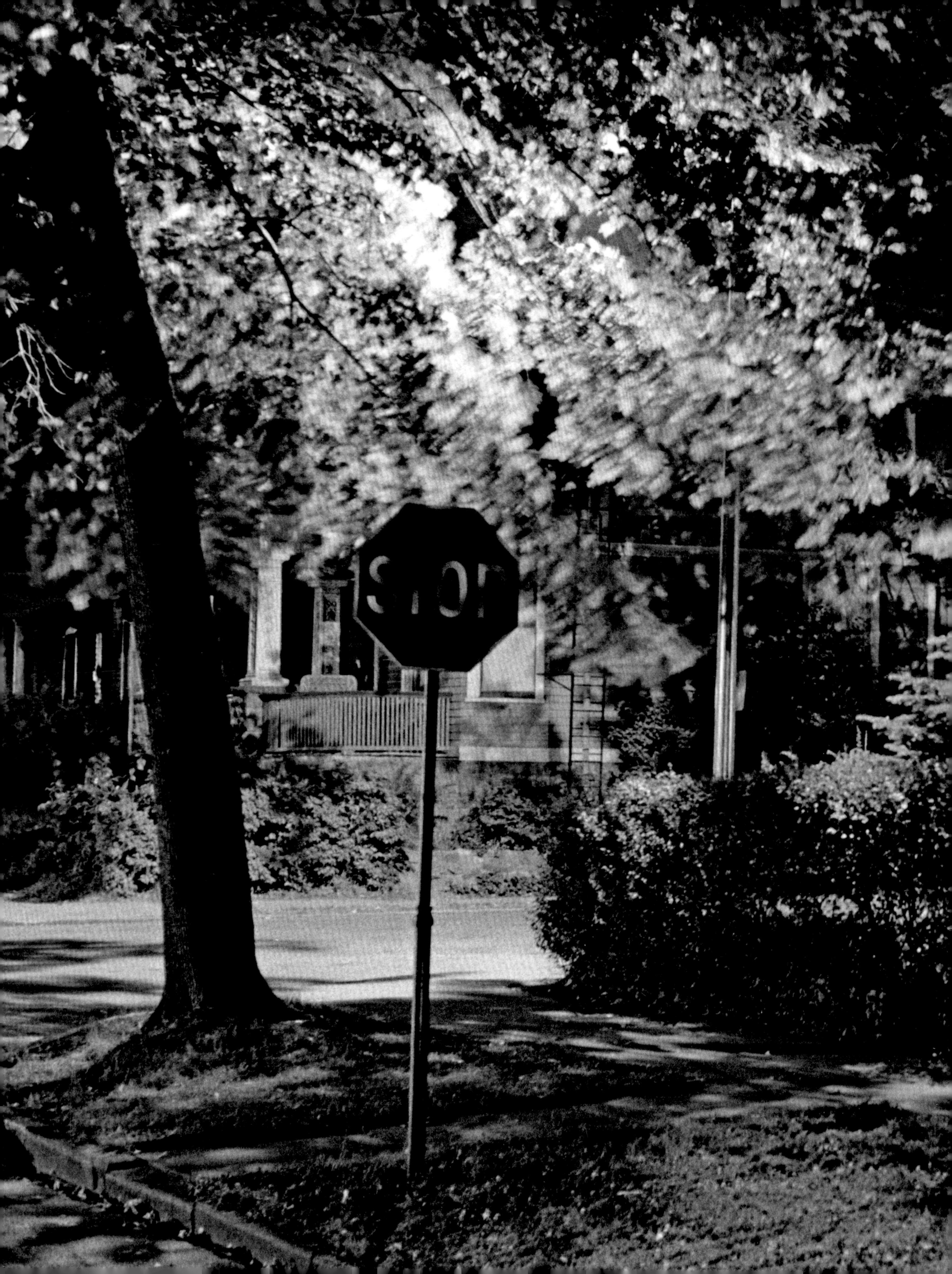
STOP

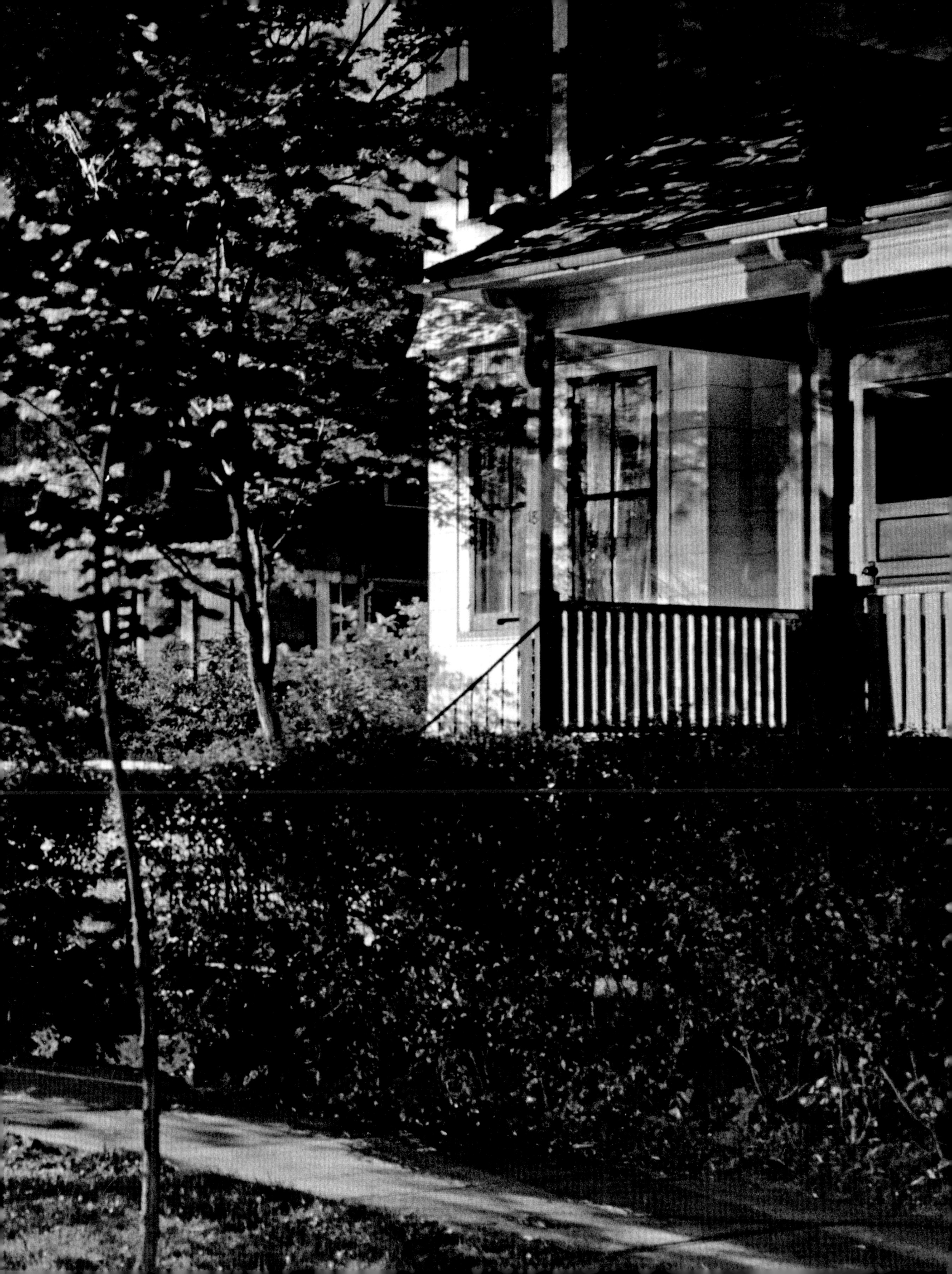

The Lonely Ones is not alone—it is the second of its kind. Photographer Gus Powell's photobook *The Lonely Ones* is, in his own words, a "cover album" of the original, written and illustrated by William Steig in the early 1940s. Steig was a regular *New Yorker* illustrator and author of beloved children's books like *Sylvester and the Magic Pebble* and *Spinky Sulks* and *Shrek* (to name the ones still on my bookshelf). In *The Lonely Ones*, Steig paired a single sentence— "I'm no good"— with a single character of Steigian tragicomic proportions— in this case, a character wearing only his underwear and tied upside down by his ankles to a rope. Perhaps Steig's refusal to fill to the margins his available white space (his characters float in a void on the right-hand page; the sentence settles to the bottom on the left), in addition to the inexplicability of the connections between his words and images, led Wolcott Gibbs, in the book's foreword, to proclaim, "this book, obviously, is not for everyone. A good many people will find it obscure and, consequently, exasperating."

But what is the value of the book that is "for" everyone? Some books are powerful because they make you believe they were written expressly for you to find. Powell's *The Lonely Ones* made me believe this; his work feels like intercepting a series of mysteriously encoded communiqués. Instead of illustrations, Powell pairs his photographs with "captions" that more resemble confessions to the self, or stern fortunes yielded by a cookie of cosmic provenance. They are messages for sure—perhaps even warnings. ("Let's not ruin it by talking.") Powell's photographs are yearningly voyeuristic, as in, *I want to see and understand what's happening here.* I look at his pictures and think genial aliens are spying on us and this is how, to the best of their deep-space abilities, they make sense of what they perceive. I sense a heartbreaking desire to connect with, and maybe warn against, a situation gone slightly or wildly wrong. But the desire to unambiguously communicate seems doomed to productively fail; that failure is communicated by the vast amount of white space in which Powell's words, like Steig's characters, float. But in this white space is where the true connection happens; this is where the viewer fills in the literal distance between the words and the image. We connect with both the visible and the implied people in these photographs by investing in them our imaginative energies. Obscurity or exasperation—of the sort Gibbs carefully cautioned against—here yields to inspiration, also a form of companionship. We befriend the lonely ones. We write their stories in the gaps.

Gus Powell
The Lonely Ones

Heidi Julavits

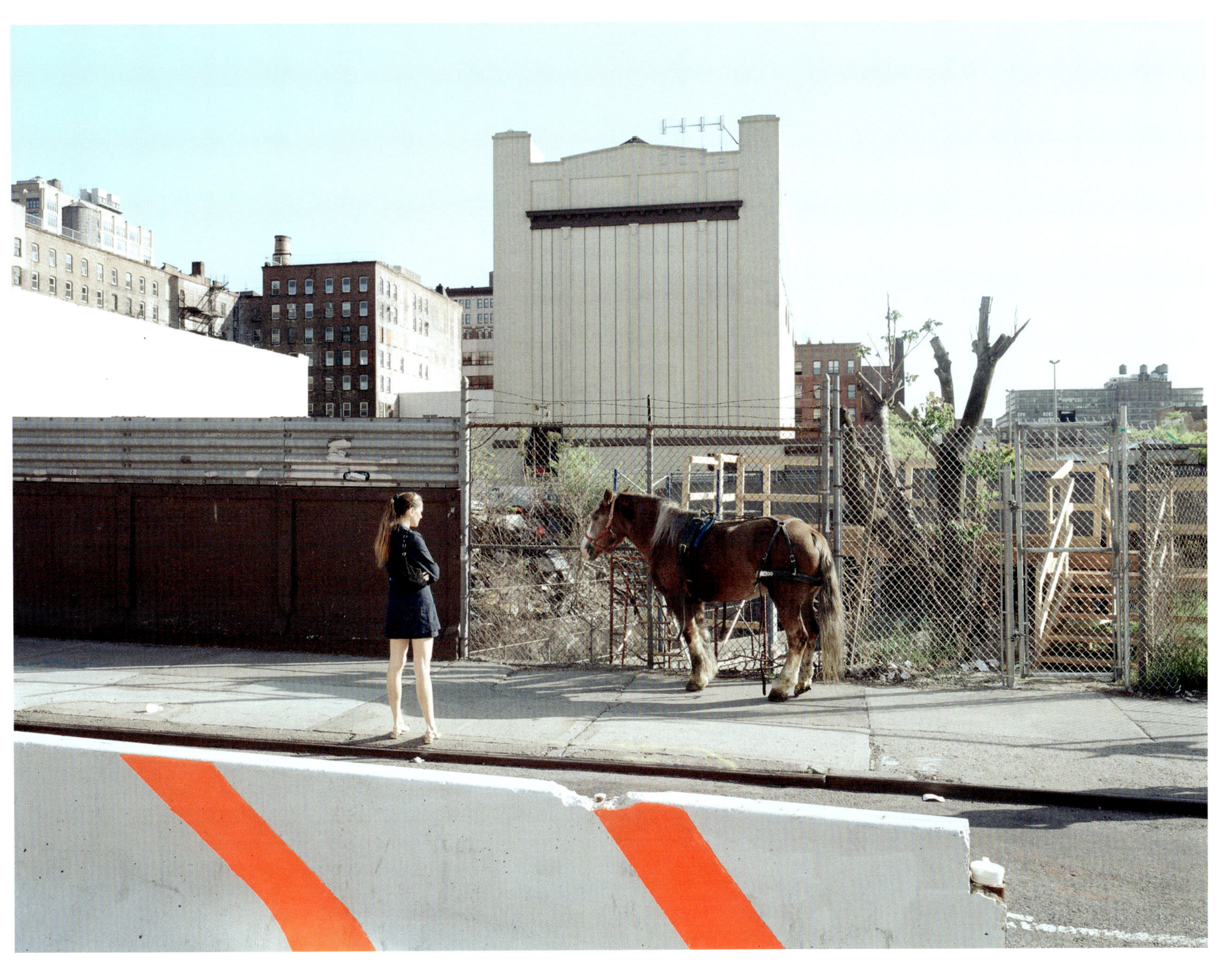

Let's not ruin it by talking.

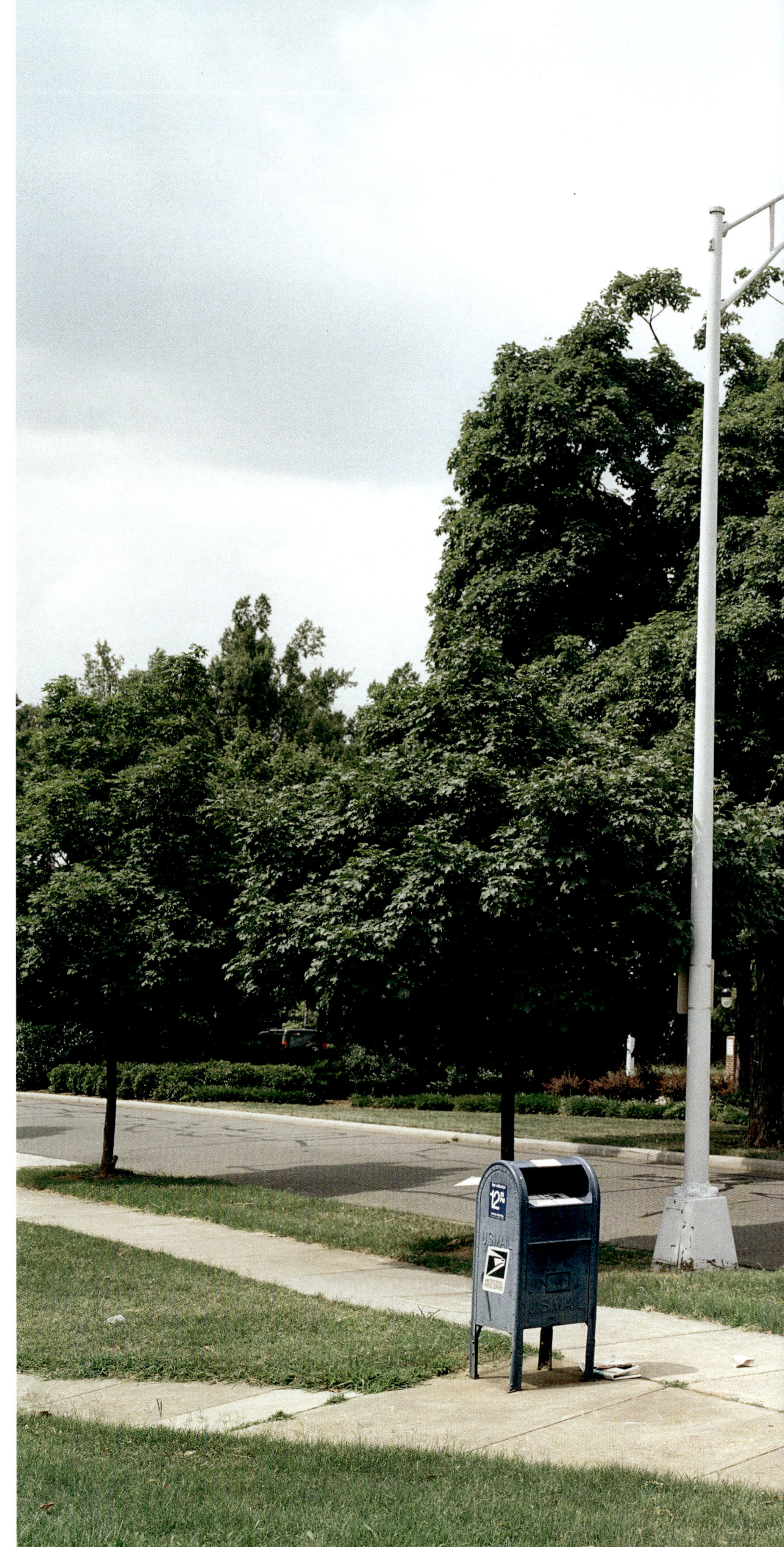

A change of heart.

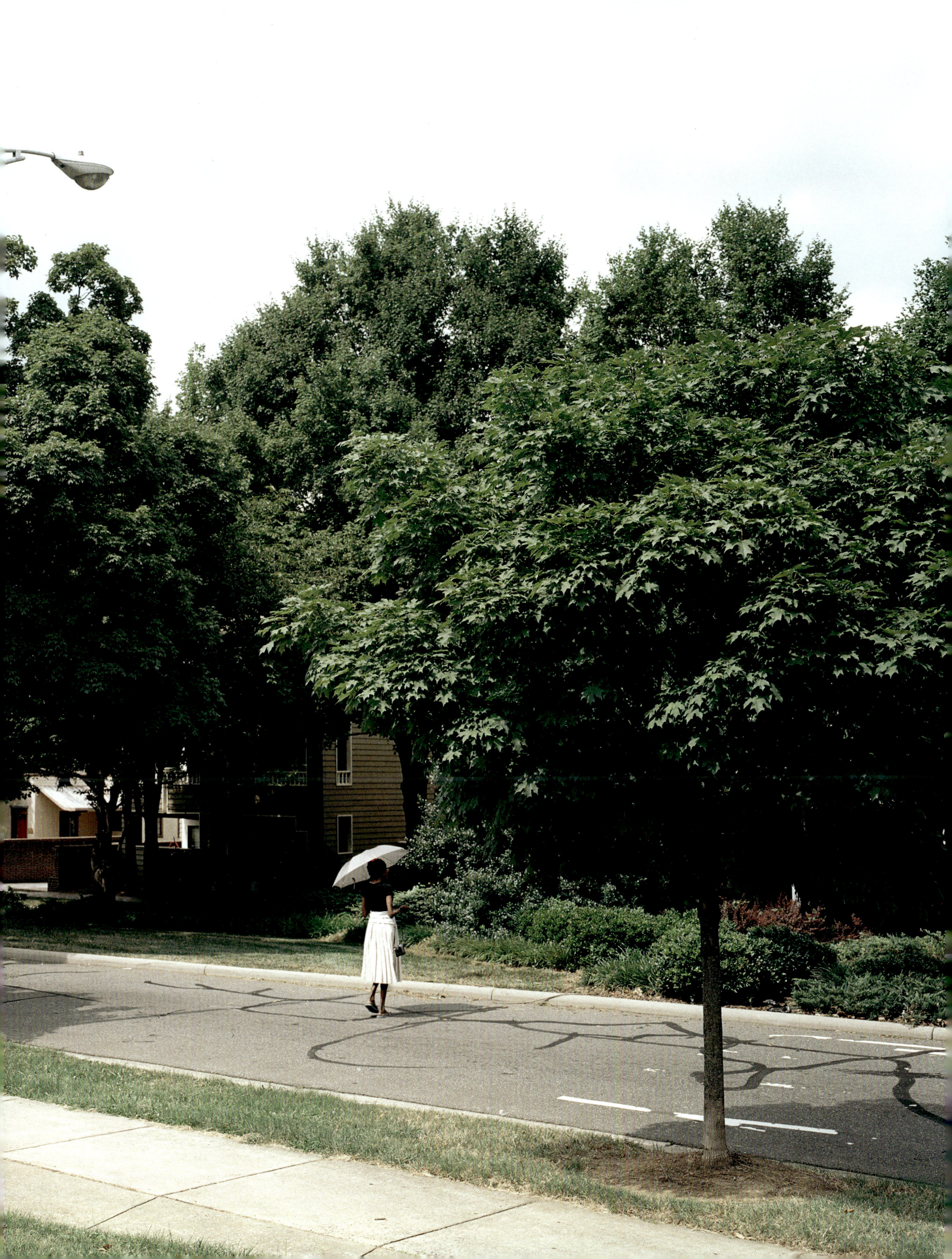

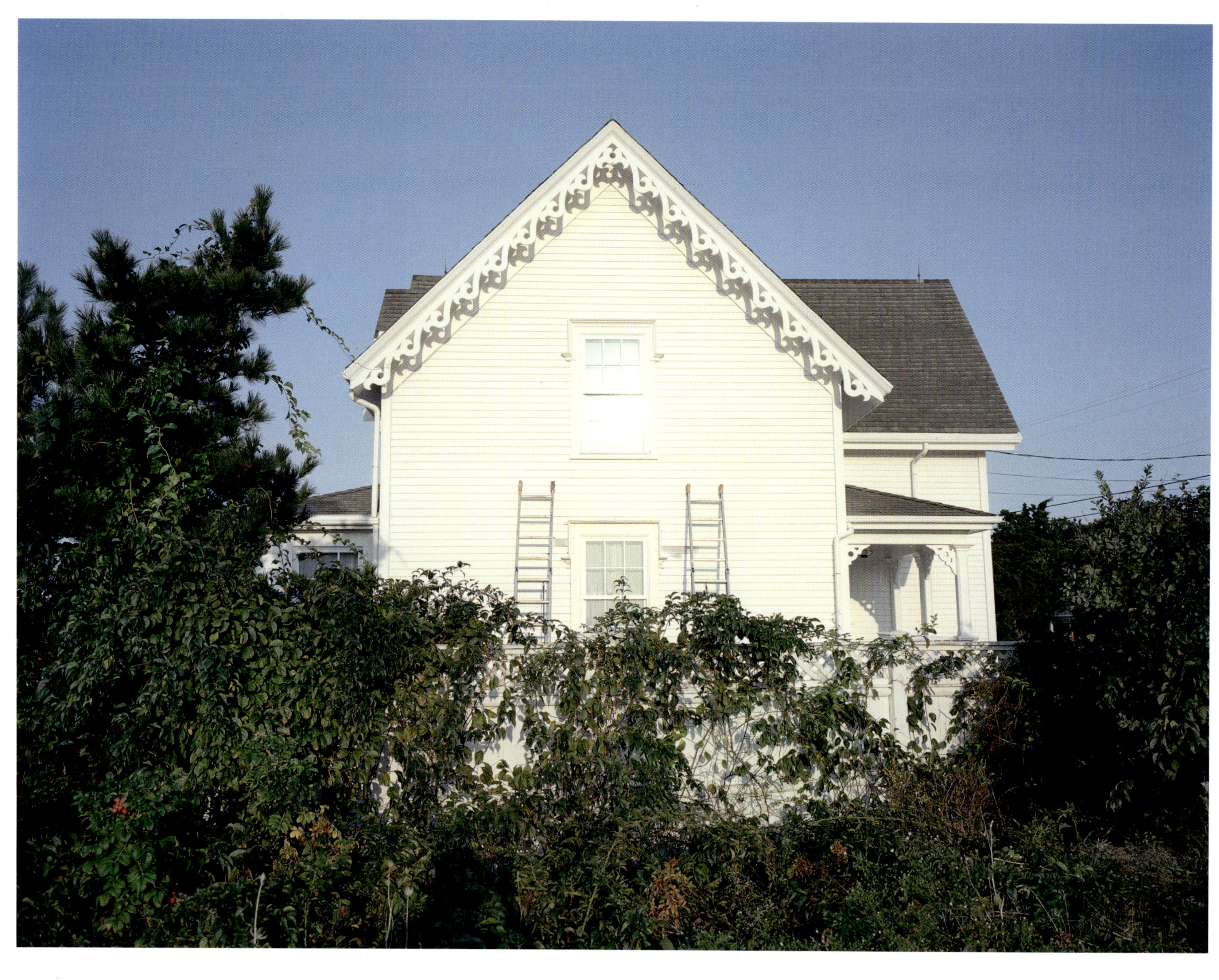

You will need a friend.

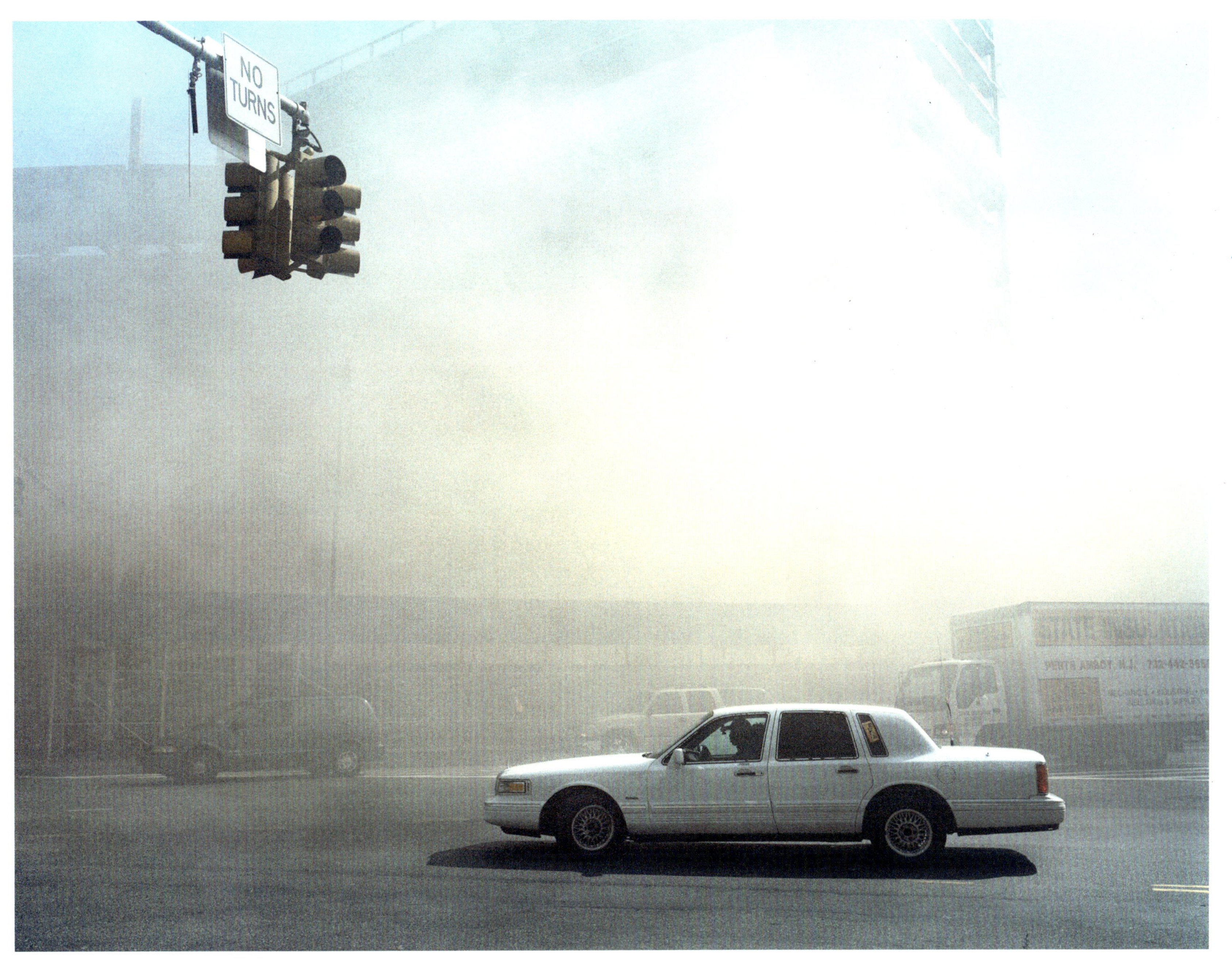

I don't think too much about happiness.

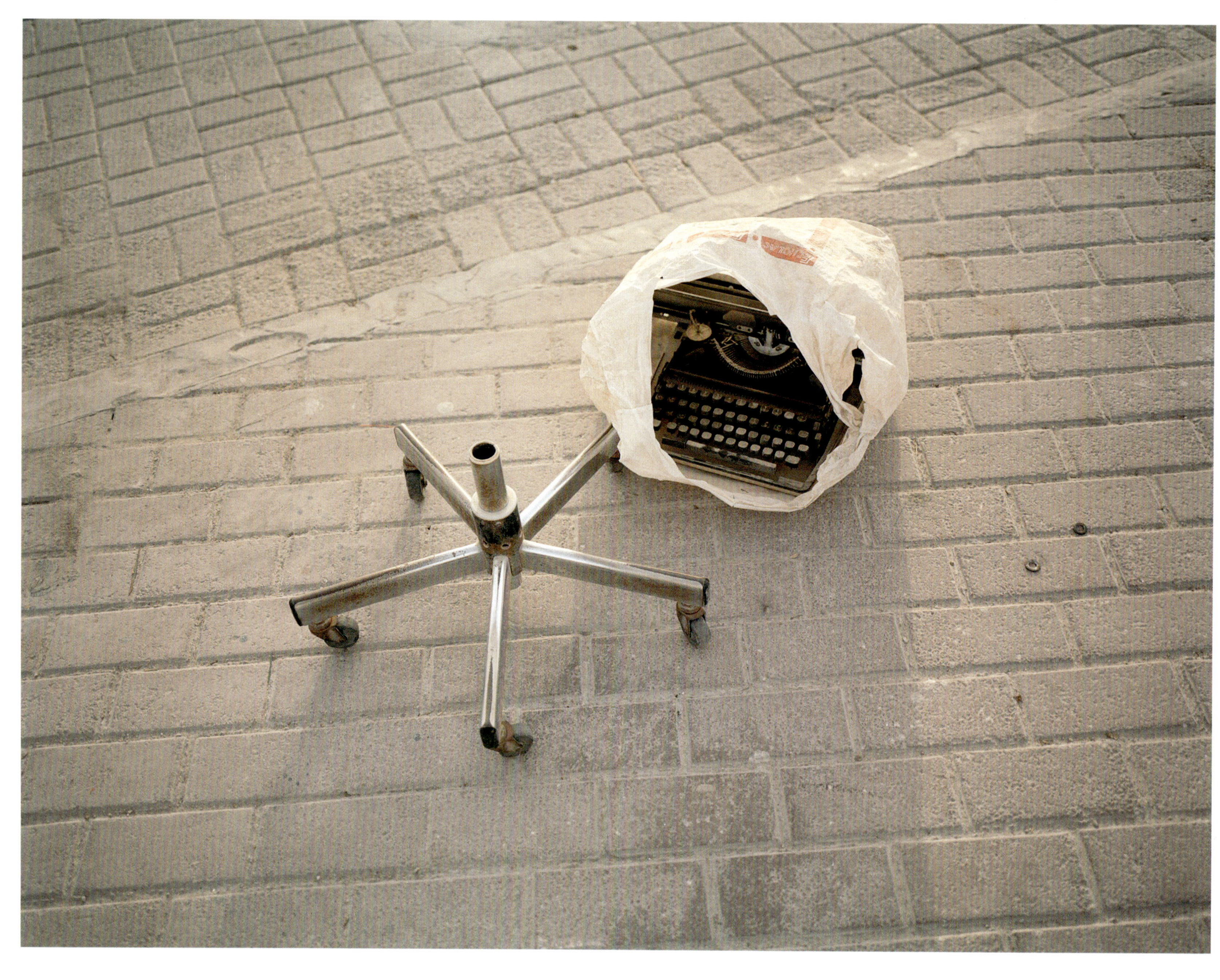

I could have been an entrepreneur.

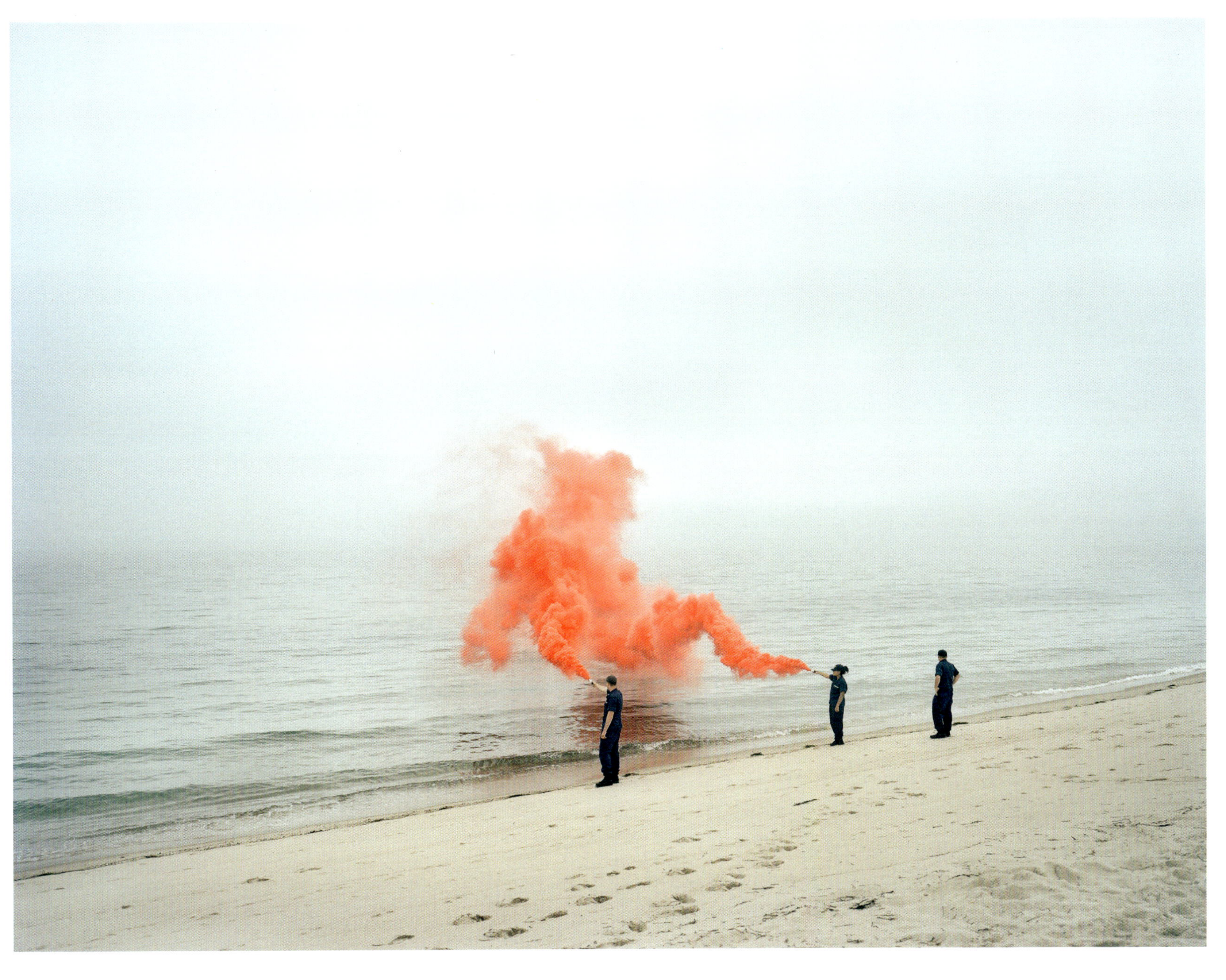

Yes.

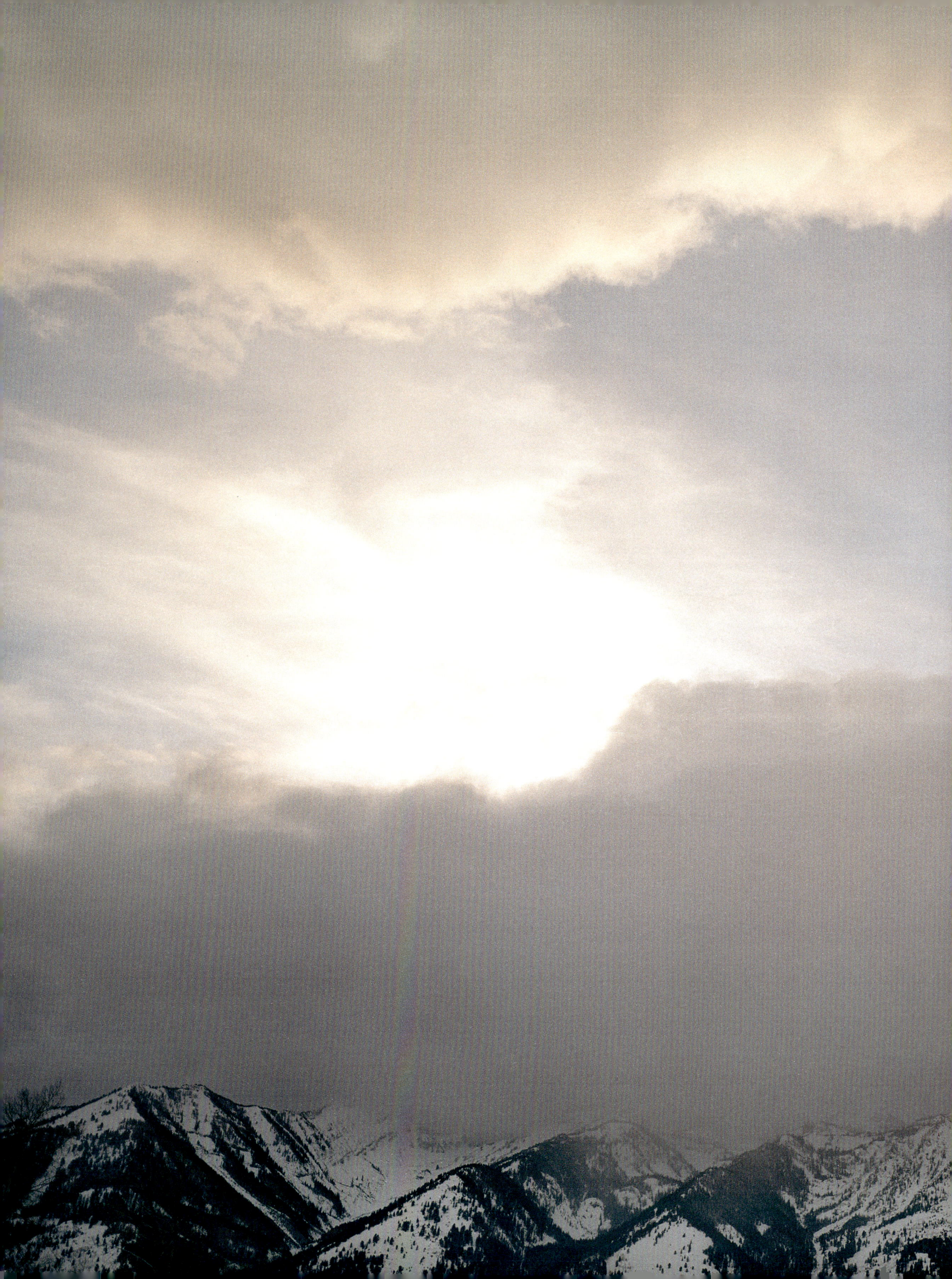

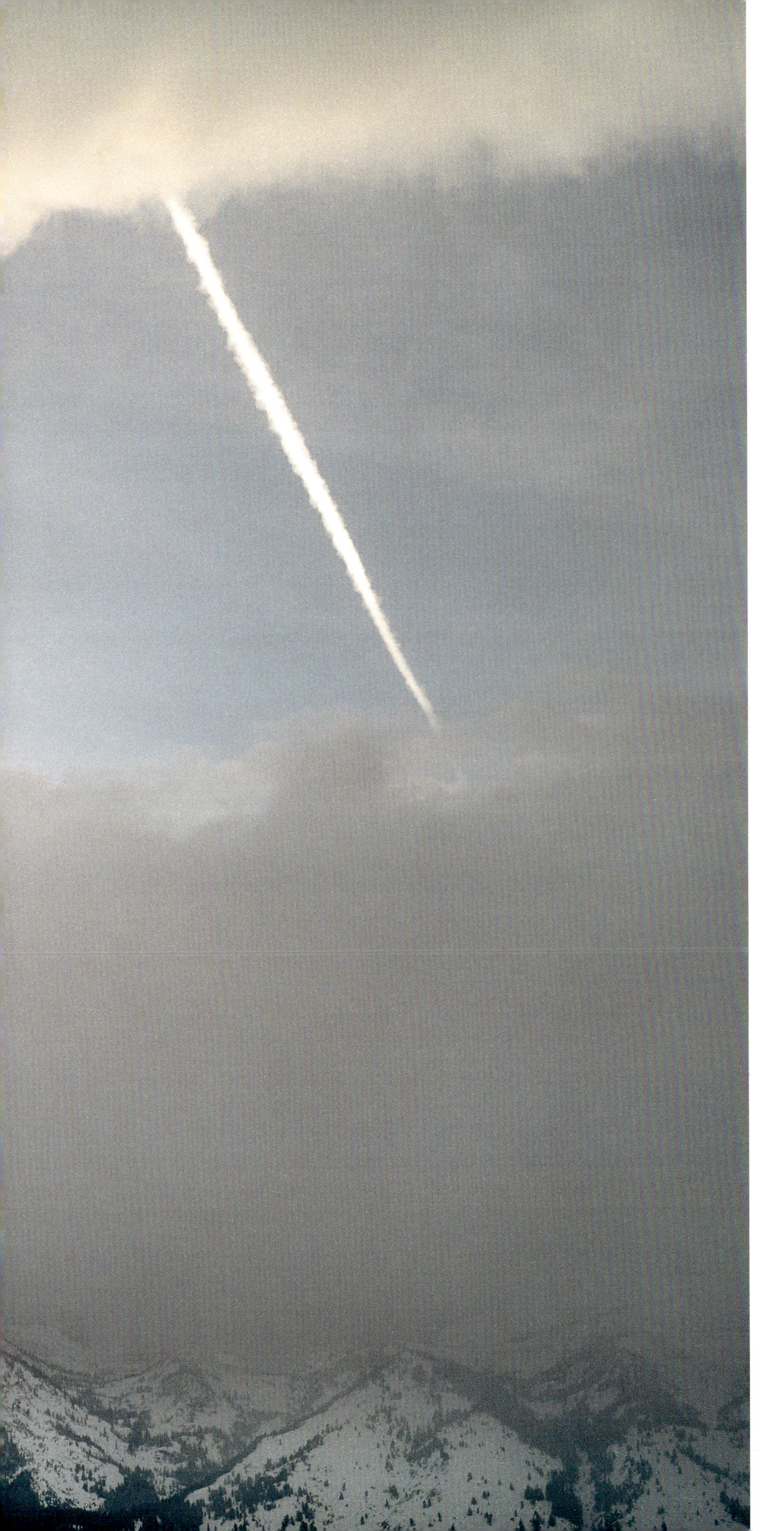

Tales were told.

Object Lessons
Germaine Krull's *Roman* maquette, ca. 1930

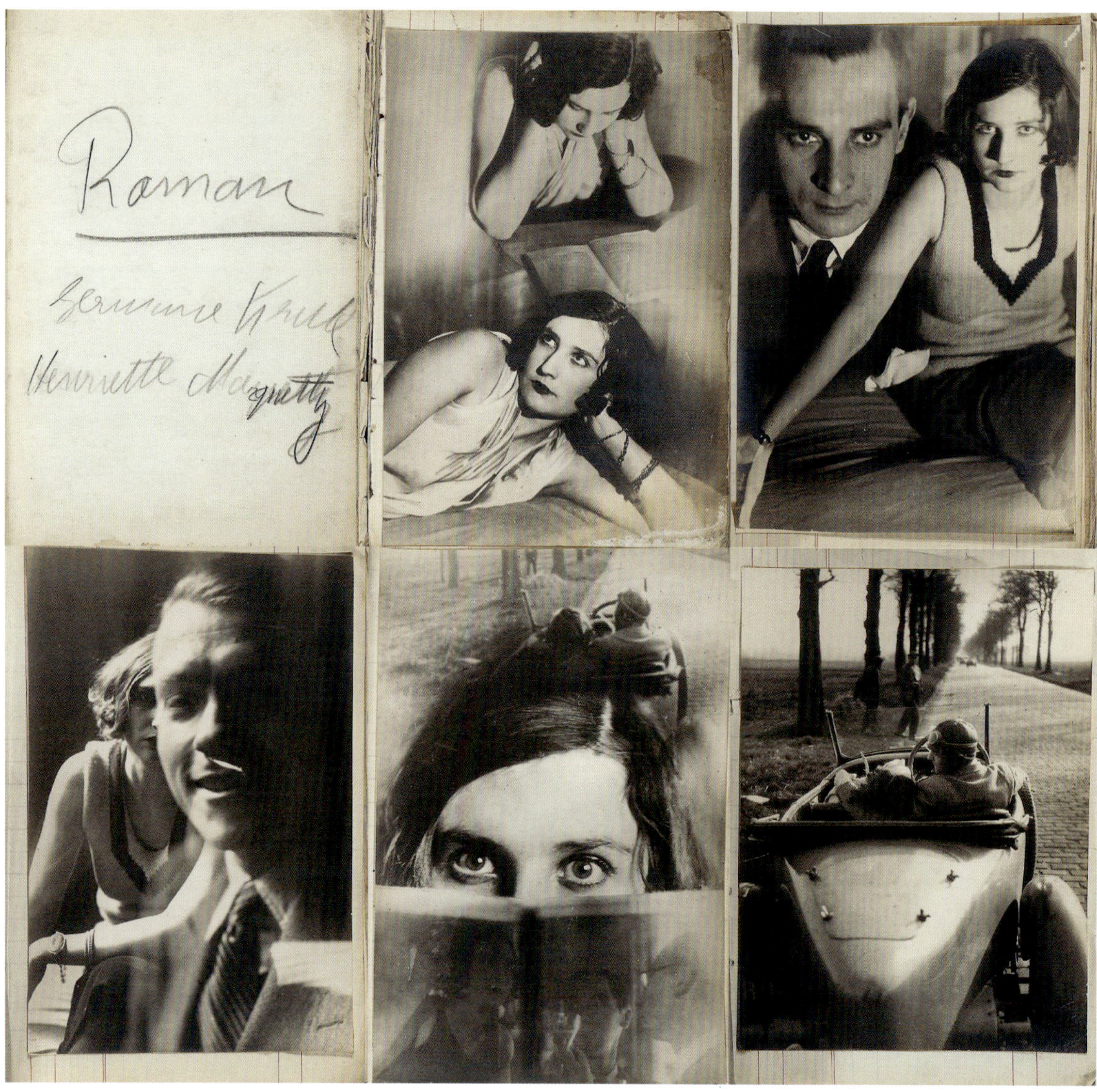

The handmade maquette for Germaine Krull's unfinished photobook *Roman* was long believed lost, along with most of the German avant-garde photographer's pre–World War II archive. In her 1976 memoir, Krull described the project as "… a book only with photographs. A sort of novel without words…. A little *roman-photo*…a fight between two boys over a girl. One was 'the intellectual,' the other 'the sportsman.'" To create this drama in pictures, Krull enlisted her friend Renaud de Jouvenel, son of Henri de Jouvenel (newspaper editor, diplomat, and former husband of the writer Colette), and her neighbor, Henriette Marquetty. Comprising forty-two gelatin-silver prints, the photo-story encapsulates many sides of Krull: her preoccupation with visual narrative and experimentation, a progressive view of gender and romance (with possible allusions to her own liaisons with both men and women), and a fascination with the car, an emblem of industrial modernity.

The project followed her earlier photobook, *Métal* (1928), which offered a sequence of steel and iron structures made in the style of the New Objectivity. Krull's interest in collaboration led her to also produce books with important writers such as Georges Simenon, the Belgian detective writer; romantic poet Gerard de Nerval; and the poet-critic André Suarés. For the detective novel *La Folle d'Itteville* (The madwoman from Itteville, 1930), she and Simenon crafted the narrative together with her photographs embedded within his prose, stand-ins for verbal description. Simenon would later write, "Germaine's Krull's photographs were as important as my words." In 2006, the missing *Roman* maquette resurfaced at a Christie's London auction, and the images from the project, seen above, alive with cinematic exuberance, reveal why the writer might have felt this way.

We may not know which character prevailed in Krull's pulpy love triangle—the intellectual or the sportsman—but the unfinished photobook reveals Krull's sophistication when it came to photography, narrative, and sequence—and with a sports car as a central prop, it conveys a desire for movement that would fuel Krull's extended photographic travels and film work in the '30s and '40s, as well as a lifelong commitment to restless aesthetic invention.

—The Editors